Women of Academe

Women of Academe

Outsiders in the

Sacred Grove

Nadya Aisenberg and Mona Harrington

The University of Massachusetts Press

Amherst

1988

Copyright © 1988 by The University of Massachusetts Press

Printed in the United States of America

LC 87–30067

ISBN 0–87023–606–7 (cloth); 607–5 (pbk)

Set in Linotron Meridien at Keystone Typesetting

Library of Congress Cataloging-in-Publication Data

Aisenberg, Nadya.

Women of academe : outsiders in the sacred grove / Nadya Aisenberg
and Mona Harrington.

p. cm.

Bibliography: p.

ISBN 0–87023–606–7 (alk. paper) : ISBN 0–87023–607–5
(pbk. : alk. paper)

1. Women college teachers—United States—Case studies. 2. Women
college teachers—Employment—United States—Case studies. 3. Sex
discrimination in education—United States—Case studies.

4. Marginality, Social—United States—Case studies.

I. Harrington, Mona, 1936–   . II. Title.

LB2332.3.A38 1988

378'.12'088042—dc19   87-30067

CIP

British Library Cataloguing in Publication Data are available.

Contents

Acknowledgments

We would like to acknowledge with gratitude the contributions to the making of this book of many friends and colleagues, including:

Members of the Alliance of Independent Scholars and all the other interviewees for their generosity of spirit, their willingness to give time and, especially, to make the intellectual and emotional effort necessary to describe the intricacies of their lives;

Jane Lilienfeld and Joann Bromberg who were collaborators in the early stages of the project, Jane in organizing our first joint discussions, Joann in helping to design and to conduct the first interviews;

Simone Reagor, Hilda Smith, Lillie Hornig, and Peggy McIntosh for helpful comments on our early planning;

Marie Cantlon, Mary Anne Ferguson, and Mary L. Shanley who critiqued the entire manuscript, contributing new dimensions to the analysis at a number of points and many valuable references to relevant feminist work;

Bruce Wilcox, Director of the University of Massachusetts Press, for enthusiasm, understanding, efficiency, and wise commentary; Linda Howe and Anita Knight for painstaking transcription; Kristin Klein for laborious footnote checking; and, of course, our families for endless patience, good humor, logistical support, and love.

Preface

This project grew out of our involvement in the formation of the Alliance of Independent Scholars in Cambridge, Massachusetts, in 1980. The Alliance, like similar groups in other areas, developed in response to the prior decade of university retrenchment which had left large numbers of scholars (including ourselves) without academic positions or with peripheral, insecure positions and little likelihood of finding anything better.

The initial purpose of the Alliance was to meet two immediate needs of this displaced academic generation—and more particularly of displaced academic women who made up most of the organization's membership. These two original foci of activity were support for on-going scholarship being done by many members, and support for career changes which others were exploring. But in the process of helping to organize such programs, we found another focus emerging and this was an exploration, highly informal at first, of the reasons why so many credentialed women had ended up—sometimes by choice, usually not—outside the academy.

In fact, this inquiry, in some sense, began at the first gathering of women who would later form the organization. The meeting of about forty women opened with introductions—each woman described herself and her situation briefly—and the effect of that round of stories was electrifying. Women who had arrived with the sense that the drama and loss in their own academic careers was more or less unique, felt a shock of recognition, hearing their experience in the lives of others previously unknown to them. It seemed clear from that one meeting, as women of highly divergent backgrounds and fields told stories with strikingly similar plot turns, that we were hearing about a generalized experience. And this conviction grew as subsequent meetings replicated the first: some women left the group and others joined, but the stories stayed the same.

In the spring of 1982, after several years of engagement in Alliance activity, we began to project a formal study of women's deflection from expected academic careers. We wanted to know why so many women were falling off the normal career track, i.e., the tenure track. We were certain there was more to it than economic contraction in the profession because disproportionately more women than men were ending up with peripheral jobs or none at all. Of course, we assumed that the root cause of special professional disadvantage for women was sex discrimination, but we wanted to know specifically how it worked, especially when it was not blatant. And we expected to find answers by collecting the stories of women's lives in academe—the detailed story-behind-the-story that we had heard repeatedly from Alliance members.

In the first phase of the study, beginning in 1983, we interviewed thirty-seven women who were off the normal career track. To identify them, we used Alliance membership lists and other professional contacts, seeking in our interviewees a diversity of disciplines, generations, degree-granting institutions, and personal backgrounds. (See the appendix for a specific breakdown of the interview pool.)

The interviews ran for an average of two hours and were taped and transcribed in full. They were conducted, one on one, in informal settings, usually in the home of the interviewer or interviewee. For the most part, we found the participants eager to talk, remarkably open and willing to explore even painful and highly personal issues. The fact that we shared their experience and thus understood the issues probably contributed to this rapport.

Because we did not know at the outset what the particularities of each woman's relevant experience would be, we did not conduct the interviews through preset questions. Rather, we identified general areas we wanted to cover, but let the interviewees' responses determine the order of subjects, the time spent on each, and the introduction of additional issues.

The areas about which we sought information were: the formation of ambition to pursue an academic career; familial attitudes toward professional career goals; graduate school experience, including professional socialization, the role of mentors, and financial support; stages of career development after graduate school, including experience of publication and other professional activities; personal life, including the relation to professional life of issues concerning marriage, children, friends, family, and community; and issues concerning the support of other women, whether in discussion groups, caucuses, mentoring roles, informal networks, or other relations. Additional issues that emerged in early interviews and that we incorporated in later ones included a variety of problems concerned with voice (see chapter 4, "Voice of Authority"), complicated questions about the subject matter of women's scholarship (see chapter 5, "Women's Work"), and issues concerning the use of power in academic roles (see chapter 3, "Rules of the Game").

The second phase of the project, beginning in 1984, consisted of interviews with twenty-five tenured women. We assumed at this stage that the responses of these women to the same issues we had discussed with the deflected group would yield different answers and that these answers would help explain the difference in career outcomes. We sought the same diversity here as in the first group and, in addition, diversity in the type of institution at which the women were tenured, e.g., Ivy League, public, private, religious, coed, all-women. (See the appendix for the actual breakdown of these categories.) We identified potential tenured interviewees through catalogs and faculty members at a variety of institutions in the Boston area. The format for these interviews was the same as for the first group.

At the end of the interview process, we were confronted with approximately 1,500 pages of transcription. We were determined to analyze it in its own terms, not to impose on it conceptions derived from the growing body of theory and observation concerning women's experience. Thus we went through a long process of naming—literally, in the margins of transcripts—the various kinds of episodes and comments in each interview, and then put together—again literally, in piles of clippings—all recurrences of the same named experience. Then we organized the recurrent patterns into larger clusters of related issues which form the basis for thematic chapters in which we interpret and explain the material in terms of our own analysis. That, after this deep immersion in the material, we found patterns corresponding in many instances to those proposed by other scholars increases our conviction that the experiences we document are widely shared.

There were strongly similar patterns, for example, in stories set in greatly separated locales. Although our interviews were all conducted in the Boston area and a majority of interviewees were from and/or educated in the Northeast or mid-Atlantic states, a substantial number were from other regions of the country and from other countries, so we were able to establish a geographic spread.

Further, the similarities run across disciplines, age groups, diversity in marital status and class origins. We assume that many of the general patterns of disadvantage run across race lines as well, but we cannot substantiate this because no minority women were among the respondents to our solicitations for interviews—a fact that probably reflects the extremely small representation of minorities in academe generally. As to the application of the common themes to the experience of lesbian women, the issue is complicated. We know that our interviewees in both deflected and tenured groups included lesbians, but none identified herself as such. Thus we have stories from these women that correspond in many aspects to those of heterosexual women, but we cannot draw explicit parallels or distinctions because the lesbian women themselves did not do so.

Given our experience of the Alliance stories, we were not actually surprised to find strong commonalities among women with widely divergent backgrounds. But we were astonished to find less difference than commonality in the stories of tenured and deflected women. Tenure, in the academic world, is the point of security, a certain measure of success. On the surface it would seem that a wide gulf should separate the experience of those who succeeded and those who were either out of or on the edges of the profession. Certainly this is what we assumed in planning the tenured interviews.

What we found, however, was that the same themes recurred. Essentially, they are themes that depict an experience of professional marginality and of exclusion from the centers of professional authority. Taken together, the stories reveal a continuum of outsiderness—literal in the case of the deflected women but nonetheless real for the tenured women as well.

In claiming this degree of commonality, we are claiming that for the academic profession there is such a thing as *women's* experience. And this is true in spite of the vast obvious differences among academic women. That is, no two stories are completely alike. The recurrent themes that we identify as important to many women clearly do not apply to all women who have entered or sought to enter the profession. But we have yet to find a woman who has not been touched in important ways by *some* of the patterns.

At root—and this is the thesis of the book—the common patterns consist of the play in all women's lives of social norms that are constructed to cast women in subordinate, supportive roles in both their private and their public lives. With these ancient norms still powerful, women's experience must differ from that of men, must be marked by strong commonalities along with more obvious wide variety. None of which is to say that the effect of the shared experience of outsiderness is wholly negative for women, personally or professionally. The position of the outsider may be a highly creative one, and this is also part of the story that unfolds here.

Women of Academe

Chapter 1

The Old Norms

Wherever you go, you will hear all around:
The wisdom of women to the distaff is bound.
Rachel Morpurgo, 1790–1871

Women are now laying claim to significant and satisfying work in the professions as a normal part of their lives and laying claim also to the authority, prestige, power, and salary that professional work commands. They are laying claim, in short, to professional equality, and the breadth of change this signifies can scarcely be overstated.

An equal role for women in the organization of society has never been the norm. On the contrary, distinct and unequal roles are sanctioned by long custom and convention, which hold that the proper sphere for women is the private and domestic one. The sphere in which women are to make their contribution is, however, not merely separate but also less powerful than the public world inhabited by men insofar as their private domain affords women no role in the formulation of public policy, in the shaping of the institutions that in turn largely shape and govern our culture. The two spheres—private and public—do not carry equal responsibility for the creative molding of the society.[1] And when we do look at women in the *public* sphere, that is, the workplace, we see that their proper normal role has been subordinate to men—male doctors, female nurses; male executives, female secretaries; male principals, female teachers; male researchers, female assistants.

It is true that for over a century there have been women professors, lawyers, doctors, scientists, engineers, and executives, and, with women's suffrage, elected officials as well. But they were clearly exceptions to the norm. A broad shift in women's status in the professions from subordinate to equal implies a substantial acquisition of new power by women and also a substantial shift in power in the society at large.

Yet, in spite of the greatly increased numbers of women entering the professions, equality between professional men and women is far from accomplished. Rather, the career track of aspiring professional women, after the first few years, diverges markedly from that of men. Further, the divergence is most notable at the higher ranks. Only a small percentage of the highest positions in any profession are held by women. And this general picture is not changing, or only very slightly. In effect, a two-tier system of responsibilities and salaries—higher for men, lower for women—operates across professional lines. In other words, women are entering the professions but they are not gaining full professional authority. They are not, in proportion to their numbers, coming to share in the social rule making—or the governmental rule making, for that matter— that is carried on in the various professions.[2]

What explains this endemic situation? And why—with women making up one-third or more of the students in most graduate and professional schools—is the two-tier system not yielding automatically to women's increased numbers? The thesis we develop here is that, as women rise in the professions, they are stymied at a certain level by the remaining force of the old social norms that in the past barred women from public life generally. The old norms buttressed the division of responsibility—public roles for men, private for women—with a variety of assumptions about male and female natures, drawing natural connections between given proclivities and given roles. Women's identity was located in the body and emotions, men's in the mind. Women gave birth, suckled infants, nursed the sick, cleaned homes, cooked meals, provided sympathy, enchantment, inspiration. Men learned, calculated, bought, sold, built, fought, wrote, painted, philosophized.

Public images of contemporary women—such as Geraldine Ferraro, Joan Benoit, and Sally Ride—exhibiting great competence in roles previously the domain of men, would seem to signal the end of old conventions limiting women's sphere. And, of course, the old conventions *are* eroding. The women's movement has been staking out, since the 1960s, new realms of opportunity and defining new rules for the relations between men and women.

But the new rules do not displace the old. Deep-set beliefs linger and the old norms have even found reinforcement in modern thought, notably from the enormous influence of Freudian psychology. Freud's own answer to his now notorious question, "What do women want?" provided a purportedly scientific basis for biological destiny and thus the effective exclusion of all but the exceptional woman from highly responsible public roles. That is, Freud located need and desire in physical being, and saw women's psychological needs and desires as stemming from that. He did not seriously consider the idea that women want personal autonomy through a fully developed mind and public authority as well.

Thus, we now have a situation in which two sets of norms coexist. On the one hand, we have new social and political commitments to individual equality, openness of opportunity, and equal responsibility for men and women, and, on the other, old beliefs in the fact and rightness of inequality, in the fact and rightness of a distinction between men and women in their capacities and proper roles. We retain—still active, still powerful—the welter of old assumptions about women's nature, and men's. And these assumptions—tying women to the physical, denying the power of their minds—set up stumbling blocks for the advancement of women in any work dependent on the trained mind, which is to say, women in all of the professions.

We trace the connection between the two-tiered structure of professional authority and the ancient exclusion of women from affairs of the mind by looking closely at the experience of women in the profession most directly occupied with intellectual power, the academic profession. Here women contest most directly the old norms denying the power of female minds, and they meet most directly the current forms of the ancient resistance to their efforts.[3] Statistics measuring the overall status of women in the academic profession bear out the two-tier observation, showing without question that the profile of women's positions and the progression of their careers vary significantly from the academic norm enacted by men. Yet more discouraging, the statistics reveal little progress since the issue was examined by Jessie Bernard in 1964 and Alice Rossi and Ann Calderwood in 1973.[4] Specifically, by 1983, women made up about 26 percent of the full-time faculty at four-year colleges and universities, but only about 10 percent of the full professors, the highest academic rank. And even this last figure is misleading; looking at universities—the centers of authority in academe where graduate students are trained and the faculty work load organized to leave time for research—only about 6 percent of the full professors were women. Most women at the top professorial ranks hold positions at teaching colleges rather than at research institutions: women's colleges, religious colleges, technical or vocational institutions, or alternative colleges and universities serving constituencies of less academically able students.

The professional inequality of women is even more readily apparent if we look, conversely, at the statistics for the lower academic ranks. Women made up 36 percent of the country's assistant professors by 1983 and nearly 52 percent of instructors, the lowest rank. Salaries are higher for men than for women both overall and at every rank, with the greatest divergence at the highest level—by 1986 there was more than a $5,000 differential for full professors.[5] To trace the conflict of old and new norms that lies behind these discouraging statistics, we borrow Carolyn Heilbrun's use of the convenient lexicon of literature. As she has remarked, the two distinct social patterns are defined in two distinct dramatic conventions—the marriage or love or romance plot, which outlines the old norms, and the quest or adventure plot, which by extension of its classic form, outlines the values and attributes of the public life to which women now aspire.[6]

The marriage plot, in all its possible permutations, defines the old norms through heroines whose lives exemplify the orthodox goals and virtues for a woman, and, conversely, through ill-fated characters who dramatize the pitfalls and vices that threaten to disrupt the happy ending—the marriage—that the plot requires. And we would emphasize here that the marriage plot applies to *all* women, married and unmarried alike, because it defines what women *should* want, the way they *should* behave, and the choices they *should* make under the old norms. Women may follow the plot successfully, try to follow it and fail, or decide *not* to follow it. But because it has for centuries been the paradigm for women's lives, the one thing women cannot do is ignore or rid themselves of the marriage plot entirely as a guide for their proper conduct and a measure of their success.

The central tenet of the plot, of course, is that a woman's proper goal is marriage, or, more generally, her primary sphere is private and domestic. Her proper role within this sphere is to provide support for the male at the head of the household of which she forms a part. Normally this will be her husband, but it might also be her father (think of Isobel Moore in Mary Gordon's *Final Payments*) or brother (Maggie Tulliver in *The Mill on the Floss*). If a woman is employed in the public sphere, her proper marriage-plot role is still to be supportive—either to an employer (in the mode of the faithful Della Street to Perry Mason) or in some cases to a cause (like Barbie Batchelor in Paul Scott's *Jewel in the Crown*).

Around this central theme of support for men or male-run institutions, any number of subplots are possible, but not another major plot. The marriage plot preempts alternatives. Not that it denies women dimensions to their lives other than support for men; it allows young women to receive and act on messages about the importance of education and individual choice in the shaping of personal interests and work. But if the main plot is to be followed, all other interests must be subordinated to the requirements of support for the central male figure in the story.

Comments from a young woman, still a graduate student in the mid-1980s, vividly portray the clear priorities of the marriage plot—and its continued hold even among women who have come of age after the advent of the women's movement. The woman, a student of ancient languages at a prestigious university, married a fellow graduate student, worked to support the household while he finished his doctorate, then moved with him several times as he began to build his career. Cut off from her thesis adviser and a research library, she made little headway on her own dissertation. "We had a tiny apartment. I had no study, no desk except the kitchen table, and why I never protested—I think I thought this was right. I became the devoted wife. I'll just have everything so comfortable for you here, we'll be so happy. We'll have your favorite sherry. We'll have your favorite cheese when you come home from class. And my own books sat in a big crate in the corner."

Two points are of crucial importance here. One is that the young woman's fortunes were subordinated to her husband's professional choices and chances. The other is that she herself endorsed this situation. "I thought this was right," she said. And this duality—women's subjection to the old norms of the marriage plot as projected by others, *and* their own internalization of them—is a key feature of our stories and our findings. Unavoidably, women follow the old scripts even as they embrace the new, which means that to a certain extent they are carrying on a battle within themselves, as well as with the outer world.

As the same young woman later remarks, "In the back of my head, I still think I have this feeling, and I don't know why it's still there, that it's the Daddies who go to work, and it's the Mommies who are left holding the bag, a kind of traditional family structure. I think, 'Why am I out here? I shouldn't have to be doing this. This is too frightening.' It's not really on my mind, it's some kind of reptilian emotion, wanting to be protected from the risks of the big world, from scathing criticism, or fair criticism, or praise or whatever."[7] Note that she expresses a longing to be protected from the world by a man in charge of the household, yet describes the traditional woman's role as "holding the bag."

The inner battle that professional women fight is particularly difficult because its terms are rarely clear. Unpredictably, women will encounter trouble that looks like a knot of circumstance that they seek to pull loose, not recognizing at its center—except possibly in retrospect—a profound conflict concerning their own identities. Often they will make decisions that compromise their new professional identities—without realizing why they have made such a choice or what its implications might be. Needless to say, the cumulative effect of several such decisions may be the virtual end of a woman's career, or the serious restriction of it—a tragic result when the woman has not foreseen and therefore has not chosen such a consequence.

How, then, do the old norms work? How do the messages of the marriage plot reach women with such insidious effect? In the stories, we see the messages carried through experience so commonplace and banal as to be almost unnoticeable. For example, a mother may emphasize the importance of marriage by urging her daughter to socialize even with young men the daughter does not like. "There was always a sense that you were failing mother," one woman said of her reluctance to carry on a high school social life. "I remember dating a fellow whom I really couldn't stand at all. I used to pretend to be asleep at the end of the date so as to avoid the parting kiss, but there was a great deal of pressure to carry on that sort of charade." Or the same message might be conveyed by a corresponding *lack* of parental interest in professional goals. A biologist recalls being greatly excited when a scientist spoke at her high school about new realms of research opening up. "I remember calling my mother, she was at her Wednesday afternoon when she played cards, and saying, 'Mother, I'm going to be a chemist.' And she said, 'Very nice, dear,' or words to that effect."[8]

A historian tells a similar story about implicit marriage-plot assumptions in her parents' view of suitable work for women. "My father is a dentist with three daughters and I spent my summers working for him and all the time I was growing up I heard him say, 'Women should be dentists. This is not a man's profession. Women have finer fingers, better motor coordination, and they don't terrify the patients.' And when it came time to talk about what I should do for a living, he thought a dental hygienist's course would be just perfect for me, and it never occurred to him I could be Dr. X., Jr. He had three daughters and he never got beyond the idea of dental hygienist's school for all three of us."

Another powerful source of instruction in the marriage plot is, ironically, the great literature that forms the basis for the academic disciplines.

This teaching is subtle, so subtle it has taken women scholars years to notice, but nonetheless it conveys the message that men and women are of essentially different castes, that there are distinctions between them that by implication relegate women to the marriage plot. A philosopher among our group, tracing her own intellectual odyssey, speaks of the astonishment she felt when, after many years in her field, her eye fell on a remark of Kant's that women should not worry their pretty heads about geometry—that they might as well have beards. "I looked at this and said, 'What does having a beard have to do with . . . geometry?' . . . It was such a revelation that this person . . . who seemed to question the most fundamental things, like causality, the self, time, space, could say something as idiotic as that and reveal this depth of stereotypical thinking. It just . . . overwhelmed me."

Pursuing this point, she went on to find similar comments in many of the great philosophers. "Hume, Locke, Kant, Aristotle, Plato, all of them, and I simply had not noticed it before. There were rarely . . . really horrible, nasty treatises where they talk about the awful creatures women are. That's there too, of course, but it's easier to handle. You say, this person's a misogynist and you can almost dismiss it, but the ones who incorporate it subtly into what they had to say. . . . Hume is one . . . they'll be writing on justice and talk about how justice is a relationship that exists between equals, which means it is not something that applies to family relationships . . . where you exhibit charity and compassion but not justice. And I had read it before and it was just astonishing that I hadn't noticed it."

Another philosopher, a specialist in theories of education, made a similar discovery—as many women scholars now are doing in fields ranging from psychology to theology. "There are education textbooks and anthologies, the history of educational thought from Plato to the present. There is a work called *Three Thousand Years of Educational Wisdom* and there is no woman [included in it]—in three thousand years. And there are people you never heard of in your life. It isn't as if they were all Plato and Aristotle. . . . There is no woman, even Maria Montessori."

The message, once seen, is clear. Women are not equal to men. Women have no authoritative place in public life. Their work is not properly to solve problems of geometry or to formulate philosophies of education. As Adrienne Rich has said, "the content of education itself validates men even as it invalidates women. Its very message is that men have been the shapers and thinkers of the world, and that this is only natural."[9] But why? Even given the primacy of domesticity in the marriage plot, why the exclusivity? Why the virtual absence of women from positions of social authority in any field during the centuries when the old norms strongly prevailed? The reason is that the old norms not only rank goals for women in order of importance—private roles first, public second—but also warn of a potential incompatibility between them.

Women's nature, in the orthodoxies of the marriage plot, is strongly instinctual, emotional, attuned—as are those of animals and children—to the rhythms of the physical world. Not for nothing are ancient female deities responsible for an earth that receives seed as they do. The old norms celebrate women's intuitional powers, their proverbial ability to understand nonverbal communication—themes that crop up repeatedly in fairy tales and mythology. What for the male requires a saint like St. Francis of Assisi (to talk to animals) or a magician like Prospero (to be in touch with the elements), women are imputed to be capable of, in their nature. Further, the marriage plot, enacted by countless heroines of eighteenth- and nineteenth-century novels, attributes to women a capacity for moral goodness greater and more natural than that of men. This capacity makes women essential helpmates for the men in their lives who have to do direct battle with the world's cruelty and with their own baser nature. Witness Mr. Rochester leaning symbolically on Jane Eyre at the conclusion of that novel.[10]

Further, the correlative point in the marriage plot is that a woman's attempt to develop other elements of her personality may undermine her inborn moral qualities and threaten her emotional and relational fulfillment. In order that she not compromise her true womanhood, the plot imposes an inhibition on the development in a woman of capacities other than those stemming from her moral nature.[11] These inhibitions operate against a full and free expression of sexuality in a woman, as well as against the full development of her intellectual capacities, her prowess in reason, and the studious pursuit of knowledge.

These strictures against the overdevelopment of intellect appear in various forms in the lives of contemporary women. One form is a mixed message concerning high achievement in school, the message that doing well academically is good but also socially dangerous. A woman who attended an eastern metropolitan public high school in the 1950s reflects on the attitudes of her comfortable middle-class family—their respect for learning, but also their reservations. "Going back to my early childhood, I took in messages about how far I could go as a woman and as a professional. . . . My parents and the rest of my family had the view that I was . . . very smart. . . . they didn't have to worry about my intellectual development, but they were worried about my social development . . .

because I was smart. . . . it was all very well to be intellectual and do well in school, that was fine and wonderful, but that was not what really mattered. The important thing was how one got along with people and how one treated people and how one related to people. It's clear to me that one reason I picked high school teaching rather than going on to teach in college right away was because it was important to me to prove both to them and to myself that I could be successful in a career where the bottom line was really personal. . . . And I was deflected from more intellectual pursuits, because I had been made to feel that that was where the real value lay."

And another woman of the same generation, but a graduate of a prestigious eastern boarding school, reports the same parental attitude. "[It] was a question of 'Don't be too big for your britches. Just because you get all A's, just don't be a smarty-pants.' Because . . . no one seemed to know what to do with this brain. . . . It was sort of an inconvenience."

Some parents went further than verbal warnings about an excessive emphasis on intellect. A linguist who grew up in a well-off Jewish family in New York City submits that her parents had actively discouraged her desire to attend an academically renowned eastern college because they feared the overintellectuality of such an environment. They preferred to send her far from New York even though this meant placing her in an almost wholly non-Jewish setting. "My father decided the Midwest was a good place for a girl, and [he thought] all my friends at high school were intellectual snobs, and so [they decided] to send me to the Midwest to become what they thought of as more normal." And indeed she attended a midwestern state university, but still thwarted her parents' designs by going on for a Ph.D. at Harvard.

Messages downgrading or ridiculing intellect in girls also come across strongly in many high school social settings, as does the message of an inherent opposition between intellectual and social capacities. A historian, in high school in the 1950s, recalls: "I actually wrote to *Seventeen* magazine when I was in high school and asked for advice about how to avoid the subject of grades with boys. . . . I was competitive . . . and I wanted to excel, and it made boys very nervous when they were in direct competition with a girl. And *Seventeen*'s advice in a whole single-spaced, one-page letter was that a really smart girl knew how to avoid having the subject come up. I felt I was really dumb." Lest it seem, however, that ridiculing intelligence in women was a feature peculiar to the unliberated 1950s, a language scholar described the same social pressure in an eastern high school a decade later. "There was a sense in high school that you were either serious or silly. . . . it was a choice, partly engrained in me from an early age, partly the result of the social climate of the high school where anyone who was best in everything was pretty much ostracized."

Later, when relationships with men deepen, the message that the power of reason is somehow at odds with a woman's true nature becomes more pointed. "I was told by another graduate student, a boy, that I was too rational for a girl. It cut me. I was well aware it came from jealousy of a kind and I well knew how irrational I'd been. What he meant was that I could argue him down. And he didn't like it. Or rather he respected the ability, but found it threatening in a woman." Similarly, "[The] young man I was dating [in college], when he discovered I had been nominated for a Woodrow Wilson Fellowship, he had a temper tantrum and said that he didn't want a Madame Curie and that ended that."

Thus the old norms dichotomize women's sexual and intellectual natures and, given this split, women are *accused* of being rational and ambitious rather than commended for it. A literary scholar comments on this general state of things in terms that recall Jane Austen. "My [male] colleagues in graduate school for the most part married women who, had they been men, would have been condemned as dull or boring. And I saw continually the choice of the nonintellectual girl as the wife, and that made me think that men did not like intellectual women."

This comment is sadly borne out in a scene from one marriage, that of a woman who had married early, postponing academic ambitions until her forties when she returned to graduate school. Her husband, not an academic, supported the idea in principle, but was appalled at the intensity of her involvement in her dissertation. "The tremendous spurt of energy I put on to finish the dissertation really terrified him. . . . it's been very hard for him all along to see it as something just natural, that a woman would want work." What is natural for women, according to the marriage plot, is to fulfill their instinctual capacities, to nurture children, to support husbands, to immerse themselves in private concerns. It defies nature for women to project themselves through their intellectual energy into the public world of ideas.

The ranking by the old norms of women's sexual/domestic role over any intellectual/public one means that women's intellectual ambitions and endeavors are often not taken seriously—at least, to the extent that the old norms have effect. And the breadth of that effect is perhaps best illustrated by the fact that women's seriousness is frequently doubted even by their professors. These figures are the putative guides of a liberating quest and yet, from them too, women receive the message, in various forms, that their true destiny is marriage, not intellectual work.

Some of the messages from professors are direct:

"What's a pretty girl like you doing in the library studying political science?" (Professor)

"What do you want to go to graduate school for? You're just going to get married and pregnant." (Undergraduate adviser)

"You're not going to get married, are you?" (Dissertation director, when asked for a reference)

"You should get out of this profession, a girl like you who is so kind and sweet and loving, get married, get a husband . . . because I really like you and all my exstudents who have gone on professionally have gotten divorced and are really unhappy." (Dissertation director with whom the woman in question had just co-edited a book)

And, of course, many women receive the same message indirectly through sexual harassment in its multitudinous and well-documented forms,[12] and also through subtle harassments of the spirit—unexpressed but still-apparent doubts about women's seriousness. A tenured professor of English recalls such an incident from graduate school days, at a West Coast university in the 1950s. She had won a fellowship for study abroad, but to take it meant she would miss her final exams. This problem was solved by her department chairman who personally organized alternate arrangements for the exams. Though grateful, the young woman in question was nevertheless disconcerted by the chairman's attitude. "In the context of this, two things came out. One of them was that at some level he felt it a duty to society—no woman was going to finish her degree but he was doing his job. . . . he really wanted to do the right thing, even by a woman graduate student. . . . it's the *even* I felt."

If the marriage plot raises warnings about the incompatibility of intellectual prowess and women's sexual destiny, it warns also of other dangers to the best fulfillment of that destiny. Identifying women's instinctual capacities as of primary importance, the plot requires that these instincts be controlled, channeled toward positive expression within the domestic sphere. The medium of control is virtue, and the necessary virtues are clearly defined in the old norms. The virtuous woman is patient, accommodating, receptive, peace-keeping, modest, nonaggressive, unselfish, and, of course, chaste. Exemplars of these virtues abound in literature—patient Penelope, patient Griselda, Caesar's wife above reproach, Esther Summerson. And literature depicts also the terrible examples of women who do not practice these prescribed virtues. These are women in whom the passions of an essentially sexual nature have run amok—the seductress Delilah or the murderous Salome. The opposite of the virtuous woman passively accepting a subordinate role is the diabolical woman—Eve with the face of a serpent. And Pandora, whose Eve-like curiosity overthrew an edict from Jupiter, loosed all the troubles of the world from a box (itself a sexual symbol) that she opened. Thus, a woman, throwing off the constraints of passivity, does not become an active, creative participant in the world's affairs, but a monster.[13]

This sense of women's otherness, of a physicality in women at odds with the scholastic order of the academy and its monastic beginnings, appears vividly in a comment on the opening to women of a previously all-male Jesuit college. One of the first women faculty members at the college, appointed in preparation for the arrival of women students, recalls: "They [the Jesuits] were worried that [the women] were going to clog up the plumbing in the bathrooms because the pipes would be full of hair and the unspeakable things that women possess, and I mean it was just amazing to observe that it was like having a new kind of animal in the zoo."[14]

In complex ways, then, the old norms contained in the marriage plot conflict with the requirements of the quest plot whether the quest is for academic or other professional attainment. The quest, classically, is a journey, actual or allegorical. In it the protagonist sets forth to find something that is missing and, in many cases, needed by the whole society for its deliverance or continued well-being. The quest as it has come down to us in its legendary form is undertaken predominantly by male figures, of whom such famous examples as Roland, Jason, and El Cid come to mind. The quest is adventurous, even dangerous, and the emphasis upon its physical exploits has characterized it as active and male, and, indeed, its heroes are frequently military.

Applied to the modern professions, the quest may be less conventionally heroic, less physical, but still it entails active, forceful service to the society. As with allegorical quests, professional service generally requires exacting training of the intellect, an apprenticeship, and then the performance of difficult tasks calling for the intelligent use of initiative, stamina, determination, resourcefulness, integrity, and, often, creativity. The performers of these tasks—Albert Einstein, Jonas Salk, John Dewey, Alfred North Whitehead, Franklin Roosevelt, Andrew Carnegie, Albert Camus, Thomas Edison—are our modern heroes. And, like the heroes of an earlier age, they are, for the most part, men.

The woman hero, under the old norms, is a contradiction in terms—or, like Joan of Arc, both an exception and a masculinized woman. The adage that "Men do, and women are," which suggests that the essential part of a woman's nature is stasis, countermands the imaginative projection of a feminine hero.[15] Like Venus, even when heroines are writ large, their scenario is generally playful or languorous. In short, the old norms define excellence for men as residing in action, whereas women's excellence is to be "far above rubies," to be chaste, and then to be faithful. Thus an individual questing role is compromised at the outset by women's collective assignment to be passively supportive. And yet, to move into the professions, to participate in the modern quest for important service, a woman must practice the *heroic* virtues, not the heroine's—take initiative, take action, effect change for the better. How can she do this?

Or rather, the question is, How can women achieve a professional persona, marked by self-possession and a serious public voice, as a *normal* rather than an exceptional choice? As we discussed earlier, it has long been possible for women to enter the professions as exceptions, which meant, in effect, following the Joan of Arc model—accepting the incompatibility decreed by the old norms between womanliness and professionalism and relinquishing claims to womanliness. Like Amelia Earhart, or, somewhat more ambiguously, Katherine Hepburn.[16] What we now see professional women struggling to do is to renounce the mind/body dichotomy of the marriage plot—and with it, the correlative assumptions of an essentially instinctual nature in women and lack of capacity for intellectual pursuit.

This effort to renounce conventional limitations on women's professional potential is reflected in the remarks of our interviewees about appealing figures in their formative years. One woman, for example, spoke of her high school English teacher as someone whose life held promise of interest and scope. "She was a bit glamorous in my view, she was haggard and slender, my mother was fat and gray. She was sophisticated, she wore bright nail polish and bright lipstick and she went to Radcliffe and I think she wanted me to go to Radcliffe. . . . She lived with a sister of hers and I think I liked the image, the image of the possibility of being single." This is an image of sexual and intellectual vitality combined in one life, not only beyond domesticity, but beyond the"spinster schoolteacher" stereotype. It is an image of an exciting and "glamorous" role to be played, the prefiguring of a heroine who will be active.

In a similar vein, with similar emphasis on the *combination* of sexuality and intellectual activity, a psychology professor recalls a college teacher of hers: "Sister N.D. was wonderful, a person of incredible integrity, and it didn't make the slightest bit of difference to me that she was a nun. Or that she was married or not married. Her life made sense to me. She was [involved in] starting the civil rights movement in Boston, she was picketing, she was getting a Ph.D. in sociology from Harvard, she had total respect. She was the most feminine nun you'd ever want to meet . . . this tiny little lady who wore Sister of Notre Dame skirts and they flowed behind her like a graceful lady in a castle . . ."

Or, to turn to literary models, we find comments like this: "I really had no models other than Nancy Drew. I had Betsy, in the Betsy books, second and third grade, and she was dynamite. She was the leader of her little group and she was very inventive and imaginative. And then when I got tired of Betsy I had Nancy Drew. She had a roadster. And she had a boyfriend but that didn't stop her." A roadster *and* a boyfriend. And having a boyfriend "didn't stop her."[17]

But in spite of their best hopes and efforts, women are frequently fated to carry on quests while practicing, to some degree, the virtues bequeathed by the old norms—the virtues that functioned in the old order to reinforce for women their centuries-old supportive role. These are, in modern terms, the virtues of "the good girl" and their common quality is passivity. To play their traditional role, women must be reactive, not active. They must maintain an open and flexible frame of mind, ready to respond to needs as they arise. The good girl is not a strategist, but much more narrowly a tactician. And, needless to say, the virtues necessary to a subordinate role are often ill-fitting to an autonomous one.[18]

Conforming to the norm of the good girl, one junior faculty member risked—and lost—reappointment to a desirable faculty position. "It had seemed as if my husband and I were moving to New York . . . and I had to tell my department when it was going to be, so they could appoint someone else. In those days I was tremendously nice and considerate, . . . and so, come May 1, I said, 'All right, I'm leaving.' And then . . . the university in New York told my husband that they weren't offering him the job after all." But her job was gone.

Another woman, tenured and with much experience in team research, speaks of the continuing inhibition she feels in initiating and seeking funds for work of her own. "I don't somehow really have problems being confident enough and sitting down doing the work that is involved . . . but to put a paper together and send it off, in fact I've never sent a paper off cold. . . . Applying for a grant of my own . . . I've never been able to do.

I've used faculty grants at the university, but never applied for outside funding."

Instructed by the marriage plot not to press an advantage (aggressive), not to have private priorities (selfish, perhaps the most formidable accusation in the battery of charges carried in the old norms), women take on staggering burdens. "I think one of the things that fed into my anger was that I was so docile about accepting difficult conditions of apprenticeship. I did the commuting. I moved six times in thirteen years to accept teaching appointments."

They make few demands. "When I did get into graduate school I was thrilled and I asked for financial assistance mainly because I knew I would need child care and they only offered me a small amount. I was incredibly grateful for it, much more so than I should have been."

They lie low. "I think a lot of the women [at Yale] thought that if they were nice, nothing would happen. We had a women's faculty group and a lot of people were afraid to come to it."

And they are treated badly. "I was bounced around from lab to lab [as a graduate student], sent to work with somebody who was totally incompetent. I think the man had had a stroke and couldn't do any new work, and ended up pathetically sending articles around to journals and they were always rejected. . . . It was very sad but four women [assigned to his lab] were made to pay for it."

The transference from the personal to the professional realm of an expectation of support and service from the "good girl" is clearly contained in the following comment from a woman serving as a department head: "The university hired a new associate dean, who was in the midst of a problematic divorce. He was a very nice person—I liked him a lot, but I was just keeping ahead of my work and my child's illness. And that January, after [my daughter's] operation the dean called me in . . . and said, 'You know, [the new man] is very upset you haven't asked him out to lunch.' And I said, 'Wait a second . . . you know I've been incredibly torn this semester.' And the dean, who is my friend, said, 'Well, look, he is going through this terrible divorce, his wife won't even take his pants to the laundry and he needs a lot of support.' I had a six-month-old who had just had major skull surgery!"

Of course, not all academic women are "good girls." Many try assiduously to avoid that constriction and enjoin their students to do likewise. As one young woman said: "I'm being a good role model for the girls. . . .

I walk in there with my miniskirts. . . . I guess [I've made] the assumption that those girls needed some role models, intellectual women who were also sexual, which had been an issue for me, and I think it was true." And similarly, from an older woman: "I am their role model, and I give them a lot of good advice and they come to me a lot. Their environment is saying, be good and stay still and I'm saying, be loud and make waves and do what you want and be free. . . . All my life I've been swimming upstream."

This is the point of tension—the conflict between old and new norms—that we seek to hold in focus and examine throughout the book because it is the central tension running through the stories we have collected. Caught between two sets of rules, women cannot avoid running afoul of one of them. If they seek to practice a profession by following the rules and habits long established by its male practitioners—competition, aggression—they offend the old conventions defining womanly virtue. But if women behave in a professional milieu according to the old female norms, if they are patient, deferential, accommodating, smiling, soft-spoken, they appear weak. Consequently, they are likely to be regarded as not serious in their commitment to work, or incapable of exerting the necessary authority. In short, the dilemma of the professional woman is that she cannot easily fit either conventional mold—not the ancient mold of womanliness, not the prevailing male mold of professionalism.

And, indeed, commentary from women about not fitting in runs as a leitmotif through story after story. Across wide variations in background and experience, and regardless of their success or lack of it in the profession, women describe themselves at different points in their careers as "not plugged in," "swimming upstream," "the only one," "an odd addition," "a fifth wheel," "weird," "an oddball," "out of step," "an anomaly," "a freak," "leading this double life." Or describing something they tried to do, they will say, "It didn't fit any existing scheme of things," or "It was not easy to assess exactly what my status was," or "Nothing fit together." Or as one woman said, half laughing, half despairing, of her attempts to fit in, "I had revised my vita so often for so many different jobs, I was losing track of who I was."

Still, not fitting in, for many women, is by no means a wholly negative or destructive experience. Especially taken together, the stories of academic women show the tensions that mark their lives to be sources of creative change. Often women do not "fit in" because, in a variety of small ways, they are attempting to fashion new roles and identities, and thereby to create new norms for themselves and for their work.

Specifically, the stories show women trying to retain values from domestic and private roles and to add to them a sense of identity that connects them more broadly to the society at large. If the marriage plot decrees that women practice patient accommodation to the will of male authorities, it also gives women practice in the accommodative techniques of flexible negotiation, which can be useful and creative social tools.[19] And if the old norms define one of woman's proper goals as the perfection of her moral nature, they also affirm a human morality and reinforce a woman's sense that humane values should be central to life— public as well as private.

Combining old and new identities, women are trying to design a life that rejects the old conventional division of private and public identities. That is, women entering the professions seek a transformation of the self—the female self—as it has been defined restrictively for centuries, and they seek a greater integration between private and public selves. Further, they seek it through their effort to reshape the norms and values that currently define professional life. Thus, as stated earlier, the entry of women into the professions in ever-increasing numbers has truly revolutionary implications, because women seek not only to enter but also to change the nature of professional work.

And yet this is not to say that revolutionary change is actually under way. Women are not rising up as an army arrayed against professional authorities uniformed in pin-striped suits, corduroy jackets, lab coats, and clerical collars. In fact, very few women entering professional life hold a vision of themselves as agents of significant historical change, with a clear agenda for changed professional practice. Most follow individual inclinations and personal agendas and they regard them as such.

But seen as a whole—the hundreds of small choices made by one woman added to the hundreds made by many others—women's lives express desire for change, an end to the tyranny of the old plots, marriage *or* quest, which leave both women and men incomplete and their society unbalanced.

Chapter 2

Transformation

To be a female human being trying to fulfill traditional
female functions in traditional ways is in direct conflict with
the subversive function of the imagination.
Adrienne Rich, *On Lies, Secrets and Silence*

The process of becoming a professional—focusing a professional ambition and acquiring the requisite training and credentials—produces, for most women, the first substantial friction between marriage and quest plots. And this is true because professionalization for women entails a double agenda. First, like their male peers entering a profession, women must undergo a process of change from lay person to expert. They must learn their trade through study and experience, acquire the credits, the degrees attesting to their knowledge, and amass a resumé of recommendations and other proofs of accomplishment. But for women, there is a second necessary process, which is to undergo change—in varying measure depending on the individual—from a passive to an active persona, from a supportive role player to a central character, a person prepared for autonomy.

We call the second element of change a process of transformation—that is, an intellectual and emotional process whereby women acquire a new identity, transcending the limitations of the identity defined by the old norms. The problem for women is that the two processes—professionalization and transformation—can make different and conflicting demands, most pointedly at the stage of graduate school when serious professional study begins.

But even before this stage (which we discuss in detail presently) the transformational process is in motion. It has to be in order to prepare the way for professionalization to begin at all, because the norms of the marriage plot restrict a woman's sense of what she can be; these inner restrictions need to be replaced with an inner breadth of identity before she can claim professional authority. Therefore, unlike men, women must now engage in a considerable amount of activity—both physical and psychological—to move past the restrictions of the old norms before they can even formulate a professional future for themselves. And this activity may impede a woman's quest for a profession, often by occupying a considerable amount of time, sometimes by creating an impression of nonseriousness at odds with the requirements of professionalism.

Of course, the degree of necessary inner change differs in different women. Some can move quickly out of the snares of the marriage plot (which, as noted in chapter 1, does not necessarily mean eschewing marriage) and into a professional quest where the main snares are external—the prejudices of others, a bad economy, bad luck. But for most women, even those who have come of age with the women's movement in full force, the conflict of marriage and quest plots is still large enough to require a serious transformational effort.

The earliest stage of transformation we call breaking the mold—a phenomenon that occurs in many forms and at different points in different women's lives. Common to all forms, however, is an inner determination not to be limited by old expectations. Most often, the initial sense of determination goes no further than a rejection of limits and does not include a specifically formulated ambition. But from somewhere—although the interviews do not necessarily reveal from where—a rejection of the given mold begins.[1]

In some instances, stories trace the rejection back to childhood. An English professor recalls, "When I was young everybody said . . . 'Are you going to be married or are you going to have a career?' . . . My mother says my reply when I was about this high [she reaches down almost to the floor] was, 'I'm going to be married but I'm not going to do housework.' [She laughs.] Later I wanted to have children, but no husband."

For others an early rejection of the marriage plot is more unconscious. Speaking of her adolescence when her intellectual interests and gifts made her feel like "a fish out of water to some extent," a Romance languages scholar suddenly remembers "one tiny incident" which showed that even as a young girl she was not following the conventional plot. "Once I went with a friend of mine out to an athletics track. Her father was an athletics coach, and we discovered these two boys—we were about fourteen years old, and . . . the boys suggested that we play tag, you know, some kind of chase game. . . . Well, it turned out that I ran faster than these boys, they could never catch me. And my friend was constantly getting caught, and I said to her afterward, 'You can run faster than the boys,' and she said, 'You don't understand that game.' [She laughs.]. . . I did not understand the game at *all!*" But probably she did not misunderstand the game; more likely, she knew instinctively she did not want to play it. Letting yourself be caught when you can avoid it is an acceptance of a subordinate place and such an acceptance is the primary marriage-plot prescription for women—which the narrator here was reacting against, however unconsciously.

Other scholars, as young girls, looked around and decided deliberately that they would not accept for themselves the role they saw their mothers and most other women playing. "I considered [the conventional life of a woman] normal behavior, except I decided I wasn't going to be normal. I was just going to get more out of things than other people. . . . I just didn't want to be bored. . . . I get bored very easily and I just couldn't stand living a life like my mother's [marriage and clerical work] where she was very good at keeping herself occupied. I don't have the inner resources and strength not to go out of my mind out of sheer, total boredom if I don't have anything that just sort of totally grips me and requires everything I can give." Or, more gently, "I always had a sense of wanting to *do* something, wanting interesting work . . . female domesticity struck me from the start as not particularly interesting, although there's no question that I found it personally very satisfying. But as a child growing up, I was interested in the world outside the house. . . . It looked to me as if men led more interesting lives." In fact, it is often the constriction of the mother's life and the mother's frustration, even depression, that spark a young girl's rejection, not of marriage, but of the marriage plot. She does not want to accept for herself that secondary, nonauthoritative role.

Rejecting the mold, however, is only the first stage of a transformational journey. Although crucial, it constitutes little more than a decision to begin, and at that it is a decision that a woman may have to make again and again as it is questioned, by herself as well as by others, during her coming of age. The next stage in women's progression toward a transformed identity is the actual setting out on a quest. And here a direct conflict between transformation and professionalization sets in for many women because, for many, the quest is still not fully defined. Rather, it consists of both an unwillingness to accept old roles and a search for a new meaningful role, but with only generalized conceptions as to what that role might be. What occurs at this stage, until the new role takes shape, is a period of veering and tacking. This is a series of moves that serve several different purposes at once. The overall purpose, as stated, is to define a satisfactory work role, but additionally, women at this stage may be engaged in continued resistance against marriage-plot claims, continued efforts to reject and break out of the conventional mold and to leave room for something new even before the new is fully defined. And because the purposes are varied, the moves are marked by hesitations, shifts in direction, false starts.

Of course, some women resolve these difficulties and find a clear direction early, especially those who adopt for themselves, with little discomfort, an established professional mode—like the biologist who says: "I wanted something which is in the mainline, where one has job security and things like that, and I even thought about it in those days [in graduate school in the 1960s] when there was so much money [for the sciences]. . . . I always knew that I wanted something regular, and real, and with all the union cards that you need and so on. Just the way it was supposed to be. I didn't want to be on the fringe and I didn't want to be a guest somewhere. I wanted to be in the mainline."

More typical, however, is a striking tentativeness in women's stories about the early stages of their careers. Frequently they preface sentences with phrases like "I sensed that . . ."; "I just thought it would be fun to . . ."; "I don't know why . . ."; "I drifted. . . ." Or they describe moves occurring "accidentally," "coincidentally," and "informally." One woman begins graduate school and then spends two years teaching at the American College in Turkey. Another takes a series of nonacademic jobs in different cities. Still another starts a master's degree as a tentative probing—and ultimately wasteful professional step—toward an academic future. Many shift and change from one field of study to another, without apparent planning toward a professional goal.

And these moves create problems for women at later stages of professionalization because they create an impression of frivolity. A woman following such a pattern ends up with a resumé that seems to portray a dilettante or someone who is not serious. But what is left out in such a perception, and what must be read into women's experience for the reading to be fair, is the barrier of the old norms, their continued power and the amount of time and energy it takes to surmount them. In short, what is left out in a reading of most women's experience is recognition of the fact that a transformational process is—of necessity—taking place.

The most common form of veering and tacking in our stories is a shaking loose from the conventional mold through a literal journey—"a flight from origins" as one woman called it. This moving out of confinement is what Kate Chopin's story "The Joy That Kills" relates explicitly. The heroine, confined (literally to her house) by an overprotective doctor and a possessive husband, declares upon news of her husband's death, "I'll go to the Sphinx, the Taj Mahal, Niagara Falls," and dies of a heart attack when his death turns out to be a rumor and he is restored to her.

For academic women, the confinement may be a cultural setting in which the orthodoxies of the marriage plot are especially strong. For example, we have many flights from rural areas, small cities or towns, either to large eastern cities or further, to a foreign country. One woman, now a tenured historian, says of her flight from the midwestern state in which she grew up, "[My parents] thought I should be like . . . the valedictorian and salutatorian of my class and both of them were good students at the state university and they went into high school teaching and married each other. It was . . . socially responsible and girls didn't do anything else." Also, her parents did not want her to go east to college and would pay her tuition only for a midwestern school. (Recall the woman from New York whose parents sent her to the Midwest to college precisely to surround her with a stronger version of the old norms than that prevailing in most eastern schools.)

Presumably safely ensconced in her state university, the future historian began her journeying first by studying languages. "I just liked studying languages. Anything that wasn't like where I grew up was wonderful, so I took German and French." Then she went to Germany for her junior year, spending the following summer in the Middle East. "I felt I had to lift off to get out," she said. After college she saved money working as a waitress in order to travel further. "I hitchhiked around the world for a year and a half," then, deciding to go to graduate school, "I cabled my acceptance to Columbia from Afghanistan." She had considered, during her travels, being a *National Geographic* photographer, or going into Middle Eastern studies, but ultimately settled on European history. Needless to say, her parents firmly opposed all of these choices and moves, including graduate school—still preferring conventional paths.

Looking back on her own experience and that of her two sisters, the historian said, "When you grow up in the Midwest . . . the horror of living there was so great that it propelled all three of us to get out. . . . We saw freedom as being out. One sister went to Hawaii, one is in California, and I'm here [at an eastern university] and half the time in Europe."

Of course, men as well as women have always rebelled against their parents and left the provinciality of small towns or agrarian regions in order to find room for some part of themselves that did not fit their environment. But, again, the press of an environment where the conventional rules of the marriage plot prevail strongly is particularly tight and restrictive for women, leaving no room for quests of any serious kind. That is, academic women who have fled from provinciality do not fall within the tradition of the sensitive artist, the painter or poet who must escape convention in order to create, or even the ambitious young man who seeks scope for large-scale activities. These women, for the most part, seek *normal* professional lives, but, unlike their male peers, they cannot find such lives where the ruling norms work strongly against a professional persona for women.

Frequently, women's flights from their origins occur not only through travel but also through imaginative projection into another culture. They travel in time to other centuries, becoming students of medieval literature or Renaissance history or pre-Columbian art. And they acquire an astonishing array of languages. "I learned," different voices say, "Portuguese, Spanish, German, Italian, Russian, Egyptian, Turkish, Hebrew, Aramaic, Celtic, Old English, Old Norse, Old Dutch, medieval Latin."

In their various travels, women move intellectually as well as literally to places that seem hospitable to the identity they are seeking. A graduate student in European intellectual history found herself drawn to Europe as early as her high school years when she went to Sweden on a student exchange. "Having come out of a situation that seemed like an absolute trap, a horrible trap . . . I was miserable in high school . . . Sweden was a rescue. . . . There was an element of snobbery in it too, but I think it was more a sense of not having been okay for such a long time, or not having *felt* okay for such a long time, that just to be in a different cultural context was exciting. . . . The intellectuality of it . . . the concerts, the music, the history . . . the nice inner cities where you could walk around, and cafés . . . this was important for making me feel okay about my own tastes and preferences and predilections . . . I think my experience of it was American culture was not kind to me, America was not kind to me. Europe was. And there was a general affirmation over there of things I was interested in that I felt I had been, not only unrewarded for being interested in here . . . [but] put down for. . . . So it felt like there was, there was a place and a connection that I had made that made me feel all right."

But although identification with European cultures may be liberating for Americans, the confinement of European social orthodoxies in turn sends questing women from those cultures to the greater openness of the United States. For example, an Englishwoman on the humanities faculty of an American university recounted spending her college years at Cambridge University in England unable to study the subject she wanted—art history—because it was not part of the traditional curriculum. Afterward she took a British civil-service job that was generally highly prized but that bored her. On leave from her job, she spent a year studying medieval art on her own in France, then traveled to Italy where she met an American, whom she married. Returning with him to the United States, she earned her doctorate at Harvard, in the field of her interest, and went on to a satisfying career. Still, she had no clear career strategy when she left her civil-service job and moved around Europe to America. She was veering and tacking, but also questing—looking for some form of work into which her talent and ambition would fit. Luckily, she found it.

Breaking the mold that prevents a woman's quest may not be as overtly dramatic as hitchhiking around the world or literal expatriation, and yet it involves great internal drama. We said earlier of the woman whose parents had sent her to the Midwest to college, that she, too, ultimately completed an Ivy League doctorate and gained a tenured university position. But she did not do it quickly or painlessly. Throughout the process she had to move against her parents' strong belief that such a path made no sense for a woman—and against her own internalization of this belief.

The conflict she felt produced a crisis when she successfully finished her first year at graduate school and was officially selected from a large group of master's candidates into the small group allowed to pursue the Ph.D. It continued until the time of her general exams, the last step in the doctoral process before writing a dissertation. "I was terrified of the exams, but I took them and passed. To do so required my seeking counseling. I really thought I . . . was going to fail, it was terrible. At the same time, I didn't feel that it was anything negative about my professors because they had been extremely supportive. . . . I think my own problems were emotional and social rather than intellectual. I think that was the point when I was making the real break with my family. They had thought getting a master's was fine. . . . Getting a Ph.D. was . . . making a break with what every woman in my family had done, and I was terribly scared. Later, I became very highly politicized and I was outraged with the system . . . and [my parents] thought I should get married, they hated [X University]." Her family correctly recognized that the Ph.D. was a radical reordering of their priorities. A master's degree is a useful tool for a teaching job, mainly in high schools. But a Ph.D. represents a decisive step into an authoritative professional role—and out of the normal role for women contained in the marriage plot.

The pressure of the old norms, and therefore the energy required to combat them so that further transformation can occur, is particularly great where conservative religious values prevail. The family in the story just told is Jewish and reflects a strong cultural tradition of private and supportive roles for women. Similarly, in Catholic families, women must often go to considerable lengths to break the hold of the marriage plot before they can move professionally. One such woman, having become highly engaged intellectually at a Catholic college in New York, found herself stymied at the time of graduation by the conventional choices open to her. She did not want to take education courses and teach. "This was something that none of us would be caught dreaming of doing. How silly, you know, to learn to cut paper and paste pictures. . . . this was really far beneath us!" Although deeply serious about religion, she did not want to become a nun. "I mean, there was nothing at all, never any part of me that *ever* wanted to be a nun, in any way." The other option was marriage. "I had been going with someone for many years, whom I didn't particularly love . . . and I was about to drift into marriage, which is what somebody like me did, and thank God . . . I literally backed out of that path at the very last minute, and through some great grace . . . some saving act because it would have been suicide. That was not a conscious act. That was leaping out, at the last minute, of the third floor window . . . because that's where I was drifting." What she did do was to join a newly invigorated Catholic lay community devoted to prayer and to social action. Of this move, she said, "I simply leapt into a situation that continued my commitment to radical, intellectual, new spirituality Catholicism, on the one hand, and on the other hand, broke absolutely, totally with my whole past." There is little literal action here, but the figurative action is dramatic—"leaping out of a third floor window," and narrowly, miraculously, escaping "suicide."

Another future scholar, while attending a Catholic women's college in the Midwest, broke with the conventions of her peers by boarding a shuttle bus to a nearby men's Catholic college. She had pursued a double major, itself reflecting the play of both marriage and quest plots in her mind. One major was literature, the subject of her eventual quest, and the other was library science, training for a career in keeping with the old norms. She went to the men's college for literature courses, thereby widening the distance between herself and the women students unconcernedly following conventional norms. "I think I was seen as sort of an oddball . . . because I was doing these independent studies and dashing off to this other college. . . . Not everyone was getting on the shuttle bus and going back and forth at that time. . . . My colleagues, especially in the library science department . . . were engaged, eyeing a library position, and were fairly organized, and I was kind of off into a corner with my graduate school plans and . . . I was a little out of step with everyone else."

The religious reinforcement of the marriage plot, and the corresponding difficulty of the transformational process, are also strong in fundamentalist Protestant families, as the following story from a woman entering college in the late 1960s testifies. "I grew up [in the Midwest] in a very fundamentalist family, and I was not allowed to dance, or go to parties, or certain things, so I was a weirdo from the word go. I was not involved socially . . . I didn't play cards, I didn't think dirty thoughts. [Laughs.] *Everything* was kept from me." As for college, her father assumed she would live at home and attend a two-year junior college in the next town. But she rejected the "very confining, very restrictive" small town, fundamentalist world—"I would just not stay in that town, I wanted to get as far away. . . ." As is true of many others, her breaking of the mold began with foreign travel—to Turkey, in an American Field Service program for high school students.

"Being a big, Scandinavian blonde, Methodist kid from a tiny little town in the Midwest, and all of a sudden finding myself in a Moslem family across the world was a real eye-opener. And that experience . . . taught me a lot about the relativity of human values and religions and everything, and consequently I think my senior year in high school was the most unhappy period of my life. I did not want to come back."

The direct result of this experience was a decision by the young woman to attend the state university where other Field Service students were going. Her parents acquiesced but then became upset when, once at the university, she stopped attending church. "My father at one point said . . . if I didn't start going to church . . . he was going to cut off the money for my tuition." Whereupon she broke the model of the fundamentalist marriage plot completely, if paradoxically, through marrying, at the age of twenty, a nonreligious young man from her home town who had already, through graduate school and college teaching, broken free of its general cultural limits. She describes her feeling at that time as consciously rebellious. "I'm leaving this town, I'm leaving this religion, I'm leaving this whole world and I'm going off on this path, with an agnostic. So there!"[2]

Often it is the question of marriage itself that precipitates a series of veering and tacking moves as a woman tries to decide whether to marry at all or what the terms of a marriage might be in relation to the quest she has begun. In the confusion that these questions necessarily produce, one principle is clear: if a woman is to leave room for a serious quest, her marriage cannot accord with the conventions of the marriage plot. That is, it cannot be all encompassing and always primary.

A young language scholar, beginning her teaching career at a prestigious university in the 1970s, solved the marriage problem at first—as many women in her generation were doing—by living with the man she loved but not marrying him. Under pressure from both sets of parents and several older faculty members, she then did marry—although in a deliberately casual fashion that signaled her refusal to accept the conventional conception of wifehood. In yet a further rejection of the norm, she said, "I didn't tell a lot of people for a long time because I was so embarrassed that I had succumbed to what I considered bourgeois conventions."[3] Other women accept the marriage plot fully until unhappiness with their role precipitates some kind of rejection. "It was an incredible relief to realize it was okay to be unhappy with being a housewife. And to sort of acknowledge that there was a way in which I had always thought of myself as an intellectual and that it was very peculiar even to be trying to force myself into this role that was really foreign to me."

For academic women, a quest for meaningful work leads eventually, after journeyings and experiments, to graduate school and to the most intense phase of the transformational process. At this point, women begin to acquire the knowledge and methodology of an academic discipline through courses, seminars, wide reading, the close study of texts, research, and writing. In the process they gain professional competence in the use of particular materials and methods as tools of understanding and inquiry—tools with which they can add to the knowledge of the discipline through research, and can teach that knowledge to others. But women, moving out of the marriage plot and into the quest plot in the academic profession, engage in study for purposes that go beyond intellectual development and the acquisition of professional skills. Internalizing the great ideas of a discipline, making them part of their own thought and values, women characteristically use their learning as a tool of personal empowerment. Their education is serving the purposes both of professionalization and of transforming identity.

The transformational aspect of learning, which is nothing less than the building of a new identity, is deeply gripping for women—a fact clear in their descriptions of initial encounters with moving ideas. A classics scholar speaks of a professor as having virtually brought her, and others, to life. "He was a superb teacher. He didn't affect just me this way. . . . people who'd been just kind of limply sitting in classrooms for years suddenly had blood flowing in their veins, and their faces lit up, and they started to say interesting things and write interesting papers. . . . And, I've never been the same since, thank God." And the words of another, about a different teacher, a different institution, time, and location, convey the same ring of excitement. "One could get lost, in a sense, in other people's ideas, in the whole tradition of human thinking. . . . there was one teacher in particular who was so good that she opened doors, she made you feel as if you were opening doors yourself, and seeing things, and putting things together. And it was so wonderful, it was astonishing. . . . that I just wanted to keep doing that."

But the transformational process, however vital, is also confusing for the woman becoming a professional in academe because it obscures her perception of the external requirements of the profession. First, it is difficult to regard learning simultaneously as personally enlivening and empowering and also as a stock-in-trade to be used impersonally for scholarly ends determined by the going practice within a discipline. Second, intense absorption in inner change tends to becloud the importance of other professional requirements, including the acquisition of external, visible credentials bestowed by institutional authorities—prizes, grants, fellowships, published articles, and recommendations from respected professors. Also important is the acquisition of knowledge about the informal working of the profession, such as the usefulness of wide networks of acquaintances among both professors and peers. Paradoxically, therefore, the very success of the educational process in drawing a woman into the realm of ideas militates against the process of her professionalization insofar as the power of ideas diverts her attention from needed external credentials.

Of course, this dichotomy of purpose can afflict male graduate students as well, but—as always for women—the pressure of the old norms is omnipresent, and it heightens the intensity of women's engagement in internal change and, conversely, their distraction from external practicalities.

Women may, for example, enter academe in the first place and choose a particular field of study following interior promptings alone, without ever asking themselves practical questions about the shaping of a career in their chosen fields. As one woman put it: "I drifted toward academe simply by figuring that the things that were intellectually exciting to me would be what I would do, which in fact doesn't necessarily follow in terms of a career, but that is the way I got into it. I loved poetry, analyzing poetry, and I tried my hand at writing poetry and indeed, I drifted into the sixteenth century, which I think was a terrible mistake, really because I like Shakespeare."

But even after a considered choice of field is made, and the significant endeavor found, the transformational process still generates a confusion of worlds; a constant skirmishing continues between professional practicalities and intellectual engagement. This is a stage of transformation we call loving not wisely—a period marked by women's virtual love relation to the subject matter of their work. That is, our stories show that women—especially in the early stages of their careers, but often much later as well—view the texts and methods of their chosen fields as all but sacred and the proper objects of loving devotion. Frequently they use love language to describe their academic work—not merely the hyperbolic phrases, "I love teaching," or "I love research," though these phrases abound, or even "I fell in love with philosophy," and "stained glass is a new field, extraordinarily a love of my own," but vocabulary borrowed specifically from other love relations.

Thus a woman speaking of her thesis, which she deferred in order to make a financial contribution to her household, muses: "I felt *jealous* of the fact that I'm not in the library or wherever, for myself. I'm on the edge of, I put in so much already, I have all this, it's silly not to bring it to *fruition* and *bring it to birth* . . . into the world." And an interviewee who characterized the initiation of her academic career as a love relation, "English gave me the world of literature. . . . I just simply became enamored of it," concludes her story with the same metaphor, but sadly changed in its eventuality—teaching a management communications course in a business school. Her love for her subject was doubly battered in this job because the course had no literary content and, further, was despised by the business students, primarily concerned with their substantive training. Speaking at the end of the school year, the teacher remarks: "I'm feeling, I think, a kind of *postpartum depression* . . . or a sense that the baby was *stillborn*, that is, it just didn't work. And it never will work, given that situation." And an art historian whose marriage ended in divorce said of her first book, a major study of modern sculpture, "I always thought of that book as my second marriage."

Of course, women hold such intense attitudes with good reason. Are they not leaving behind, through new access to a larger cultural heritage, an identity caricatured as catty, fickle, garrulous, irrational, lightweight—the second sex, as Simone de Beauvoir has termed it? But an intense, loving relation to work has its dangers. A person who is devoted to a subject only for the love of it is an "amateur," in the dictionary definition of the term—"one who cultivates any study or art . . . for personal pleasure . . . instead of for money." A professional academician, on the other hand, is paid for services—teaching, writing—based on the knowledge gained from study. Women graduate students deeply engaged in their subjects of study are thus in some measure both amateurs and professionals, and, inevitably, they encounter the conflicting requirements of two roles.

An art historian draws this distinction explicitly by contrasting her scholarly work, pursued on her own, with that of her husband, an internationally known professor at a prestigious university. She was married while in college, and after college, began her independent form of study. "I immediately proceeded to do with art history what I wanted to do with it and that is to pursue any intellectual questions and any issues about art, any study for its intrinsic worth . . . without thinking at all about a career goal. . . . And at all points in this pursuing it for its *intrinsic* worth, we often joked that I was the family intellectual. My husband was pursuing an academic career and couldn't just do things for intrinsic worth and had to do things that were required of him *by* the profession." She is saying, that is, that the requirements of the profession at some point compromise work pursued out of love, or an internal sense of the worth of a subject. And one of the benefits of not having a conventional career was freedom from this amateur/professional conflict.

Others, however, sharing her loving relation to work, but also preparing for the practice of a career, encounter difficulties. One well-known phenomenon among women—and one that appears in our interviews— is the extremity of their reaction when their work is rejected, an extremity that can prove detrimental to professional advancement. For instance, when an article or a book is rejected, professional wisdom calls for resubmitting the work elsewhere, revised or not, but many women, deeply wounded by the rejection, put the work in question away, sometimes for years, sometimes forever. This phenomenon is often explained as demonstrating women's lack of self-confidence or an indiscriminate, stereotypically feminine emotionalism. We suggest instead—on the basis of our stories—that it should be seen as pain at the rejection of a love child— work that is not simply a product of labor but virtually an extension of the self. And as it is the chosen self, the transformed self that is expressed in written work, rejection strikes at the center of the woman's new and deeply valued identity. Her commitment to that identity, her love relation to its product, vanquishes professional considerations.

In one of our stories, an Arabic scholar, having finished her dissertation, was elated to learn that her department was submitting her work, with strong recommendations for publication and even some money to support it, to the university's press. But when several months passed with no word from the press, she called, only to be told in an offhand way that her work would not be published because there was no market for the Arabic literature she analyzed. The editor she spoke to remarked, again casually, that a book expanding her introductory remarks on the politics of the Near East would be publishable, but not one on literature. It was a stunning reversal of expectations, as well as an infuriating devaluing of the work itself. "And instead of taking it home and sending it to a university press that publishes that stuff, I just took it home . . . never submitted the manuscript again to anybody, never looked at it, never did anything, and that was the end of it. . . . it was a toxicity . . . for me the whole thing stands for an exhausting, maiming sort of thing." Though certainly in this case an especially costly physical and financial toll during the writing period needs to be acknowledged, perhaps the woman's sense of being maimed, or sickened by something toxic, can best be understood by juxtaposing her exuberant feelings on entering graduate school: "I loved Arabian literature, I loved literature, I loved the Near East, I loved Sufi poetry, and I wanted to go on teaching." The love expectation with which she initiated her career is the obverse side of the poison metaphor, the connection between poison and love a familiar one from literature.

A second tale involves another Ph.D. thesis, this one the focus of departmental factionalism—specifically, objections from one thesis committee member. This excerpt demonstrates the same recoil from the created work after its failure to win approval, and the same domination this reaction exerts over other, pragmatic considerations. Additionally, the story discloses the great cost of the struggle not only to the candidate, but also to her female adviser, who was mediating in the department on behalf of the thesis: "I literally couldn't stand to look at it [when it was over]," asserts the candidate. "The day that I passed my thesis defense would have ordinarily been a day of celebration. It was a bit of a tradition that my adviser would have a little party for the dramatis personae, and she had done this for a few of her other students who had been awarded Ph.D.'s. But she said to me in so many words, once I had passed the dissertation defense, 'You know, I just don't have it in me to celebrate. I'm relieved this is over, I'm glad you got your Ph.D.' But it was clear that she really wanted things to be over and done with. And I couldn't blame her. In some ways I felt the same way. I went out to dinner with my husband, who insisted that we have at least a little bit of a celebration, and I got drunk, which is very unlike me . . . because I felt so depressed."

This narrator had achieved her credentials, had successfully completed a long and arduous course of study, but felt "depressed" rather than triumphant, because her thesis, a creation of her transformed identity, had been turned into a political bone. The conduct of her female adviser, somewhat surprisingly, accords with her own; the experience has been contaminated for both of them. And although the professor is older and more practiced, she does not offer advice about the importance of the degree itself and its empowerment—rather, she too would seem to place the reception of the love child above the bestowal of the degree. Furthermore, the recipient of the degree put away her thesis for years, rather than revising it immediately for publication, which is the common and professionally advantageous procedure.

The simultaneous play of amateur and professional purposes also has consequences for both the nature and quantity of scholarship for many women. There is a high price to be paid in the professional world for holding out for "significant" work, for not being satisfied with competence as a criterion for publication, for not taking visibility as a goal. Nevertheless, through a variety of stories about research and publication runs this thread: the interviewee's desire to "make a significant contribution." This means, however, in the competing world of the professions, fewer papers, fewer addresses at meetings, longer-term research, books that occupy an inordinate amount of time, and, as we shall show in a later chapter, books that frequently are maverick—interdisciplinary or out of the mainstream of the discipline. In this way the excitement of transformation lingers on; in this way the amateur's love remains. But in this way too women impede their professional progress by not supplying quickly enough the credentials their institutions require.

Disdain for the pedestrian project, even when such work would be useful for credentialing, appears clearly in the following comment. "I was in the map room of the library yesterday, and there was a man in there talking with the honcho in this room, the director of maps or whatever he is, and this map librarian was saying to this young guy, 'Let me suggest a topic you might be interested in working up. . . . I really think this would be manageable for you, and you'd have no problem seeing this in print.' And the guy took out his little black book, and he wrote down the information. . . . it was something I thought was so boring to listen to, I turned my mind off thirty seconds into this conversation. But can you imagine a woman doing that?" This observer couldn't credit such trivial motivation as a basis for initiating work; it was neither significant, substantial, nor internally directed.

If the obligation, then, is primarily to the demands of the material, certain externally directed practices appear shoddy and self-aggrandizing. Thus, the "going to meetings" or to "the marketplace," almost a sine qua non for practicing professionals, becomes a task distasteful to perform: "Giving papers at the professional meetings, I did that once, it was OK . . . that paper, but it represented to me, it took on a kind of symbolic meaning. It has to do with the fact that you're supposed to get up and sell yourself, by giving a fifteen-minute talk and what can you say of any significance in fifteen minutes?" If we pause briefly at this statement to notice its many false starts, its sentence fragments, we can see in the very form of the answer the conflict it describes.

Other women allude to the same conflict by contrasting their own distaste for the expedient choice along the career path with the choices they see being made by male peers. "The male students in graduate school had the ability to keep on fulfilling the letter of the law in any circumstance until they finally won. Rather than worrying about whether they were making a contribution to scholarship . . . they just simply barreled ahead through the whole thing. And if somebody told them they didn't like the shape of the dissertation or that it shouldn't be done this way, . . . they might change it or just go back home and turn it in all finished. None of that made a difference to them, I think. I think in that way they were different." Another reports on her recognition, also as early as graduate school days, of divergent approaches to their subjects between men and women: "I had to write eleven papers in one semester, all on different things. My sense of commitment was such that I couldn't bear that. I really felt 'If that's what you have to do to be a professional, I don't want to become one.' Now this may be a feminine reaction . . . an unwillingness to make compromises with reality . . . I felt that I was just doing one picky little thing after the next." A third woman, suggesting that men are more calculating, admits about her choice of dissertation director, "He had a fine mind . . . but [was] not the best possible adviser. I picked the most brilliant man I could find in my field instead of somebody that might have been more pragmatic. And perhaps easier."

The experience of art historian Barbara Erlich White (not an interviewee) certainly fits this mode of focusing on significant work and not professional advantage. As an untenured assistant professor, she embarked on a massive study of Renoir in spite of the fact that there was little collected documentation of his work. Her book, *Renoir: His Art, Life and Letters*, took twenty-three years to write and embroiled her in a sex discrimination case when she was denied tenure early in the project for lack of publication. With the book finally out in 1984, she commented, "I'd like to spend another twenty-five years on Renoir. I can see doing this until I'm a real old, old lady."[4]

In sum, appearance—the appearance of being a scholar—is shunned for the reality. A sharp line of demarcation is observed. Women respond to the inner demands of the disciplines more than to the demands of departments and institutions. Their notion that they are answerable to an internal clock does not take account of tenure committees; if, as one academic woman confided, she "wanted to write something that would last," she is pacing herself by eternal time, not by the academic calendar.

Yet, to be professionals, women must use their subject matter for purposes and in ways defined as useful or valuable by their respective disciplines. They must develop, to some extent, a detached relation to the material as a tool for carrying out the social, that is, larger, functions of the academy. And as a practical matter, they must also use the material for their own advancement in the profession—they must demonstrate their prowess in shaping material to professional ends. But often the love relation to the subject matter is so powerful for women that it subverts external professional goals. The governing modality in language and gesture is love, not focused ambition.

Then there is an additional problem, also arising from the transformational experience and the lover's or amateur's stance, and this is the reluctance of many women to place a monetary value on the loved material. Here is a young woman talking about the meager salary she receives as a part-time university teacher, the only post available to her: "The Puritan in me says I'm really very lucky and that they probably shouldn't be paying me any more than they are. . . . if you work it right you can have all this time, this freedom. Freedom of choice of what you do. No one is looking over you. It's a wonderful life, career. And maybe it isn't worth what they're paying me. Yet, when I look at the person who sits across the hall from me and makes three times what I make, doing much less work, seeing fewer students, correcting fewer papers. . . . but I'd do it again, I love it."

And this is not an isolated reaction. Women, knowing the weak job market in academe, continue to pour into graduate schools. A professor notes of a former student: "I know a student right now who just got into the Institute (art history graduate school) and I've given her the bleakest, blackest picture of what she is going to have to go through to actually become an employed person in ten years. She doesn't have any money and she is going to have to borrow right up to her eyeballs to do it; but she really just loves doing it and I think she knows she will live poorly and maybe for a long, long time."

Certainly many women do continue to feel ambivalent about the relation of money and work throughout their careers. And this is particularly true of married women whose salaries are not crucial to the family's welfare. A historian-archaeologist, asked whether her forthcoming archaeology book (now out) will be lucrative, says: "Well, they haven't negotiated that contract yet. I don't have any idea what the returns would be, or what I should ask for, or what is appropriate, or anything. . . . they're going to do it right, they're giving it a beautiful format, and I trust them. I know that editor. Where I fit into this as far as returns are concerned, I mostly see as professional. If there's some money, I'm going to be very grateful."

Perhaps the most interesting, compacted view of the amateur/professional tension in this story is the sentence near the closing of the statement—"Where I fit into this as far as returns are concerned, I mostly see as professional." But is money not a professional return? Why is she dichotomizing money and profession? *Whatever* women's economic status—comfortable or strained—our interviews disclose an ongoing uneasiness when intellectual and financial remuneration impinge on each other. The power of the transformational process to displace, for many women, the mundane considerations of professional practice should not be underestimated.

To sum up, the difficulty we have been tracing here is the contribution of the transformational process to a conflict about professional identity in many women. That is, transformation in itself is a vital, almost magical, process of growth and change. But when this internal change in persona through learning becomes confused with the external change in status through credentialing, trouble ensues. What has been a medium for growth becomes a source of professional difficulty as the lover of learning, or amateur, resists becoming a seller of learning, or professional.

Of course, this is not an insoluble difficulty. With time and experience, women can sort out the conflicting claims of the amateur and the professional and make conscious choices for one or the other. The problem for professional advancement, however, is that during the sorting-out period a woman may seriously jeopardize her professional future by not making the right moves at the right time in what is a tightly structured, temporally directed and highly competitive career setting.

There is also a related problem stemming from the transformational process. The conflict generated by women's engagement in transformational learning on the one hand and professional credentialing on the other contributes in many cases to an appearance of nonseriousness. And this appearance unfortunately reinforces the assumption, widely held by male authorities, that women are not fully serious in the first place. Given this ever-present doubt, what is needed from women is overwhelming evidence of strong professional intent and capabilities. But often, women who are deeply involved in the material of their disciplines do not supply the right evidence, or at least not in recognizable form. Rather they send signals that are misperceived.

Here is a historian recounting a frustrating conversation that she had had with a male historian about her work. She had talked of recent projects with great enthusiasm, which she felt her male interviewer had misinterpreted as flirtatiousness. She speaks here of venting her dismay in a talk with an older woman colleague. "I said to her, 'Doesn't one ever get out of this box of being categorized in a certain way?' And she said, 'No. . . . I think you . . . have to realize that what he was relating to was not your whole persona, this person who was very involved with an idea she was trying to express to him . . . talking in a very dynamic and alive way, as one person to another person. You weren't aware of the fact that he, as a man, is very much more likely to attach a sexual connotation to that kind of dynamic and lively and exciting quality that we feel when we're sharing ideas with one another.' She said, 'What I feel emanating from you is a love of the ideas you're sharing, the students and faculty you're involved with. But it's a love of which sex is only a very small part. And that's the only part he was able to tune in on.' "

Perhaps the clearest evidence of women not being taken seriously—of their strengths not being perceived as such—is the prevailing division of academic labor. Throughout the college and university world, women are allocated primarily to teaching functions, and often low-level teaching functions at that, rather than to the more prestigious writing and creative research functions.[5] This hierarchical ordering is widely justified in the male-dominated academy by invoking the common cultural assumption that women are "natural" teachers, that such positioning agrees with their own preference. This attitude, clearly a remainder of the marriage plot, grounds the "natural" gift for teaching in the "naturally" nurturant qualities that are, supposedly, sui generis in women—and that are irrelevant to the discipline and creativity required in serious research.

Certainly, women often do display outstanding personal devotion to the substance of their own discipline and to the art of teaching itself. But, we suggest, there is an explanation for their behavior that accords far better than the nurturance theory with the evidence of our questing stories. We submit that the lure of teaching for many women is the desire to reinvoke the transformational experience, their own experience of growth and change, for others. It is not, that is, simply an extension of the nonintellectual gifts of mothering transplanted to another, professional, scene, but something far more radical—women invoking change in others.

This answer throws into relief both women's awe of the subject matter, its power for change, and their own powerful impetus to transmit it. "Perhaps it was being in a Catholic college, teaching," ponders a non-Catholic academic, "but the word that crossed my mind was 'mission,' a sense of mission." Or in the words of another academic interviewee, "I have a sense there is some kind of moral commitment that should go with academia." And a professor of Romance language and literature, when asked about a viable future for her graduate students, replied: "Well, I think it is a question, but I think that the world would be done a disservice if people stopped thinking seriously about literature, that's the emphasis I put on it. . . ." Articulating even more specifically a commitment to change through learning, an English professor says of her inner-city university: "[It] has a very diverse student body. It has a lot of adults, it has a lot of returning women, it has a lot of working-class students, people working their way through school. . . . It has a lot of very bright, very uneducated people who are just the kind I love to work with. You can really open up their minds. . . . What more can I ask?"

Another teacher of English states that she herself was drawn to the profession by the powerful impact on her of two outstanding teachers, one in high school, one in college. "I think I had a real motive in that these two teachers had done so much for me. I saw both of them as effecting transformations [her word, not ours] that were almost lifesaving, and hence, being a teacher who could do that for somebody was very attractive. And I certainly saw myself in that role."

Again and again this is the gist: I'm a medium for change. This self-conception imparts a sense of power that redeems many unsatisfactory situations, both in the smaller and larger picture. As the interviewee quoted earlier goes on to say about teaching part-time in a non-tenure-track position: "I would not continue forever doing the kind of part-time teaching I'm doing. I resent it in lots of ways. I do get weary of reading low-level composition work when I'd like to be doing some other things more. But at the same time, I know that I'm an effective writing teacher and still, in a different way than perhaps I thought when I was twenty, I do see myself effecting transformations [again, her word], even in students who have not as much potential perhaps as many freshmen you would encounter." Like the professor who claims she went into philosophy to become "more competent to change the world," these women attest to the ongoing force of their inner revolution.

What these last passages have in common is a highly serious interest in and dedication to the idea of change. Though women as a gender are usually depicted as conservators, guardians of the culture, or, even more reductively, its embellishment, that passive role is in large measure a result of their disenfranchisement, not of their selection. The "excellent women" of novelist Barbara Pym, women who serve worthy community causes, lack opportunity and can project change only through interior fictionalizing. But those women who are professionals want to be practitioners; and we affirm that the seemingly nonserious choices by women, made in the beginning stages of their careers as they veer and tack and then become engaged in amateur/professional conflicts, are, in fact, parts of a highly serious process—the process of transformation—which produces, in the end, a high degree of professional dedication and purpose.

Chapter 3

Rules of the Game

*She never knew whether it was her turn or not, the game
was in such confusion.*
Lewis Carroll, *Alice in Wonderland*

As we have seen, women's entry into the academic profession occurs in part through the workings of a transformational process that makes intense intellectual claims and raises complicated moral questions. Here we look at an extension of these questions as they arise, both in graduate school and throughout women's careers—specifically, the range of issues women typically face in dealing with the institutional structure of academe.

All institutions operate through a set of formal and informal rules. In academe, the rules for entry into the profession are fairly straightforward; they consist of the requirements fashioned by graduate schools for advanced degrees in the various disciplines. The rules for employment and professional advancement, however, are harder to define, varying with the kind of institution, the region, and the times. Further, in all places and times, there are rules emanating from a variety of sources—some decreed by tradition, others by the governing instruments of particular colleges and universities, still others by union contracts that have replaced the older system of professional norms promulgated as desirable standards by the American Association of University Professors.

In addition, in the last three decades, employment patterns and practices in academe have been subject to new rules and practices stemming

41

from governmental policies. Since the late 1950s, when the federal government began to provide significant aid for higher education, the size of various fields and therefore employment opportunities in them have grown or shrunk depending on federal funding. And since the 1960s, the federal government has involved itself in employment practices concerning women and racial minorities by prescribing rules against sex and race discrimination.

To negotiate this maze of rule and custom in the successful building of a career is extraordinarily difficult for all young professionals. That is, men and women alike making their way in academe must run a hazardous course, and few are perfectly adroit at what is, in important part, a political process. But, as we have noted in other contexts, women entering the academic profession encounter the usual range of difficulty and then an extra margin that is unusual, either in degree or in kind.

Women face special problems from the outset because much of the time they are working without essential support. First, and probably most important, they suffer from undercapitalization. And, because learning the institutional rules and putting them into practice is an arduous, time-consuming process, the lack of money to buy time and release energy can be a serious handicap.

The specific reasons for women's financial disadvantage vary, but in general they are traceable to the remaining hold of the marriage plot which categorizes women's professional education as unnecessary—a luxury. One woman says, "It was understood that if there was money for professional school, it would go to [my brother]." For another, the problem was simply her father's belief that graduate school for women was foolish. He thought going to college was "normal" but graduate school was "a waste of time since he didn't feel that I would finish and that I would marry before I finished and that it wasn't a very wise decision."

Graduate school administrators notoriously act on the same principles these parents followed, giving effective priority to young men and awarding fellowships to women mainly in return for teaching. But women who depend on teaching for their support then take on heavy teaching loads because stipends are low, and, as a consequence, have difficulty finding time for their own course work or dissertations. If these women are married and have children, a heavy teaching load is even harder to maintain because it requires child-care expenses—which many schools do not take into account in assessing financial need.

One woman, describing an angry interview with a graduate school dean, vividly evokes the desperation she felt when caught in the tuition—

teaching–baby-sitting bind. "I ranted and raved to him about financial aid, and how all these years, my single colleagues had been getting their noses wiped for them with money, and that I had been, you know, not only paying full tuition, but child-care expenses and never got a penny from the university except for my teaching work, which I considered *my* work, and not their apprenticeship because I had already done a lot of language teaching. And he said to me, 'Well, we have to make some decisions about what things we will support, and what things we won't, and child care is not one of them.' And I said, 'My single colleagues, you know, get their room and board paid, their meals cooked.' Well, he explained that they don't care about your child-care expenses, even though it's as essential if you're married with children as room and board is if you're single. . . . And age is a question. He made it clear that a twenty-six-year-old man or woman, who is single, is a much better investment than a thirty-seven-year-old woman. It just isn't worth it to strain that much, you know, with old women. Okay. I was so angry that for the first time in five years there I burst out crying, which you should *never* do. . . . *never*, never shed a tear if you're a woman. I was *furious* . . . but I cried out of defeat . . . I really was whipped by that point.'"

The problem of support for child care is a continuing sore point for women because, although policies vary from university to university, the assumption often prevails that a married woman whose husband is employed does not need aid. But if there are children, the costs of child care are often higher than one salary can sustain, especially if the woman student buys as much time as she needs—which she frequently does not do.

A sober calculation of the actual time and money required for serious professional preparation appears in a most unusual story in which a woman administrator counsels a woman student about fellowship support. The student, a historian, was returning to graduate school after the birth of two children when she met with the administrator's insistence on calculating the practical as well as intellectual aspects of this step. The returning student should plan to free a substantial amount of time with child care, the older woman said, in order to organize regular contacts with others working in the same field, to attend extra lectures and seminars, and to have time for informal meetings with peers and professors. And this was excellent advice, crucial for overcoming the usual pattern of isolated work on the part of the married women who dart to class and to the library and then home to keep child-care costs down when they are not subsidized. But, as the woman adviser in this story pointed out, the monetary costs of buying time may be far surpassed by the professional costs of isolation, including lost intellectual and informational exchange as well as lost opportunities to build useful networks of acquaintances. The advisee in question, from the vantage point years later of a tenured professorship, declared of the advice she received and had followed, "this was the beginning of the change."

Unfortunately, however, such a change in the fortunes of many women is not possible because the money is not there. And it is not there, in part, because of the remaining power of the marriage plot. Who will endow fellowships or scholarships devoted to the professionalization of women when a strongly prevailing norm defines women's place—even in the workplace—as properly subordinate to men? Women have no business, under this norm, seeking authoritative positions in their own right. If they choose to do so, they can do it on their own. And so they do, but with serious and debilitating consequences—in addition to professional disadvantage.

One such consequence is substantial debt. "That was the main problem . . . the pay for part-time teaching was so low that you had to do so much of it to just break even, and then you had no time left [to work on the dissertation]. . . . I don't know how long I was in that situation, but for a long time. . . . then I started getting into student loans, of which I have $17,000, and I didn't—I was a mess. . . . I feel as if so much energy and money and time and everything else has gone down this hole. . . . I don't know how to invest in it further. . . . You know, for instance . . . people are always asking, is this dissertation going to be a book. Well, I don't know how it can be a book—I have $17,000 worth of loans to pay back now. . . . Should I spend another two years, three, or whatever it takes to get this into book shape, meanwhile doing what?"

And then there is exhaustion, a word that recurs frequently in the interviews. "I was teaching two freshman sections while I was taking courses for the master's. And then I fell ill, I was quite seriously ill not long after I was married, and had to drop a whole semester really. . . . it may have been pure exhaustion." And similarly, "I was teaching full time, three courses . . . which was quite a bit when trying to do dissertation work and still trying to do housework and shopping. And it never, it really, even though I thought this would be a sharing kind of thing—we were both going to be academics and we would shift everything else between us, it never really was that. I found I shouldered everything. . . . And I nearly went over the edge that year just trying to do everything. Just exhausted all the time. . . ." From a language scholar writing her dissertation while teaching and expecting a baby: "The baby was due in January, came in February. . . . And I was serving on three or four faculty committees, and writing and teaching, and advising thirteen students. So I just got tired all the time, chronically tired." And from a woman with children and insufficient financial support, finishing a dissertation under a deadline to avoid further fees: "People congratulated me—I looked like a cadaver. . . . the last twenty-five pages of the last chapter, I was actually throwing up, I was running from the typewriter to the bathroom because I had been, you know, stricken with nausea in my exhaustion." When women work in this fashion without sufficient subsidy of time, ineffective career planning and career moves are virtually inevitable.

Another important form of subsidy that women notoriously lack is professional counseling—guidance and instruction in the actual rules of the game. And here, our interviews amply bear out the virtual truism that women suffer chronically from lack of professional mentors—that little time is spent by graduate school professors on the careful professional counseling of women. We have many stories of male professors who prize the work of women students but who do not take the next step—that of treating such women as if they were future colleagues, helping to launch them advantageously on their professional way. Women professors are more likely to intercede with practical help, but, of course, there is a dearth of tenured women, especially in the prestigious schools where much of the nation's graduate training takes place.[1]

The result for many women is that, on receiving the doctorate, they have little clear idea of how to plan a professional life. They do not ask themselves the classic career-minded question—Where do I want to be in five years? With only a vague, long-distance vision of scholarship and teaching in mind, women tend not to plan intermediate five- and ten-year strategies. Rather, they take smaller steps, almost literally feeling their way along. An anthropology professor with a doctorate from an Ivy League university says, "I don't think I ever thought in terms of building anything, I didn't know anything about careers. I had no more conception of what a career was than . . . what it would be to be an astronaut. I had no conception. . . . I knew about research grants and I knew that you worked on grants and I was interested in research and all I wanted to do was to work on . . . research jobs that were interesting and exciting challenges."

Lacking instruction in general career strategy, women frequently remain unaware of specific steps important to their advancement. Throughout the interviews, the words "naive" and "innocent" probably occur more frequently than any others, as women—of recent as well as earlier generations—recount career setbacks they incurred through ignorance of the rules of the game. For example:

A woman in Romance languages, who finished her degree in the 1960s—with highest honors from a prestigious university—submitted her thesis for publication, had it accepted, then rejected due to a change of editors. Preoccupied at the time with a new baby, she said, "I wasn't even unhappy. I didn't realize that this was probably, you know, the death knell—that I'd *have* to have that book. I just was not on the ball. And I find it so hard to understand now, but I didn't realize what the hell was going on." She did not resubmit the manuscript. In fact, her intellectual interests changed and eventually she wrote a completely different book which was published, but too late to help her secure a good position. Faced with an academic future of part-time or service course teaching, this highly talented woman left the profession altogether and went into business.

An English literature scholar did a lot of full-time teaching even before finishing her dissertation in 1982, but never really had the chance for a tenure-track position. "I just took teaching jobs, one-year replacements, and I wasn't very canny about discriminating between a kind of . . . job that would be dead-end and a position with more tenure-track potential." She continues to conduct research in and lecture on her field, but is obliged to earn her living in other ways.

A biologist was shocked when she first encountered outright misogyny in a departmental conflict. She had simply not believed that she would be subject to sex discrimination. "What really happened to me then was that I got radicalized in about ten minutes, because all of a sudden I saw [she laughs]—it happened really fast. But what happened was that all of a sudden I understood that these women who were department secretaries and technicians and all of these people, I had something in common with them. Before that I had thought I was going to rise to these great heights and I was going to be like the men, there were not many women doing what I was doing and I just thought I was going to be like the men." This is another woman who eventually left academe for business.

A musicologist-composer, still working on her degree, is not sure of the steps to take to get her music performed, and also not sure why she does not know. "It puzzles me why I don't know some of these things, because I don't quite know if I am asking questions enough. I don't know exactly what it is." But she does know she is not getting enough support from her adviser. "I think my adviser, his heart is in the right place, but he doesn't understand—it's not that he doesn't understand what's needed, he doesn't think that it ought to be needed, if you know what I mean. . . . [He] thinks that you have to make it on your own . . . that you shouldn't need a lot of support from other people because you're going to have to be up there in your garret by yourself. Anyway, that's just another way of saying that he doesn't recognize all the support he has himself."

Of course, in linking lack of political awareness in women and their consequent career setbacks to lack of counseling and guidance, we are relying on negative evidence, which is always open to question. But there is positive evidence as well that the role of the mentor is important to women's professional development. Recall, first, the story of the woman who received strong advice at a crucial point about the importance of spending money on child care to buy time for serious professional engagement.

Another woman tells of critical help she received during a recent, and positive, process of tenure decision. "I was very lucky to have a female chairperson who took me through tenure the way you would want a mother to stand by you as a guide, who really cared about you but wanted you to have your own independence. And tenure is normally for people here a pretty horrible process."

Many interviewees speak of the help given them by older women scholars, not necessarily their thesis advisers, in getting their first articles published, helping them to get grants, or steering them toward their first job. And, of course, established scholars serve as public role models and advisers as well. Here is Emily Vermeule, professor of classics at Harvard University, speaking at a baccalaureate service to the graduating class of 1985 and addressing one aspect of the rules of the game for women. She outlines, at first, the problem for women in finding ways to respond to male colleagues whose behavior conveys their contempt for women. "Perhaps, sometimes, you will have been passive, even subservient, on occasions when you could have been more active, out of a cultural courtesy toward your male colleagues. This natural courtesy of yours will be met, in a surprising number of work and graduate school situations, with a discourtesy so pervasive you may not recognize it for what it is. You will at first perhaps be genuinely surprised at the expectation that you must be stupid and incompetent because of your sex, and that your gender puts you in the servant class." Then she concludes with the firm admonition: "Your best style is to be yourselves at your best, a pretty impressive creation. And do not accept that discourtesy which denies your talents to you. Never believe it."[2] Note, as an indication of the continuity of these problems, that this warning and advice are being given to seniors at Harvard in 1985. As Harvard graduates, these are young women in a position of unusual professional advantage and, as 1985 graduates, they are children of the women's movement, brought up in an ethos of liberation and equality. And yet they are still being warned against the dangers of doubting themselves.

The importance of this message also appears in stories about a more ambiguous, less-recognized mentoring function that appears to have a profound effect on the formation of women's careers. This rather mysterious process consists of words or actions that convey to a woman that she is being taken seriously. It is a validation exactly the opposite of the doubtfulness or outright mockery of a woman's capacities for seriousness to which Emily Vermeule refers. And, like expressions of doubt or denigration, being taken seriously can have surprisingly potent effects.

A tenured philosopher marked, as the turning point in her professionalization, informal and indirect but still deeply meaningful gestures of collegiality by a department chairman. "[He was] a very interesting man . . . a funny combination of sort of old world, paternalistic courtesy and . . . remarkable liberation. I think because he was simply not uncomfortable [with women]. His own wife was teaching political science and was a very strong woman. And one of the things that he did that was so nice was he would invite people to his house for [discussions] and people would come with their wives and husbands. There were a number of other women in the department actually, and the undergraduates. . . . So there was a kind of respect for people's capacity to think intelligently no matter what you were. And that was not expressed as a matter of principle, it was something that was evident from the fact that you would go there for dinner and somebody would talk about philosophy and there were other women there and they were treated with respect. . . . It was a de facto thing that was very impressive and I think it is one reason why I did really become professionalized because it didn't seem like an insuperable obstacle."

At the career juncture this woman is describing, she had completed her doctorate, having had several children along the way, and had followed her academic husband from West Coast to East Coast, holding part-time or replacement positions wherever she happened to land. And she had no overall strategy for developing a career beyond making the best of such circumstances. In fact she joined the department she refers to in a part-time position, which was all she wanted because of her children. However, after several years of "being taken seriously" she began to think of herself in more focused professional terms and, without being guided in an explicit way, she began playing by the rules—attending professional meetings, giving papers, then applying for and receiving a year's fellowship to work on a book, which was ultimately published. And all of this activity resulted in a tenured professorship at a different university. Many other stories, beginning in the same way but lacking a similar extension of collegiality, do not take the turning this one did. Rather their narrators continue in a pattern of shifting part-time jobs teaching introductory courses at pitifully low salaries.

The phenomenon of conveying to a young woman a serious sense of her own capacities, can also occur at earlier stages when ambition is just beginning to form. The following story is about a woman in college—a Catholic women's college—talking about her career plans with an English professor—a nun. "I remember talking with her . . . and saying, 'Well, I thought I would be a children's librarian,' and having her say, 'I don't really think that's good enough for you,' or something to that effect, and being quite amazed at that, not quite understanding what she meant. This seemed like a fit, and safe, I suppose, place for me to spend my intellectual coin, and to hold onto what I had treasured in childhood. And yet, I've thought of it since, that sentence, just because I think it's typical of my aiming too low in my view of myself and what I might be able to do in academia . . . or might be able to take, or what I ought to offer to the world of ideas." What she did was to enter a doctoral program at an Ivy League university to pursue the enlarged vision of life she had been given.

This and other stories underscore the point made earlier that women academics who do receive helpful career advice or direction often receive it from other women. But then there is another, sadder dimension to the role of the woman mentor in contributing to the advancement of younger women and that is the relative weakness or insecurity in many cases of the mentor's own position. One interviewee, somewhat disappointed with the lack of involvement with students on the part of a notable woman in her graduate school department, acknowledged the difficulties faced by this would-be mentor: She was "very much the embattled woman scholar who is being as impersonal as possible lest being personal [would stamp her as] too feminine." And two women scientists who had worked in laboratories headed by women spoke of strain and lack of support stemming from the lack of power or relatively low level of funding the woman adviser commanded. "In fact I was working for someone who was much more insecure than I thought and then I discovered her grant money was unbelievably tight. . . . And it was a combination of pressures on her. Financial pressures for more grant applications and trying to put out the work with totally inadequate staff in the lab and not much time and the whole thing. . . . We got into a messy situation."

What then of graduate school or early professional situations in which women find no attentive mentors, no confidence-building support, no senior guides to instruct them in the institutional rules? What can they do? Many have made their way through difficult situations by drawing on the support of women peers. "What saved me was a thesis group . . . we formed, a dissertation group of people in women's studies. . . . I actually called it together because I was the most desperate and had nobody to really help me with my work. . . . And there were probably ten of us in this group and we met for two years, once a month. And that's what pulled us through. That's where I got my professional evaluations, people in that group read my stuff." And five of the ten, including the speaker, ultimately published books out of the work the group had supported.

In story after story, then, the factor of support—received or not received—appears to be critical to the course of a woman's professional development—which raises the question whether this *should* be the case. Or to put the question as it is often framed: Why do women *need* so much support? So much attention? So many support groups? And then the implied question: What is the matter with them? Why are they so uncertain, so dependent on praise and encouragement?

From our perspective, there is nothing the matter with women, nor are they peculiarly dependent by nature. Rather they enter competitive professional worlds from different starting points and with heavier burdens than their male peers. The starting point is different because women still face questions as to *why* they are entering a professional domain and whether they are prepared to pay the price it exacts, whereas for a man such entry is accepted as natural. And women bear heavier burdens because they carry the same sorts of individual disadvantage as men— matters of class, race, education, health, appearance—but in addition they carry the weight of the old norms that foster suspicion, in themselves and in others, about their professional capacities. That is, professional women do not start out on a par with men and then lose ground; they start with extra disadvantage, which is the reason they need extra support.

As one woman put it: "Very often we have been conditioned so that we don't reach out as far as we're able to reach out. But if someone either pushes a little from behind or pulls us a little bit from the front, or just says the right word at the right time, it can give us just enough to get us over the next hurdle. . . . We do have to have extra help overcoming the stereotypes. This is why I'm so incredibly emphatic about support systems . . . among ourselves. . . . A lot of us are extraordinarily well endowed and we just need to have the understanding that we really can do something with it. What I have found is that as I have broken out of the stereotypes, the real binds that I've grown up in, is that I've become alive. . . . I didn't know that I had the strength that I have. I didn't know that I had the verve for living that I have [and] again support systems . . . that's going to help you make the break."

Our stories confirm, then, the general proposition that women—until recently only exceptional participants in the professional game—do not know its rules and need strong support and highly attentive career counseling. Further, it is clear that the academic profession itself does not supply adequate support and guidance to young women. But it also appears that with the advent of the women's movement, women increasingly provide substantial support for each other. They seek and share practical advice, provide moral and emotional support, and even intellectual guidance through such mechanisms as thesis-writing groups and study or support groups at all career stages. More formally, the women's caucus, established in conjunction with the professional association in various fields (e.g., the Women's Caucus for Political Science and the Coordinating Committee for Women in the Historical Profession), offers information, lobbying strength, and an opportunity for extended networking.

Stories of effective support from women peers occur in other professions as well. Women graduates of Harvard's law and business schools have formed an "old-girl network" that meets regularly in New York City. And the Committee of 200, founded in 1982, is a national organization of women in the executive ranks of business and industry whose contacts with each other allow useful exchanges of information and support. Further, women now have the benefit of substantial advice on the politics of career development in a variety of books or articles—advice that is especially helpful in demystifying the unspoken assumptions, the unwritten rules that young professionals do not know unless they are told.[3]

Yet, we also see that women entering the profession in recent years, presumably armed with a wide range of sophisticated advice and support, are still often stymied by political obstacles in much the same way as their

less-sophisticated predecessors were. Several of the stories above chroni-
cling some form of political naïveté involve women still in graduate school
or with recent degrees. The question is why.

Our sense of the depth of this question changed markedly from the
beginning of our study to its end, and it began to change when we found it
difficult to settle on the right language to describe the difficulties with
institutional politics that women's stories frequently revealed. Clearly we
were seeing lack of knowledge about politics, i.e., the rules of the game, as
well as lack of skill, but in many cases the lack of knowledge was coupled
with something like a refusal to know, a shunning of political issues. In
other words, women call themselves "naive" and they mean that they did
not—or still do not—know how to play the academic game, but they also
mean that they rejected—or still reject—the idea that playing games to
advance themselves is necessary. They believed—and still want to believe—that people advance in the academic profession primarily through
merit. And by merit they mean true merit that includes quality of mind
and moral commitment as well as performance in writing and teaching.

Further they believe that true merit will somehow be evident and
recognized by professional authorities without self-advertisement. They
eschew academic politics—the technique of gaining the notice and support of important people—assuming that such game-playing is, if anything, self-defeating because it is the opposite of merit and integrity.

We call this complicated form of shunning politics the merit dream and
it appears prototypically in the following story from a medievalist. This
woman was taken completely by surprise by the nonrenewal of her three-
year, tenure-track contract—her first appointment after completing graduate school in the late 1960s. She had published several articles and had
just won a fellowship for the revision of her dissertation, but she had not,
apparently, convinced her colleagues of her professional seriousness. The
reason, she surmised later, was that she did not spend much time with
them. Rather she organized her schedule to do most of her work at home,
to minimize the time spent away from her small child. "I do think tac-
tically I was very foolish. I didn't make an effort to get close to anybody. I
didn't . . . in the parlance of the business school, I did not seek a mentor
and I should have done it. . . . I never even knew a decision was immi-
nent. I assumed that there would be an automatic renewal, that I didn't
have to get busy lining up the troops for another three years. . . . I should
have been more present, I think now, looking back. I don't think I looked
serious. I should have talked about my work all the time. . . . I should have

been more conscious of the need to make that effort." But, she concluded, "I didn't even think of it. . . . I can't even say I made the wrong decision. I didn't make any decision, except, sort of, unconsciously. I never even *said* if I don't hang around, if I don't talk to this person and that person . . . I'm running this risk. It never dawned on me."

Another woman, a classics scholar now in her forties, describes a similar reaction to a strikingly similar experience—a surprising non-renewal of contract to a tenure-track position at a prestigious university. "There's a terrible battle going on here," she says. "It's deeply part of our culture today, between the reality or the essence and the appearance or the image. And I think that the academic world is hooked into that. And has bought it. And it's the same thing there as it is anywhere else. I have often felt that people I was competing against, or people at the same career level as I, were very consciously manipulating the image. And it's not only the image. Along with that goes making the right contacts, saying the right thing to the right person. . . . That's where I think that I, that I was held back by this sort of *purity*, that I think of as my refusal to . . . play that part of the game."

Note that the classicist speaks of her "refusal" to play the game, not any lack of knowledge of the rules—although there is some indication here, and elsewhere in her story, that she did foresee the full consequences of nonpolitical behavior. That is, while half-recognizing that a game was going on, she could not fully credit its importance. Publishing little, but laboring assiduously on a long-term, complicated project, she expected that somehow her dedication and wide knowledge would be recognized and rewarded and she was deeply shocked when it was not.

A story from a historian of the same generation depicts a young woman entering academe with the merit dream intact, then discovering the distance between dream and reality. In this case, however, the woman neither denies the reality nor plays the game, at least as a faculty member. Rather she leaves teaching for administration. "It became very clear to me that people in the teaching profession were—there was so much politicking, so much backbiting and posturing, about all matter of issues, whether it was internal politics or academic issues and all of it heavily disguised with the language of the academic world that was supposed to be. People would take positions and defend positions that would *clearly*, by my evaluation, be motivated by their personal interest, but they disguised them in language of academic values, academic freedom—you know, eternal truths. And so I felt . . . that most people in the academic world lived in a fantasy world. . . . that happened when I was teaching. And one of the reasons . . . I didn't have any trouble when I worked in Washington [in an education agency] was I felt it was decidedly refreshing. Here were people who were clearly politicians, they weren't pretending to be anything else. . . . I felt in contrast that people in the academic world were often doing nothing but politicking and were kidding themselves about it."

The point here is that the hold of the merit dream is such that even women who recognize its falsity find it difficult simply to set it aside and play by the accepted rules. One interviewee, a philosopher, makes this point explicit. Recognizing the actual rules of the game early in her career, she responded by deliberately remaining on the edges of academic institutions where the rules did not apply. "I started out in the fifties getting my Ph.D. right immediately after undergraduate education. . . . And felt very early that the likelihood of my belonging in any kind of institutional structure was slight. I had a very realistic view of what the university was like and what university politics was like and I think some knowledge about myself and my varied interests and thought of the possibility of working part-time as a very positive thing and an opportunity that my husband also wanted. And we were able to manage for a while, in the sense that he could work part-time and I could work part-time and we could be outside of the institutional framework. . . . I never saw myself as wanting a tenured position with all the responsibilities, the committee meetings—what I saw then and still see as the corruption that comes with power. And I didn't know if I would be able to swing it. . . . I think there was very much the sense of a unit, my husband and I . . . and both of us being anti-institution and seeing the teaching as a way to make a living, but as a way that was separate from having an intellectual life and being an intellectual."

But anti-institutionalism is not a practical approach for most people, because peripheral work is insecure and poorly paid. In fact, the couple in the story above could not "swing it" outside the institution and one of them, the speaker's husband, eventually took a regular, full-time faculty position as an economic necessity. What happens, then, when women seeking regular positions at regular salaries encounter the rules of the game and clearly recognize their importance early in their careers, early enough to use the rules to advance themselves? What effect does the merit dream have on this encounter with reality? No single answer emerges to that question, but our stories do reveal one clear part of the varied picture: the power of the merit dream is still evident, even among politically sophisticated women—women now in their thirties who went through graduate school when the women's movement was in full swing. That is, even women who seriously want a faculty career and who are fully cognizant of the rules are reluctant to play by them.

One younger woman with a recent doctorate in English literature articulates more clearly than most the paradoxical position of knowing the politics of the profession yet not wanting to deal in politics. In fact, this conflict has long been an important and painful issue for her because her husband, a tenured professor well known in his field, has served throughout their marriage as a live-in example of "how to do it" and has also frequently urged her to take the practical steps necessary to advance her career. And she has made attempts to follow this advice, but only sporadically and half-heartedly. Throughout her interview, recounted in a long excerpt here, she returns to this theme.

"I know them, I know what the rules are, I know what the requirements are. My husband tells me at many opportunities, far too many opportunities, what the rules are. And I think, the most stress in our marriage comes from that problem. That is, I for some reason will not play the game. I know the rules, but I'm dragging my feet. I'm just not sure why. And it's so frustrating for him to see me not getting my credentials in order . . . getting the dissertation out, getting chunks of the dissertation out, getting the stuff out." To this point the young woman has been talking about the credentials necessary to land a good tenure-track position at the entry level. A few minutes later she reflects on what she would have to do if she held such a position and wanted to gain tenure. "Now you can't, as we all know, be considered [for tenure] without a book or a string of articles. . . . I guess that I see the six years of tenure-getting as a continual process, as demanding I make choices that would be for tenure. For example, writing certain things and not others. Going after tenure would mean not editing the [X] letters [her keenest scholarly interest]. It would mean pumping out other kinds of articles. For display. I mean, it's a line on the resumé. And I feel uncomfortable about many of the choices. It would be so calculating to write what is required as opposed to doing something that you really thought was useful, necessary, and worthwhile, worth doing. . . . I am not a promoter of myself as much as I could be. I've discovered that again with reference to how I differ from my husband. He's an excellent promoter of himself . . . [and] at first I was really pretty turned off by the kind of path he followed, the kind of competitiveness that he exhibited. . . . [He] is terribly efficient and very sensible, very savvy about the profession, about choosing a topic that is doable and getting it done. I think he's quite amazing, I really do. . . . I'm in awe, and I suppose jealous of that ability. . . . I don't bring to my work the same dedication or calculation or cold-bloodedness. I get frustrated, I get down, I get sick of the whole putting-my-credentials-in-order syndrome, . . . [not] doing a project for the sake of doing a project . . . doing it to get it on my resumé so that I can be employable. And that's sad. . . . I think I'm fighting that all the time. If my husband wants to play that game, he plays that game, but more than that. He's in it now, so he's playing his own game. He is picking projects he wants and he's loving it, he just loves it. And I can't or won't play on my side. . . . I suppose you could describe his productivity and success in a kind of cynical way. He played the academic game. Or you could say he was savvy enough to know what was required and he did it. It depends on how you look at it, and I can look at it both ways [laughs]. I can admire, or I can have contempt for it, and I feel that ambivalence a lot of the time. . . ."

Thus, as we suggested above, women's seeming political naïveté has more to it than a lack of tutelage. Behind the apparently naive behavior is a deep repugnance for academic politics, a repugnance that remains even when the naïveté is gone. Why, then, is this so? And why is such repugnance strong enough to outweigh, in many instances, prudent requirements of self-protection?

One answer to these questions, we believe, lies in the dismay expressed by the classicist quoted above, that the academic world is no different from any other in the importance it accords to image or appearance. Clearly, she—and many other interviewees—think it should be different and thought it *would* be different when they entered. That is, to deal in images is literally to play a commercial game, to produce and package a product for the primary purpose of selling it. And women are strongly disinclined to treat the knowledge and wisdom they have acquired in the academic world as a kind of trading commodity. As we have seen in the preceding chapter on transformation, to become a professional, for women, is not simply to acquire a marketable skill, but to acquire a dignified, empowering identity, frequently for the first time. And whenever the academic game requires dealing in images or carefully packaged products as opposed to "worthwhile" projects, it threatens the very identity that women have so painstakingly created. In short, having experienced the inspiriting power of ideas valued for themselves, women are appalled to see ideas reduced to commodities and the academic world reduced from a life-supporting sanctuary to just another place of commerce.

Of course, women do not stand alone in their dismay at the trivialization of academic work through political manipulation. Many men of the academy express similar sentiments and avoid political engagement where possible—as in the philosopher's story above in which both husband and wife sought to separate an intellectual life from institutional pressures antithetical to it. But the issue is of sharper significance for women than for men because a professional identity for women is still precarious. It is not yet taken to be natural. Women must wrest their new identity from the contrary pull of the marriage plot and can never be wholly safe and comfortable in the new relation they have established to others. And until the marriage plot loses its hold and the naturalness of a professional identity for women is not in question, it will remain harder for women than for men to use intellectual skills politically without an intolerable sense of threat.

We suggest, then, that it is not the politics of self-promotion as such, but specifically the presence of politics in academe—the ground of life-enhancing transformation—that women find deeply repugnant. And we have further evidence for this conclusion in the fact that the same women who find it impossible to promote themselves politically within academe have no difficulty in doing so elsewhere. To take a striking example, the young woman who could not emulate her successful husband in playing the academic game decided instead to follow her own scholarly interests outside of academe while earning needed money by writing popular romances. Having made this decision, she then began, quickly and efficiently, to learn the rules of the romance game. "I systematically set about to study the romance. You can do that [laughs]. I bought a novel from each of the . . . thirteen series and read them, analyzed them. You can analyze the things. The formula becomes very clear after about twenty pages in any one of them. . . . And I wrote to eight publishers for their guidelines, which they very willingly sent. The hero has to be so old, the heroine has to be so old. . . . There are certain virginal series where the heroine remains a virgin through the whole thing, or other series . . . in which the heroine can have sex at various points, and it's *very* programmatic. . . . So I set about, I spent ten days and wrote ten pages a day and got a hundred pages together. I revised fifty of those pages and have sent them out to eight publishers. . . . It was a lark, it was fun because I, I was really kind of cold-blooded about it. That is, I was doing it entirely for money. . . . I could write four of those things a year and spend the rest of my year doing what I want to do. . . ." This is precisely what she could *not* bring herself to do in academe . . . cold-bloodedly to write and publish work that had no intrinsic interest for her. But when such an approach had no significance at all except to make money, she produced fifty revised pages in ten days, and sent them to eight publishers. There is no trace of such bold and determined behavior in any part of the story of her academic life.

And yet the dilemma remains. In order to secure a professional position in which a woman with doctoral training can practice her new competence, engage in the work she loves, exercise the authority she has gained over subject matter—in general express and enact her new identity—she must to some degree play the institutional game. But how can she do this without putting at risk the very identity that is the point of her professional life? As things stand now, there is a constant tension for women in this issue, a tension that can be seen in the experience of those who *have* committed themselves to engagement in the established structures of academe—which means playing by the rules as much as necessary.

On the one hand, it is clear that once women decide to play the institutional game, they are well able to learn and use a variety of political rules—such as the following:

Find out what's going on. "After I had been [in graduate school] three or four years, a women's reading group was formed and I promptly joined that. We met about every three weeks and discussed something we had read, and it was usually light reading because nobody wanted to add a big load to what we were already doing. But that was a real sort of inside line to what was going on there in graduate school. I hadn't had it before. . . . when you're commuting you're out of it and this women's reading group was a big help, because they sat around and gossiped about the professors and what was going on. . . . You learn an awful lot that way that you don't learn any other way."

Gain practice in political skills—for example in volunteer work. "I was the president of about every other organization in town at one time or another while my three children were small. . . . I had a lot of experience managing people and running meetings and learning how to present things."

Assume opposition. "[It] helped to know that there was no such thing as consensus. That you couldn't please everybody all the time. And also that there were people in power who . . . can see what you do as dangerous, or trivial. It takes awhile to get used to that. But I'm used to the idea that not everyone . . . will think that my particular version of something is a good one."

Be persistent. "Professor X [on being approached to direct a dissertation] said he was extremely busy and he wasn't sure he could take on another thesis at that time and yet I knew I was one of the best students there, certainly at that time one of the top two or three best. And I didn't see why he should discourage me, and other people told me that he should welcome me and I wanted him. I really needed him as an adviser, so I just kept pushing and he finally caved in and accepted me. I was so glad I did because he has turned out to be a marvelous adviser, very supportive, very helpful."

Learn to say no. "I see several of the women here, not just in this department, who are too involved in committee work. They're asked to do it and they do it. They become a public servant, as we know women do. They find it hard to say no, and I guess that's another piece of advice—learn to say no. And learn to ask, 'What's in it for me?' Which is very selfish, but if you're going to get tenure, you've got to keep your eye on the main chance."

Use contacts. "When I wanted to get some administrative experience before I returned to teaching . . . [my thesis adviser] came up with a good contact, another ex-student of his. . . . It was the old-boy network. And it worked like the books say it does!"

Choose your fights. "I guess since I've gotten older, I see the danger with [fighting sex discrimination] although I still do it and you have to be very careful. You have to choose, you can't turn everyone in all the time. And I've learned to choose when I think it's important."[4]

On the other hand, for many women, following these and other rules is always a matter of strain, of overcoming a contrary impulse to rely on the standard of merit alone. And the strain itself sets up another burden, another drag upon straightforward professionalization—and another source of possible deflection from that course.

Furthermore, even when women achieve secure professional positions as a result of playing by the rules, questions about politics remain. Several stories from women who hold tenured professorships and department chairs reveal their strong misgivings about using the institutional authority to which they have gained access. That is, some women in a position to control the game to some extent themselves are still uncomfortable with the rules and exhibit a reluctance to use them, at least in the mode and for the purposes that are usual in academe. And this reluctance leads, slowly and by no means surely, to their seeking to change the rules. A tenured university professor speaks at length about her ambivalence toward the authority she holds; we include most of her remarks, largely unedited, to convey both the issue and the disturbance, the conflicting pulls that surround it.

"I find it very, very difficult to get ahead personally if it involves competition. . . . [It] is important for me to get ahead, I think I am a fairly ambitious person. I'm somebody who does strive to better myself, but I think that it's always within the context of cooperating with other people. I think I was particularly aware of it during the two years I was in administration, where I think that there is an awful lot of competition on the job, competition both within offices and between offices. And you see people often trying to make a name for themselves. In administration you need to get recognized to move ahead and to get recognized you have to do something that's particularly outstanding that is going to call attention to yourself and some people seem to go about that in a very personal way, trying to call attention to themselves perhaps even at the expense of the other people. I've always found that that was impossible for me to do. That what I enjoy doing is cooperating with other people and facilitating the sort of getting ahead for a group of people as opposed to me as a single individual getting ahead. . . . I think it is a real problem, it has been a real problem for me. I'm very aware of it now trying to chair the department, that people expect you to be an authority figure. They expect you to sort of stand above the rest. And there is a certain amount of that that comes with the role. I don't do anything, I command that kind of attention by being a chairperson. And yet I think that is a style that I am not comfortable with, and I often wonder if I'm going to be successful in this kind of position given my emphasis on cooperation, my desire not to be that authority figure. I don't like competition that requires that in order for one person to win others have to lose. . . . That's the negative use of power. I think and I like to believe that it is possible for individuals to get ahead without there being a cost to others. . . . And sometimes I think that I may not ultimately succeed in this world because of that. And I think that it is very, very difficult. There is a part of me that doesn't want to engage in that kind of competition. There are some times that I think I carry that too much to an extreme and that it would be better for me if I weren't so sensitive to the losers."

Asked about using power in a way that is enabling for others, she goes on: "That's certainly the way that I try to use it. But I also know that I constantly find myself running against a set of expectations that I'm not quite meeting. The odd man out again. And I have found that to be very much the case in administration as well, in that I was very aware of the extent to which competition is at the heart of the way people interact with one another. Always sizing one another up. I feel often that men come to new situations, I mean if you take a look at a committee that's been brought together to work on a particular task and if you look at the group of people who come together for the first time and sort of listen to what's going on, underneath what's being said, you hear an awful lot of sizing one another up, trying to establish position in a pecking order, and I was very, very conscious of the extent to which that was going on, especially in administration. . . . Or take a colloquium, when you go to speak somewhere or someone comes to your department to speak, if you listen to the questions that are being asked afterward, they're not just questions, they're assertions—I know more than you do. Look at me, aren't I the knowledgeable one? . . . But I don't feel I have this need in quite the same way that other people do. . . . I wonder if being associated with a minority group, whether it is being a woman, or being a black, an Asian, doesn't make you much more attuned to the extent to which people need to assert their status, vis-à-vis you, and you in turn try to assert your status, and I have a certain distaste for that. . . . Sometimes it is very necessary and I can see how it can lead to success. For me the cost is too great. Or I prefer to define success in different terms."[5]

Here the issues of personal aggrandizement and the use of administrative authority to gain desired ends are combined in an overall sense of frustration with the spirit and purposes prevailing in a certain university, if not the academic world more generally. And the woman speaking identifies this alien spirit and purpose with men—although not with all men, as her remarks about minorities make clear. Rather it appears that the constant sizing up, seeking attention, establishing a pecking order, represent for her a mode of behavior of dominating males and she cannot quite bring herself to use it.

Another tenured professor, also chairing her department at a large university, describes the same conflict but resolves it differently. "I learned a lot from being chair of undergraduate studies [at her last job] because I was the only woman. There were thirty or so departments and we had chairmen's meetings so the dean could tell us what had to be done. One couldn't help but notice and pick up on what was appropriate language and what was not appropriate. . . . There is a way men talk about work with others . . . and a lot of it has nothing to do with what they're talking about, but just a certain mode of speech. I didn't have qualms about using it because I recognized it as the voice of the oppressor . . . and I think that the best I could do as department head and as chair of undergraduate studies before was to use that mode of speech to get what I really wanted. For the oppressed."

Thus another issue emerges, related to but larger than personal discomfort with political self-advancement. The larger issue has to do with uses of authority that are oppressive—practices that both preceding narrators identify as traditional male uses of authority. The first speaker's preference is to work cooperatively, which means to distribute power equally in making decisions over who gets what. The second speaker has more tactical concerns. She is working within her university for the advancement of oppressed groups which she identifies in other remarks as "women" and "minorities." And to gain that end she is prepared to use power tactics—"the voice of the oppressor," as she says. But both dislike and oppose the present distribution of authority in the academy and the practices that buttress it.

Not all tenured women, of course, engage so directly in large questions of power. As one recently tenured literature professor said, "the old network and the old way of doing things are so tremendously entrenched, and so many people are vested in it for whatever reasons, that the most one can do is to deal with, case by case, whatever you have any influence over." Another, a tenured historian who explored the possibility of moving into administration in order to influence policy, finally decided not to involve herself in "that hassle."

The problem facing all women who hold substantial authority is that, for millennia, women have been subject to authority held by men, and those women who now share authority do so in systems still controlled by men. And these systems still operate in practice, if not in theory, on the premise of women's inequality. Thus women exercising even the modest authority of a department chair in a university do so within a system that, if unresisted, would continue to operate in myriad ways that are disadvantageous to women. Without resistance, the prevailing rules of the game would presumably continue to result in women holding only 6 percent of the full professorships in research universities and 52 percent of the instructorships. How is a woman in authority to operate in such a system? Different individuals sort out the difficulty in different ways and arrive at different resolutions. Some avoid authority altogether. Some reduce issues to narrow practical dimensions. Others, seeing the larger picture, are immobilized by the scope of conflict. And still others deliberately use the language of the "oppressor" in aid of the "oppressed."[6]

Present at some level, however, throughout the stories of most women is a deep mistrust of social authority, and a deep uneasiness about holding it because, we suggest, its historical use has been hostile to women. Yet until women hold authority equally with men in all social institutions, the rules of the game in those institutions will continue to work against the possibility of women's full participation in them as professionals. Women must use the rules to change the rules and that is a game fraught with tension and hazard. There is tension in the deliberate use of speech to manipulate ("There is a way you talk . . . [that] has nothing to do with what you're talking about"), when women are strongly committed by the transformational process to deal in substantive meaning. There is hazard in seeking change when any deviation from the norm places women at risk of not seeming "serious" in their professional purposes, offering grounds for not being taken seriously. This tension between women's mistrust of authority, and the need to exercise it in their own interests— and the larger interests of the academy—runs through the experience of professional women generally, whether or not they consciously confront issues in these explicit terms.

Chapter 4

Voice of Authority

> **But I suffer not a woman to teach, nor to usurp authority**
> **over the man, but to be in silence.**
>
> 1 Timothy 2:12

> **That woman's days were spent**
> **In ignorant good-will,**
> **Her nights in argument**
> **Until her voice grew shrill.**
> **What voice more sweet than hers**
> **When, young and beautiful,**
> **She rode to harriers?**
>
> W. B. Yeats, "Easter, 1916"

We have just seen that women have trouble securing a position of authority for themselves within institutional structures and in this chapter we will attend to the difficulties women have in developing a voice of authority, despite long training and experience. A strong, clear voice is necessary to the practice of the profession, both literally in the classroom and figuratively in written research. But our stories demonstrate that women trained or training in specific disciplines—that is, following the quest plot—still report feeling "inadequate," "uncomfortable," "an impostor," "mute." To state views boldly in public debate, to challenge the intellectual views of others, still pose problems for professional women.[1]

Why should this be so? Why do women find persistent difficulty with forms of public assertion? Why do they refer to silence, apology, diffidence, hesitancy, as characteristic of their discourse? One powerful reason is that a voice of authority is exactly the voice the old norms proscribe.

According to the old norms, women should not speak with authority, because they should not be holding authority. Rule making, or speaking with authority on any matter of social importance, including the subjects of knowledge pursued in academe, is properly the province of men. Women may contribute to knowledge in various secondary roles, but the final, authoritative word belongs to men. This ancient norm has been enforced through the centuries by the promulgation of negative images that attach to women who challenge the norm, and praise for those who uphold it.

Consider for a moment the speaking images of themselves women inherit from history, mythology, religion, literature. On the one hand, women are stigmatized as shrew, vixen, bitch—i.e., female animal in being and voice. This, they are informed, is what they become if they risk being strident or contentious, traits that justify suppression, as in *The Taming of the Shrew*. Yet, simultaneously, the opposite and equally destructive image is dangled before them: the fluffy, loquacious, irrelevant Blondie of cartoon and film. The message of these images is that, without question, vocal women are either silly or nasty and, in either case, unloveable.

By contrast, the praiseworthy woman of the old norms practices the virtue of silence, even against her own strong urge to speak. Carolyn Heilbrun underscores the centrality of this point in comments on Lyndall Gordon's biography of Virginia Woolf. "Mrs. Gordon understands that Woolf was, like all women, trained to silence, that 'the unloveable woman was the woman who used words to effect.'" And she quotes Gordon as saying, "Women felt the pressure to relinquish language, and 'nice' women were silent. Mrs. Ramsey [in Woolf's novel, *To the Lighthouse*] smiles at her husband 'silently'."[2]

Similarly, Phyllis Rose, in her compelling study *Parallel Lives*, documents Jane Carlyle's unhappy acceptance of silence, the reduction to letters and diaries of her own writing after marriage to her mentor, Thomas Carlyle. The contemporary feminist poet Adrienne Rich titles her book of essays *On Lies, Secrets and Silence*, perceiving those three modes of speech (silence is, after all, the withholding of speech) as the real choices available to women. The fiction writer Tillie Olsen titles her book of essays, *Silences*. Elaine Showalter in *The Female Malady* documents the effective silencing of women by gender-based diagnoses of women's complaints as neurotic hysteria. And Heilbrun concludes the book review cited above by pointing out that women writers attempting to write truthfully about their own experiences have a particular problem because women have been "muted by centuries of training."[3]

Even when women seem to contradict this injunction to silence, upon closer consideration we see them to be vessels, actresses, mediums. If we think, for example, of the sibyls, of whom there were thirteen in the ancient world, we recall that these supposed prophets were all mouthpieces of the god Apollo, not the authors of the messages they transmitted. Their function bears more resemblance to Trilby's or Verena's than to a god's.[4]

Marriage plot and quest plot are poised here, at grips with each other. To be loveable, the goal of the marriage plot, a woman must be silent. To express professional knowledge and wisdom, the goal of the quest plot, a woman must speak, and speak authoritatively. To presume that as women enter the professions in ever greater numbers, the injunctions of the marriage plot will simply fall away, automatically removing the struggle between plots, is to indulge in wishful thinking. Rather, the attitudes that enjoin the apologetic or stilled voice of the old norms (the restaurant called The Silent Woman in Maine emblematizes, with its logo of a headless woman's torso, the calumny that the only silent woman is a decapitated one!) remain and influence conduct, even though they are inappropriate to new lives. That is, women must struggle, consciously or unconsciously, to resolve contradictory norms and this struggle unavoidably compromises the development of the voice of authority that normally attends professional empowerment.

A major problem for women, then, in developing a voice of authority, is that they encounter resistance to authority in women from the moment they begin to claim it, thus inheriting self-doubt as an unwanted legacy from the past. A young woman who attended graduate school after the beginning of the women's movement attests to this insidious fact. "The message was still there that 'Oh, I see, you're going to graduate school. . . . you're going to find a husband. That's what your whole aim is.' I sort of felt doubt creeping in. I was very apologetic." Here the old norms are carried and spoken by random acquaintances but still have their effect: they raise doubts; they produce hesitance.

Further doubts arise in graduate school—the place where the highest authorities in the profession practice and where women in authority are next to nonexistent. The same speaker continues: "I still see the academic world as a bastion of masculinity and power. I feel like a little moth against the light, banging and falling."

If not all women internalize this degree of self-doubt, few can escape the omnipresent sense that their professional lives are conditional. Instead of feeling that they belong where they are, women graduate students frequently feel that they are tokens, a position that imposes its own burdens. Here is a recollection by a tenured professor of history. "I was determined that I was going to get all A's. . . . I can remember coming home after my first hour exam, and I had been out of school for a couple of years, just devastated, certain I had flunked . . . and I think more devastated in a public way, a sense that it would have been more than a personal defeat. I had the sense I was setting an example out there in some way."

And knowing that you are flouting subliminal distrust, needing constantly to prove your worth, undermines self-confidence in even the strongest women. In 1918, Dr. Alice Hamilton, soon to become the first woman appointed to the Harvard Medical School faculty, writes to her cousin, "It is the end of my sixth year here, and I cannot think of one thing that has gone well and I know that the fault is nobody's but mine, that I came brashly into a milieu to which I was not adequate, and tried to fill a place which needed more brains than I have. . . ."[5] More than sixty years later we hear the same doubt in the remarks of a talented graduate student in the humanities: "I felt that some day they were going to find me out. You know, that feeling that it's not quite true, that my I.Q. was really 60."

A Romance languages professor sums up succinctly this chronic sense of self-doubt. "The need for approval, the need to succeed, the amount of self-doubt that I have experienced in getting tenure, that my female colleagues have experienced, seems to me to be very much a product of the fact that we were raised as women [she's in her late thirties] in a culture that demanded excellence of us but never quite expected that we'd be as excellent as anyone else so that we walk around not quite as sure as other people that we are as good as they are." Her words evoke an echo of Orwell's famous formula in his satire, *1984*, "everyone is equal, but some are more equal than others." Here is a double message, indeed. And women's need for reassurance proceeds from their felt knowledge of this professional vulnerability.

If women must seek authority as outsiders, as carriers (for themselves and for men) of two sets of social norms—what specific effect do these burdens have on women's speech? How can we trace this problem in the tones and cadences, the dynamics, of women's voices?

In their early educational years, women often report remaining silent in a coeducational classroom—the conjunction of social and intellectual worlds. "From being somebody who would blabber in class, in my fresh-man class when I wasn't interested in any of the boys in the class—now I couldn't open my mouth. . . . it had something to do with that old con-flict." This woman was in part heeding the old adage that "boys don't make passes at girls who wear glasses"—at intellectual girls. Her own desire for a professional self, which in fact took her all the way to Scan-dinavia to study, is silenced because she perceives silence as the way to aid her social interests. Thus a conflict is set up early—silence to further social ends, speech to develop intellectual goals.[6]

Another interviewee, who serves on the admissions committee of an Ivy League college, informs us that even today the commonest description of the female candidates is that "they're shy. They need drawing out," according to their recommenders. And these shy college applicants turn into muted graduate students. A senior faculty member says, "Men are much quicker to take an authoritative stand and the women are still being deferential and apologetic. The women are still doing nods and smiles." (Notice the gerund "doing" here—a gesture, not a sound.) Distressingly, what we see is that women, faced with professional situations that de-mand authority, demand rebuttal, still attempt to please, to be winning, to be placatory, to be all the things for which the marriage plot has prepared them. It is a psychology of the dispossessed—winning a place by ingratia-tion and self-abnegation.

Another syndrome, complementary to deferential "nods and smiles," is overcompensation or running scared—investing more time, greater effort in their work than is objectively required. An American literature scholar discloses: "All the way through graduate school I would have to say I was very, very insecure, and probably worked two or three times harder than I needed to." This insecurity is echoed and amplified by a classicist. "I was always running so scared. I was terrified. They're not going to like it, I'm not doing good enough work, they think I'm not really serious because I have a family, and I have other obligations. My career pattern isn't like theirs. I'm too old, older than the average man would be, entering an assistant professorship."

Another woman, despite teaching at the college level for many years subsequent to her marriage, confesses: "It took me twelve years to finish my Ph.D. because, first of all, I was scared to death . . . because at my age I had to go through the generals [Ph.D. examinations] and it took me another two years to take my generals which I could have taken in two months. . . . " That is, this woman's actual experience inside the profes-sion still did not dispel incapacitating self-doubt.

Thus running scared results in a work load that is heavier than necessary because the requirements are perceived unrealistically, perceived as insuperable, at each level. As a Spanish scholar describes it, her notion was that "you have to be good at everything, you've got to give tremendous service, you've got to write a book, everybody has to say you're excellent at everything. It's harder for us to say no in the department than for a man."

The salient point about the insecurity expressed here is that it is unrelated to the abilities and experience of the subject; it is, rather, the result of social forces and their internalized messages, the old norms dictating the impropriety of an authoritative voice for women. Another unfortunate effect of these unrelenting forces is the diminution of women's voice through the common practice of self-censoring. One woman reflects retrospectively, "I ought to have learned that there's such a range of ability out there that the standards I set for myself were ridiculously high and punitive." And another: "I discovered that I couldn't quite come to terms with the idea that whatever I did would be good enough, *although* I knew very well I did better work than [male colleagues], knew I had a better mind, a better prose style."

Sometimes a real writing block sets in, as this French scholar remembers. "Unless I felt [my work] was wonderful, and the very, very best I could do, I wouldn't submit anything that anyone else could read. . . . I was afraid of not being good enough. He would pass a lot of people, but it was difficult to be considered very, very good by him. And rather than be seen as something less than very, very good I couldn't write." The refrain of "I decided it wasn't good enough," "I didn't submit it," "I redrafted and redrafted it thirty-seven times," appears in dozens of stories. Originating in anxiety over the question whether the quest is the appropriate plot to pursue, self-censorship continually stills women's voices by its unreasonable demands.

A related reaction is apologizing, a mode of discourse many women adopt when they do speak professionally. The prefatory disclaimer, for example, is common—"I just thought I'd mention," "I know it's a minor point but. . . ." Such remarks aim at self-effacement, the denial of self, at the very moment when the speaker is supposedly making a professional contribution. One experienced professor comments: "When a woman, particularly over thirty, is about to give a paper you can allow—I look at my watch—I can pretty much time it. If allowed to go on, maybe seven minutes of apology about why this may not be exactly what she should have done and how if she'd had more time she could have done it better, and if she does badly on something, she says, 'I just didn't get it, and I should have worked harder, and I'm sorry.' "

And Adrienne Rich observes the same phenomenon: "Listen to a woman groping for language in which to express what is on her mind, sensing the terms of academic discourse are not her language, trying to cut down her thought to the dimensions of a discourse not intended for her (for it is not fitting that a woman speak in public) or reading her paper aloud at breakneck speed, throwing her words away, deprecating her own work by a reflexive prejudgment: I do not deserve to take up time and space."[7]

For some women this reflex of apology, of self-deprecation, shades into an automatic reaction of imposing self-blame in the face of negative judgments of their work, or career reversals of any kind. A historian recalls with chagrin her willingness to accept blame for the rejection by one committee member of her thesis, when she had not yet learned the reasons for his judgment. "When [my thesis adviser] called me up on the telephone to tell me that one of the readers had raised enormous questions about my dissertation, my first reaction . . . was a very feminine and characteristic one. I started to say, 'Well, well, it's all right, it's all right,' and my adviser was furious with me. She said, 'It's not all right. You've worked very hard for this. You shouldn't have to rewrite your whole dissertation.' "

A sociologist who now has tenure in a Boston-area university confides, "I even blamed myself for what I perceived as my lack of success in the job market in the 1970s"—that is, at the beginning of a severe economic retrenchment in the academy. And a philosopher, comparing her own with her husband's attitude when both faced negative thesis reviews, tells us: "I think that it is a difference between men and women, that he assumed the negative review was the reader's fault, and I would assume it was my fault. It took me a lot longer to do my dissertation than it took him." This, unfortunately, is the point for many women: such basic apprehension about what is normal for women to expect causes career delays, many of them irreversible.

Yet another difficulty visited upon women by the old norms is the burden of avoiding contentiousness and confrontation in public address. If women are suffered to speak, they should provide the mellifluous note in a strident society—peace-keeping, soothing. But contention and confrontation need not signify the onset of hostilities; they can very properly be the instruments of intellectual argument and political amelioration. Traditionally, however, the old norms inhibit women from speaking out, questioning, challenging, criticizing. In short, women are supposed to accept whatever authoritative word is delivered to them; they are not supposed to raise their voices against authority. If they do, they are likely to be quickly stigmatized, as we noted earlier, as shrewish, shrill, whining, or complaining. Of course, the old admonitions do not completely silence women, but they do curb boldly assertive speech.

Several stories testify to women's ease with verbal contention only when they are not speaking on their own behalf—that is, in circumstances outside the prohibitions. "In my present career [as library coordinator for a large urban school system] I do bludgeon and scream and yell and I'm very assertive. But you see I'm doing it for other people. I'm making these libraries for children. . . . I'm not doing it for my self-interest." Another, faced with an adverse contract decision, explains why she didn't protest: "The only way I can really [have a confrontation] is if I don't care a lot. It's an act, in other words, and I have to be pretty conscious that it's an act. I find it's remarkably effective. . . . I have been stunned at the way people back down. . . . But it's not something that comes naturally to me. If I really mean it, I'm incapable of doing it."

Interestingly, even when a *woman* is domineering or overpowering, her female colleagues find it difficult to mount vocal opposition, as one scholar illustrates with an anecdote. "I feel as if in many ways we have to buy into this male game to succeed. I just came back from a conference in which two of the women who were not directing the conference, but who made themselves controlling in the group, were playing what I call a bitchy male academic game with the other women . . . putting people down [about their conference papers], assuming they knew more about the material than the people who were actually writing about it, making people defensive, so that they couldn't quite make comebacks, because they had asserted their power from the very beginning, not taking criticism themselves, remaining impassive when people criticized them. . . . and the rest weren't like that, but sure as hell weren't very good about dealing with those two women. And I am still trying to work out why it is that we took this and didn't make a fuss about it . . . and I think women in general really have a hard time confronting people. It takes a kind of aggressiveness that a lot of us don't quite have, however assertive we may be intellectually."

But another woman faculty member points out that women, conscious of the problem, sometimes lean over too far in the opposite direction and end up overcompensating for underassertiveness. "I think women [in the classroom] perhaps overcompensate in the direction of rigor, they're afraid that one of them will be the soft touch or this sweet nice lady has a few little ideas and so overplay the other side a bit . . . but I try to be very, very helpful." A Slavics professor, speaking to the same point, admits she has not found the ideal balance: "As far as my scholarship goes, I would say I rarely speak out, but when I do, and I think I have something to say [arguing with the content of a professional paper at a meeting] then I go overboard in the other direction, which is probably part of the same thing. . . . In other words, I think I'm more strident and arrogant than I would normally be. . . . I'm overcompensating . . . because I don't want to retreat. . . . I come on very strong."

A variant of women's tendency to avoid contention is the reaction of speechlessness in professional situations which telescope the gulf between women's own understanding of events and that represented by male authority. As women describe it, it is an experience of being struck dumb on meeting incomprehension. It marks the difficulty of the outsider trying to convey to the insider the actual nature of her position and perceptions—a difficulty that may become insurmountable when she realizes the necessity for doing so abruptly, suddenly, through some turning of the plot. Then she sees that she is not operating through shared assumptions, and yet much is at stake. One woman reports on such an incident. "I had asked to see [the department chair] to ask him about my chances of getting financial aid and to try and lay out what my husband's financial situation was, but he was extremely busy and distracted [and rejected the appeal without listening to the circumstances]. I would say that it took me fifteen years to learn to ask for anything, as a self-respecting woman."

Another, recalling her response to an unexpected nonrenewal of appointment, says, "I was so amazed . . . that I couldn't even discuss it. I didn't know what to say. I didn't have any thoughts or arguments ready. . . . I was publishing articles. . . . A month later I had a book accepted. . . . No effort was made [by the department] to find out. The department didn't know me. I wasn't a politician sitting around the lunch table dropping big names . . . letting people know I knew the editor of this and that. . . . I had two young kids and that's why I wasn't at the lunch table all the time." This career turning focused for her the great disparity between her own conception of herself doing meaningful work, and the view of the department that she was not worth reckoning with. Inaudible leads to invisible.

And, significantly, such speechlessness or muteness does not seem to depend upon temperament, but is imparted by the position of being a defendant—inexpressiveness can befall a forceful woman facing professional misinterpretation. A historian relates how her intensity during a job interview was misconstrued, probably costing her the position: "I certainly came on very strong in that interview because I wanted the job very badly. And I guess I scared a few people. . . . I didn't know how to respond when the interviewer called me 'a tiger in the classroom.' . . . I could have answered something like, 'I'm very forceful and dynamic, but I think I also have enough teaching experience to know how to nurture students . . . and bring them along.' But those words were simply not there."

In other instances, women have refrained from speaking out on their own behalf, not so much because they cannot quickly find language to describe their situations, but because—as outsiders—they have no ready measure of the retribution their speech might provoke. That is, the general prohibition against protest threatens hazy, unnamed consequences and women literally do not know how far they can go. For example, confronted with an article based on her research to which her senior professor had affixed his own name as coauthor, one interviewee failed to remonstrate. "He had a bibliography a mile long, and the last thing he needed was another article to his name. . . . I didn't really know what to do about it. . . . I was a graduate student, I had passed my orals, but I hadn't finished the dissertation and I wanted above all else to get my degree and I was intimidated by the whole thing, even though [another professor] was completely supportive. I wound up capitulating."

Faced with a potential conflict, the woman deferred to male power, not out of a willing collusion with power to publish an article but because she did not know what might happen if she protested. What are her rights? Her professor's rights? What court of appeal has she? And, finally, of course, what power has he over her? All this being unknown—partly because women do not know the rules of the game, partly because it is unclear how the rules apply to women—the doctoral candidate finds it safest to withdraw from the dispute.

A musicologist tells us much the same story from *her* experience: "Even now [after graduate school], I still feel I'm at the mercy of the faculty of my university . . . because they're the ones who'll recommend me. A couple of years ago I went to a conference on 'Women and Music' and I got an enormous amount of flack from my adviser about that. . . . I've gotten to the point now where I go and do it anyway. . . . In fact, it's never backfired on me, but it took me a long time to figure out that it wouldn't. And I'm still not quite sure that it hasn't in some way. It certainly led them to identify me as a radical feminist."

The qualities of speech we have been discussing—silence, muteness, apology, self-blame, diffidence, hesitancy—are so inextricably linked to most women's speech that they are very difficult to extirpate. Even tenured women, who must have been practitioners for nearly a decade past their training to reach that professional level, manifest the same conflicts over voice to the point that, in various situations, they prefer avoiding public speech where possible. For example, a woman who has been chair of her department tells us: "I'm reluctant to speak up in the question period at conferences. . . . On a one-to-one basis I come on very strong, but in a group I do not and it may be a woman thing."

Others explain that they prefer the written to the spoken voice, because in this form they can project authority and influence without engaging in confrontations that raise confusing issues of appropriate response. A scholar of literature, now deflected from the profession, tells us, "I preferred to get reaction [to her work] at arm's length. I like submitting an article to a journal, getting it accepted or rejected that way." What seems remarkable is that another woman, a well-known critic at one of the nation's most prestigious universities, advances exactly the same sentiment. "It took me awhile to develop a voice. . . . I speak softly and may be unable to interrupt people. . . . Publication was easier for me because it was done in my absence. I mean I didn't have to become aggressive personally. Lecturing has taken me a long time . . . to project authority. . . . Publication isn't like interrupting somebody. . . . You submit manuscripts . . . there's a lag. . . . You don't have to present yourself in person. . . . That's the easy part. That part I'm confident of." Clearly the split between intellectual confidence in the form of scholarship and the projection of personal authority is not automatically bridged by such intellectual success as the last speaker had already won.

For some women these difficulties with voice extend as far as the classroom, where the necessity to assert authority may arouse serious anxiety about its acceptance. In the following story, a woman who left a tenured teaching position for administration describes this anxiety graphically—anxiety that is the more unexpected in light of the fact that the speaker holds degrees from both a highly rigorous college and an Ivy League university. "Day after day [teaching] depressed me if something would go wrong. At course evaluation time my heart would be beating harder and I would go, 'Oh, God, not again,' and then the [student] evaluations would come in and usually they'd be fine, good, great, and then there'd be one kid who said something horrible and I'd be thrown for a loop. At the university, teachers have alternating schedules, like a Monday, Wednesday, Friday teaching schedule and Tuesday and Thursday you don't teach . . . so you go to meetings or do research on those days and I found through my teaching career, when I woke up in the morning and pried my eyes open, I would try to think what day it was. If it was a teaching day, I'd go 'Ugh,' and start to go back to sleep again. If it were not a teaching day, I would be hopping up, ready to go. Since I'm in administration, I feel that way every day. I feel fine. I'm ready to go. So I think I was a little diffident about exercising authority, uneasy about hurting the [students'] feelings, uneasy about calling on them if I suspected they didn't know the answers. In a way, I was failing them by not being more authoritative toward them."[8]

Two forces seem to be at work in this situation of classroom anxiety: women both want more than most men to be liked by their students, and fear simultaneously that their students will not accept their authority. Both forces are exemplified in the following statement contributed by a tenured Slavics professor: "I would say that I notice [a problem with asserting authority] most in the grading. . . . It's very difficult for me to give students bad grades. . . . My male colleagues say, 'You know, why are you agonizing? They don't care anyway.' I have to admit to myself, I'm afraid they won't like me. . . . I'm afraid that the students will not put up with the same sort of absolute judgment that they would from a male professor. I fear trouble; I go overboard trying to explain to people why I gave a C plus. This is particularly true in things like literature. That's why I like to teach language, because it's easy to maintain objectivity." The clear implication is that she fears she will not be liked *if* she exercises rightful authority. She does not believe that her authority in the classroom is a given, as most males would. And she is more concerned than her male colleagues with forfeiting the acceptance of her students. In short, because of the marginality of their presence in the academy, women are still justifying their judgments. Whether the students *would* withhold favorable opinion or not, she is acting upon the assumption that they would.

The story of women's search for full authority in the society, however, and of a voice in which to express it, is not one of disadvantage only. It is, as discussed in the context of "Rules of the Game," a story interwoven with the current uses of authority—in the academy and elsewhere. In part, the hesitancy that is characteristic of women's professional discourse stems from hesitancy about the proper definition of professional role. For what purposes should a voice of authority be used? This is a question that must be answered before a confident voice of any kind can take form.

The discovery that the classroom is a place of power that can be put to various uses can be unsettling. "When I became a teacher I realized something . . . that I don't think people talk about very much. . . . I mean the first day I was up there in front of a class . . . I was aware of the power I had. I was practically blown away by it, and always felt very ambivalent about that." This statement, by a philosopher of education, recalls her early days teaching in grade school, before she received her Ph.D. and became a tenured professor, but both the recognition of power and her ambivalence remained in her later career as well.

Most broadly put, the question of power and voice runs thus: If women want to be accepted in a professional orbit, should they retain the tentative and yielding voice prescribed by the marriage plot, which wins approval within *that* plot? Or should they, on the contrary, use the assertive voice employed by those already in power? This is a voice that delivers its messages with the expectation that they well be accepted as true—a voice that delivers truth through hierarchies, from those who know to those who do not know. This is the professional tone that has traditionally carried with it the recognized resonance of power.

And when women do not employ this voice they seem not authoritative, not professional. One interviewee, herself an established member of the academy, pinpoints the trouble. "The ways in which women express themselves are offputting to men . . . because they talk a different language even when they are talking about literature, and it seems frivolous or it seems off the point or it seems personalized. . . . And [men] don't feel congenial about hiring somebody who talks in such a different way." But by not adopting the male model of professional speech, women may not be manifesting a lack of serious address to their disciplines. Rather, they may be challenging old modes of authority—rejecting authoritative assertion as the mode for pursuing knowledge and expressing it. The tentativeness of their speaking style may express a belief that what can be known *is* more tentative than firm assertion makes it seem.

Certainly our stories suggest that many women react against the prevailing mode of academic discourse because they feel it actually undermines the integrity of its subject matter. For example, a scientist among our interviewees wrote—under contract—a textbook intended for the junior college market, only to have the publisher reject the finished text in response to objections from junior college faculty to whom galleys were circulated. The objection was that the language of the text was not sufficiently scientific, that the author seemed to be "talking down" to the students. What the woman in question says she was aiming at were simplicity of language and clarity. "I was always trained to choose the simplest and most precise word that will do the job. And elegance lies in that and this is not what the people in the community colleges want. Because when they see that, they think you're talking down." Asked for an example, she says, "When I was writing about rickets, I looked it up. I said, 'That's a strange name for a disease, rickets.' Well, rickets was an old Dorset word—rucket—a breathing sound that a child deformed by rickets would make, and the original word was Anglo-Saxon. And there is a malformation of the ribs called the rickety rosary in classical texts, which I think is a lovely name. There is a series of little bulges along the ends of the ribs that is part of the general malformation and I used the old term 'the rickety rosary' for it. The community college people were absolutely furious. They called it baby talk. The present term, derived from the old term, is *rachitic* which is really mock-Greek, and that's the only term they think I should use, without mentioning the other. But I think, if you can find an Anglo-Saxon word, like the first one, what fun! . . . And I think the essence of really understanding a subject is to be able to talk about it so lightly you can make jokes about it." This woman's approach to science, in other words, is to demystify it—both to convey meaning clearly and directly, and to treat the subject matter as an integral part of ordinary life, not something distanced from ordinary experience by pretentious, impenetrable technical vocabulary. She went on to say that she had been advised "to take out all the short Anglo-Saxon words and put in three-syllable Latin words" but that she could not bring herself to do that. "It embarrasses me. It would embarrass me to put those things on paper." But in demystifying, she is also undermining the authority of specialists who are the custodians of a particular subject. And for teachers of science at the junior college level—specialists whose authority is marginal to begin with—the threat of losing authority through simplicity is particularly acute, as our interviewee acknowledges. "The community college professors are in a very difficult situation. They are looked down on by the real biologists. . . . And they are also looked down on by the medical people because they are not training doctors. They are training paramedics and nurses. And they fight very, very hard to hold a position and they do that with words, and I'm in the position of undermining what to them are the words that make them what they are."

This same motif of wishing to be clear, understandable, to demystify the subject of experts, recurs frequently. One Near Eastern expert, herself adept in many obscure tongues, claims, "I want to write an updated, *readable* history of ancient Egypt. I want to write a book on the religions of that area that's readable . . . good introductory and theological material."

The word "readable" is selected also by a literary critic who says, "I've had a number of people tell me, thank God, my book is *readable*. Along the way I've developed a real antipathy toward many kinds of academic scholarship, toward the deliberately arcane, toward the contorted theory making . . . so I was very clear I didn't want to be that kind of scholar in my book." Another woman, a philosopher, discusses her difficulties finding an appropriate style and tone once she departed from conventional academic writing. "The trouble was that I didn't want the book to be a really scholarly book . . . and so it's not full of a lot of documentation and footnotes. The result is that the professionals don't like it, but I tend to think rather abstractly and so the ideas are obscure enough so that it is not really popular either. And so it sort of falls between the two." Later we will be looking at this same sense many women have of "falling between two stools" or "two camps" when we discuss the kinds of research academic women choose. But here the difficulty was that the writer wished to communicate to an audience that was not just academic, but an audience of "normal, intelligent people."

What these comments share is a sense of mission based upon belief in the educability of the general public. And stemming from this is a shift away from the purely academic to a more widely accessible mode of discourse. Thus a French language and literature scholar, whose translation of an extremely difficult work in psycholinguistic theory was about to be published, asserts: "I was a true translator. . . . I was moving it from one literary language to another, French to English, but to some small extent, from one jargon to something closer to real language, as I see it."

Thus women strive to find a voice that expresses what they know, but when they speak "in a different voice," to use Carol Gilligan's phrase, they do not sound authoritative. And while they are implicitly challenging the current grounds and uses of authority, they are denigrated for sounding silly, for using "baby talk." The problem, then, for women who reject the prevailing model for professional discourse is to find a counter-model that commands respect. How can women become insiders and acquire an insider's voice of authority while questioning insider values? Where is the model for new forms of discourse? Not readily available, is the predictable answer.

One English professor notes about a female predecessor, a noteworthy scholar respected in her field: "She had an almost southern, digressive style, you could say. I didn't like that as a style although I admired her mind no end, her insights no end. I think it was almost a fanciful style . . . and I like something evidential, clear. . . ." Another English professor, also tenured, similarly rejects a woman who might have been a role model. "I was very critical of her; she was mostly what I didn't want to be. She was very defensive. . . . I think she was comparing herself to male graduate school professors she had had and tried to be as thorough in the material as they were. . . . But I felt sorry that she couldn't understand that we would have learned more from her just talking off the top of her head, she knew so much more than we did." Significantly, in both cases, what is being rejected is the delivery—one overly digressive, the other overly formal—not the substance or any intellectual limitation. What these two women criticize is the inadequacy of their female academic models to provide them with a useful voice of professional authority.

Even without clear guidelines, however, one form of alternative voice emerges in a number of stories, a voice eschewing the authoritative lecture in favor of the more open-ended discussion. For example, a Renaissance scholar describes the pedagogical mode she disavows: "So many of my teachers at graduate school, the ones I particularly loathed, came with yellowed notes and just said, 'This is what I wrote down twenty years ago, here it is, and be quiet and listen.' And you know, you fell asleep in those classes. Why did you bother to come? . . . And I never wanted students to come because it was politic to come." What sort of classroom environment is she seeking as a professor? "Momentarily, in the classroom, you were out of the scholar's cell, and you were passing on, or eliciting, or communicating what you had found there to another group of people. . . . I always loved a class discussion, I never enjoyed lecturing very much . . . just that sense of exploring things. . . . The course I set up for myself was becoming the catalyst."

Other stories also disclose this deliberate turning from lecture because it is authoritarian and distances the student from the material and the professor. We interpret this as an outgrowth of the transformational process, which we have identified in chapter 2 as a wellspring for women's teaching. As we noted there, women regard teaching as a direct means to transform others through the power of ideas and intellectual training.

Many of these reactions set in in graduate school, when women had direct experience with some authority handling the material in a way that denied individual interpretation. Conversely, one woman recalls with gratitude a professor who actively encouraged student engagement. "She built up what was good in people, building up out of the morass of their words what was fair, without distorting it, so that the person really saw that their contribution had been heard . . . then she would take the contribution and put it together with that of the other students. . . . just a skillful discussion style."

Or, as others phrase the figure they project of themselves, "Not a showman, not flashy, just solid," and "able to bring together the subjective and the objective, the emotional life and the intellectual life." This last quotation describes this speaker's male mentor in graduate school, one whom she chose deliberately to emulate. For, of course, not all men eschew discusssion and discourse for lecturing, nor do we mean to suggest that. Neither do all men impose a unilateral interpretation of the text upon their students. But the authoritative style is the dominant academic style, and our stories chronicle strong resistance to it among women.

One tenured English professor emphasized the point that, finding no suitable models, women are under the necessity of inventing new modes of address for themselves. "I really think I made myself up . . . not out of whole cloth, but as a composite. I remember an undergraduate professor I had. . . . His vocabulary was very exact and precise and broad. . . . I was impressed with words that I had never heard before come tripping off his tongue. . . . but he lectured which I'm not interested in doing. . . . My own teaching style is getting more like another style I borrowed . . . walking in with a formula you've thought up, batting it around, getting counterexamples. . . ." Another woman, who was interested particularly in pedagogy, found her model in the writings of Martin Buber: "What drew me," she recollects, "was his description of the relationship between the rebbes and their disciples. . . . It was a dialogic relationship."

These comments emphasize the pedagogical truth that both teacher and student must have a vehicle for expressing intellectual engagement and excitement. In the lecture, only the teacher possesses the vehicle. Many women prefer not to lecture at, but to have discourse with. They seek not transference of information, but transformation. This vision, using voice as a medium for transformation, is a potent incentive for developing a different discourse.[9]

Still, developing a congenial classroom style is only one part of the general problem of finding a voice of authority. That voice must extend beyond the classroom to address colleagues in meetings, in journals, and in books, and also to address the public in writing and speech. And the problem is larger than the issue of definitive pronouncement versus open inquiry. It extends also, and deeply, into the subject matter of academic discourse.

As we discuss at length in the next chapter, women enter their academic fields with a range of social experience different from that of men and therefore with perspectives on knowledge that diverge from the prevailing focus of the various disciplines. For some, these divergent perspectives are subtle or unconsciously held. For others, the divergence is wide and deliberate because it is based on their conviction that traditionally defined knowledge is skewed by patriarchal values and practices. These women seek, through the pursuit of women's studies, to add to older understandings of their fields the previously excluded experience and contributions of women, and to rethink past certainties built on assumptions about the natural inequalities of mind, character, and power of men and women.

But it is difficult to find a language in which to express divergent perspectives. And this is especially true for scholars engaged in women's studies because in deconstructing old systems of knowledge, they are undermining the foundations of their own training, and in reconstructing something new, they must name phenomena hitherto unnoticed.[10]

What one frequently hears, therefore, in feminist exchanges, and even more in personal discussions—including our interviews—is a good deal of hesitant, fragmented, even agitated speech. Unfinished sentences, a succession of words tried and discarded, fast speech, raised voices, pauses, shifts in direction, emotive hand gestures—the opposite of the clear, fluent, assured articulation of thought by the great professors who are the models for the public presentation of ideas.

Without question, agitated speech does not command authority. Its very fragmentation denies certainty and the thoughts it offers are often not fully and clearly worked out. It can easily be dismissed, disparagingly, as incoherent or emotional—typical of women.

And yet such exchange is frequently laden with meaning—not the meaning of certainty but of questioning. The participants offer ideas before they are fully formed so that others can add to them, and so that others will feel free to offer their own tentative conceptions. The more usual academic practice, testified to by interviewees speaking of running scared or self-censoring, is to withhold ideas until they are complete and polished and clearly defensible. But the feminist enterprise is so far-reaching and so urgent, that certainty and polish are as yet impossibilities.

Further, this ongoing search has from the beginning been communal, advanced by exchanges of insight, a conversational discourse, open to—indeed, dependent on—contributions in unfinished form. And it is also dependent on attentive listening—women's ancient skill, here used not to take direction from others but to join with others in defining new directions. In short, the language of feminist exploration is inevitably probing and tentative, and the participants in the exchange, therefore, have little choice but to abjure precision and fluency if they are to contribute.

Yet addressed to a broader public, agitated speech sounds not creative, but unserious. Thus women, speaking from different perspectives, trying to convey different premises, different conclusions from those prevailing in their fields, face a double barrier: the old norms counseling silence, and a chilling expectation of misunderstanding, of disparagement of efforts to alter the discourse. The result, for many (although by no means all) is a muted public voice, speech tempered by indecision about how best to confront incomprehension or resistance, words left unsaid, authority unclaimed.

Finally, we suggest, there is one more iceberg in this frozen sea of speech, and that is the underlying fear on the part of women that dire consequences will befall not just themselves but their society, if they claim authority equal to men's. As a young literature scholar reflects: "this physical, congenital, female fear comes up and cripples them, keeps them from really writing something good because they don't want to shake the social order. They don't want to threaten. They don't want . . . to take responsibility for being adult women with brains. . . . They stand behind a man who's going to keep the world away."[11] And for whom they keep the quotidian away. This is what Jane Carlyle had to do with Thomas, and Mrs. Ramsey with her professor.

These women accepted the ancient division of labor by which men organized public affairs and women tended to the hundreds of small relations in the family and in the community that keep the social fabric whole. And though women now want to widen the scope of their lives, and to share public authority with men, they still fear, at some level, that doing so will rend the fabric it has been their long responsibility to preserve. Thus women's voice of authority is, to some degree, contingent on a broad redefinition of social responsibility, a redefinition of male and female roles in all spheres of life. It is certainly not simply a matter of speech training, of learning tricks of style and projection. Rather it is an expression of a role, a status, and a purpose, and the difficulty for women in redefining all of these and commanding respect for their redefinitions is as large as the old norms of the marriage plot are powerful.

Chapter 5

Women's Work

By "women's work" in the academy we refer to the fields women choose to study and teach, and the subjects they choose to write about, as well as the methods, the approaches, they employ in this labor. We realize fully that, in adopting such a term, we are claiming that women's intellectual work differs from that of men and that this claim is the subject of a fierce academic debate—and an ancient one.

Ever since Plato proposed to include women equally with men in the ruling elite of his ideal republic, and to provide the protorulers equal education and training for their task, questions about women's intellectual aptitudes have been in the air. Do women think differently, perceive and respond to experience differently, from men? Do men have greater capacities than women for understanding some subjects—mathematics, for example? Are women less capable than men of analytical, abstract, theoretical thought? Are they more capable of drawing on emotion, feeling, or intuition in handling the same subject matter? And underlying all these questions is the larger issue: whether any such differences are significant enough to establish one or the other sex as intellectually superior—and if so, which one.

The answer supplied by the old norms is, of course, that women's intellectual aptitudes are indeed different from and inferior to those of men. In this long-standing view, women are emotional by nature and subjective in intellectual approach to subject matter. Their minds are ill equipped to employ objective principles as tools of analysis, to place the materials of a subject matter in logical relation through the use of such principles. At best they are proficient in forms of creativity such as light fiction or poetry, which allows the direct expression of emotion, or water-color landscapes, which need reflect only the surface of what is perceived. In short, the creativity of women is seen under the old norms as limited to self-expression. It is assumed that the intellectual capacities of most women do not extend to intellectual work that requires deep probing, or the grasping of nonapparent attributes of objects or the logical relation of complicated ideas.

Further, as discussed in chapter 1, this belief in the inferiority of women's minds has been invigorated in the twentieth century by Freudian conceptions of women's nature as primarily expressive, emotive, responsive to biological functions and needs. In the Freudian view, women, undisciplined by the oedipal experience, do not generally have the capacity to become active and instrumental beings, taking full responsibility for serious public work.

To put it the other way around, the old norms, reinforced by Freudian theory, decree that women's proper work—the work that fits their natural capacities, their emotionality and physicality—is indeed responsibility for direct, daily human need: caring for the physical and emotional needs of the very young and the elderly; nursing the infirm at home or in hospitals; ridding the home and workplace of dirt and waste products. And there is little question that this arrangement, by which women are not only relegated to the private sphere but to the lowliest tasks in that sphere, retains a certain force. In a study of how couples share household duties, Laura Lein of the Wellesley Center for Research on Women reported that "husbands tend to take on the tasks that are high in gratification, such as bathing the children and bedtime stories, while wives end up with chores that offer little positive feedback or opportunity to socialize, such as cleaning bathroom fixtures."[1] That is, the remaining presumption that women are somehow of a lower caste is signaled by the fact that they, like the "untouchables" of India, are consistently assigned the basic maintenance tasks of the society.

With the advent of the women's movement, however, the centuries-old, tenaciously rooted belief in the innate limits of women's intellectual capacities has been under insistent attack. The predominant counter-theory rests on the assumption of essential equality in the intellectual strength of men and women, with historical differences in intellectual accomplishment ascribed to limitations imposed by the old norms on women's education and experience.[2] But the claim of equality is not the only challenge to the old invidious distinctions. Another line of attack on the old norms is a theory that accepts significant differences in the minds of men and women but finds it is women, not men, whose capacities are superior.

The proponents of this latter approach challenge the validity of the intellectual tradition that places logic and the rigorous use of objective principle—linear thinking, it is called—at the pinnacle of intellectual achievement. In this view, the intellectual asceticism valued in the old tradition, its vigilant exclusion of emotion and subjectivity from thought, are far from laudable. Rather, for these critics, overly objectified, overly logical thinking excludes from understanding vital elements of human experience and truth; its intellectual product is found to be desiccated, partial at best, whereas the deliberate inclusion of sense and emotion in the process of understanding the world produces a fuller, truer picture. And the conclusion of this school of thought is that the capacity to integrate reason and feeling, objective and subjective judgments, as well as a willingness to rest in ambiguity if necessary, are greater in women than in men.[3]

To enter such a field of fire at all with observations about distinctive qualities in women's intellectual work is a risky business, fraught with the danger of being misunderstood. Thus we open the subject of "women's work" in the academy guardedly, and with insistence on the following general disclaimer: Nothing in the evidence of our interviews, nor in our broader experience, suggests that there are clear-cut characteristics that are common to the work of all women and that distinguish women's work, as such, from the work of men. Rather, great variations run through the work of women as well as men, and the work of both is strongly marked by variances other than gender, most notably, by variance in intellectual generation.[4]

What we *are* claiming about women's academic work, in the face of such variations, is that common patterns do appear, not as absolute qualities marking the work of all women, but as clusters of similarity, propensities to do similar kinds of work. And we see these commonalities as deriving from the common experience of women who set out on a quest for professional authority in a cultural climate still significantly defined by the marriage plot. This experience sets up perspectives and interests that unavoidably affect how women carry out their intellectual work—from the academic disciplines they enter, to the questions they ask and, often, to the values they apply in reaching answers to those questions.[5]

The most significant commonality in the experience of women academics is the stance of the informed outsider. Women in the late twentieth century are informed about the world and their society by their inclusion in most of the education and experience of their brothers—often in the same schools, the same sports, the same travel, many of the same freedoms. But, with the old norms still powerful, the woman seeking to use her knowledge in roles of serious public responsibility remains an outsider. She holds authority on sufferance, under the perpetual suspicion that she will not be able to fulfill her demanding role, perpetually subject to the accusation that she should not claim serious authority at all. Surrounded by male colleagues, she is perforce "other." Thus she sees her world from the dual perspective of close knowledge and psychological distance—which is classically the perspective of a questioner or critic.

And this is one observable pattern in women's scholarship—the examination of familiar subjects critically, from an angle of vision that differs from that of prevailing authorities. Such scholarship may take the form of explicit social criticism—an examination of the structure and uses of power in this or other societies, and a call for change. Frequently, as noted in chapter 4, such an examination occurs within the rubric of women's studies; here the woman scholar calls into question some part of the historic distribution of power between men and women, as well as the history of that distribution as it has been conventionally recorded, through a male lens. Or, starting from a general conviction that women's nature and place is wrongly defined, wrongly understood, the woman scholar may use the materials of her discipline to explore new parameters of women's identity.[6]

But women's critical vision takes less obvious forms as well. Often women scholars work in their disciplines without explicit critical intent but—given their outsider experience and status—still not in sympathy with the interests, the foci, the certitudes, prevailing in their fields. They may engage in the prevailing discourse, or they may ignore it, but sooner or later, they are likely to go off on questions of their own—thus implicitly if not explicitly, expressing values counter to the established definition of the subject.[7]

These, then, are the issues we trace: the way in which women's particular social experience produces work that differs from and ultimately challenges established scholarly patterns; and the way in which the old norms that create women's outsiderness simultaneously undermine the credibility of their academic work and the seriousness with which it is taken. And, as in the other chapters, we see here too the doubts and insecurities that women internalize about their own work, as well as the political difficulties attendant on their supposed aberrance.

The aspect of women's academic work almost universally taken as evidence of their intellectual inferiority or "softness" is their habit of choosing humane subjects—the "soft" (here synonymous with "easy") scholarly fields—in numbers strikingly disproportionate to their male colleagues. By the end of the 1970s, when women accounted for about 28 percent of the total Ph.D. recipients each year, they received 48 percent of the degrees in English, 63 percent in French, 40 percent in psychology, 40 percent in fine and applied arts, 29 percent in biology, and 27 percent in history—that is, in the "soft" subjects, or subjects like history and biology containing "soft" areas. To look at the "hard" subjects in the same period, women received only 18 percent of the degrees awarded in political science, 13 percent in economics, 17 percent in math, 15 percent in chemistry, 10 percent in computer and informational sciences, 7 percent in physics, and 4 percent in engineering.[8]

And furthermore, women continue to flock to humane subjects in graduate school even in the face of the severe contraction of teaching positions in these fields—and in the face of inevitable accusations of dilettantism. A young woman studying ancient languages recalls constant remarks in her early graduate school years about the pointlessness of her choice. "I remember my official stance somehow became apologetic. 'Yes, isn't this peculiar, you who are in government [she laughs] or you who are in physics or you who are going to medical school?' And I do remember early on being really annoyed with myself for doing it, but taking a sort of jokey stance . . . hiding behind sort of the clichéd flightiness of the intellectual . . . somehow not being able to stop apologizing at parties, and being really the butt of people's remarks. . . . I'm not sure they realized how much of a put-down it was, but what they were conveying was, 'How typical of a woman, how typical that you are dabbling around in this little area, that you still are not taking yourself or the world seriously, or you wouldn't be doing this, you'd be doing something else.'"

The question is why they aren't "doing something else," or rather, why they do not distribute themselves in the various academic fields in numbers generally proportionate to those of men. On the face of it, it would seem that for large numbers of women to study esoteric or unworldly subjects is, indeed, an indication that they are not taking the world seriously, but are using academe as a refuge, a place of beauty and private enjoyment. Such women appear to be opting out of the very engagement in worldly affairs that would expand their influence both in the academy and in the society. They appear uninterested in gaining the authority necessary to bring about change and therefore uninterested in change as a goal. But, as we have seen repeatedly in other contexts, the appearance of unworldliness in the directions women follow in academe is deceptive.

For one thing, women do not usually drift into "soft" or nonpractical subjects; in fact, many interviewees describe serious explorations of other subjects, including the so-called hard fields, before settling on literature or language or art history or music. One woman studied nursing as an undergraduate, married and raised a family, then returned to college with the thought of earning a degree in clinical psychology. "But I got there and took some courses in it and took courses in English literature and decided that I was just not that interested in science no matter how clinical it was . . . whereas I was absolutely enthralled with English and with writing. I just wanted to do it enormously even though I knew it was impractical."

Another woman majored in political science in college and was greatly drawn to political theory and constitutional law but was put off by an emphasis within her department on political organization—"lobbying and pressure groups and all the dirty side of politics." Asked whether she found active political practice repulsive, she said it was more that she felt no response to it at all, that she felt "blank" and "noncomprehending." That is, she comprehended the subject academically, earning good grades, but the material held no keys to understanding for her. She turned in graduate school to philosophy, of which she is now a tenured professor. Still another worked for some years with an activist group aiding the poor, but on entering graduate school, she chose to study language and literature. "By that time, I was really sure of who I was. I was a literary person. I was not a politician. I was not a revolutionary. I had a personal sense of myself."

If, then, women's choices of literary and other impractical subjects are carefully considered, the question still remains what the grounds for these decisions are. What serious purposes draw women to "impractical" fields—that is, purposes beyond the conventional ones that have always drawn scholars to them? Again, we are looking at the disproportionate

numbers of women in these fields and reasons for the disproportion—
reasons other than the usual explanation of frivolity.

The key to the question, we think, lies in a common characteristic of
"women's" fields—literature, languages, art, psychology—which is that
they examine human nature, human experience, human capacity and
creativity, directly. The "hard" social sciences, on the other hand—political science, economics, parts of history—study the nature of groups,
social systems, organizations of power. And the sciences, except for biology which is a scientific field women choose, do not examine human
nature at all. We suggest that many women shun nonhumane subjects,
either deliberately or instinctively, not because women are unworldly, but
because such subjects do not touch issues vital to women's experience of
the world. Math and the hard sciences deal in abstractions. And the social
sciences are generally preoccupied with groups and systems that do not
include women, or in which women have little influence, or that are
studied and recorded without reference to the particular experience of
their women members. Thus, subjects that seemingly examine the levers
of change in a society actually offer little promise of analysis or change
meaningful to women.

What women *do* find meaningful, on the contrary, are subjects through
which interior change is possible—enlargement of individual scope,
shaping of individual identity, interior liberation—for themselves, and for
their students. Again, we suggest that it is the material of personal transformation that is gripping for many women precisely because they are
interested in change. That is, such women enter the soft subjects, not
seeing them as romantic retreats, but as arenas for the kind of change that
seems most direct, most accessible, most certain—ultimately the source of
change in the society at large.

One English teacher describes her vocation as based on "a strong conviction that [studying literature] is a very basic, central, and important
activity . . . central to one's sense of self . . . to one's own capacities to
respond." Both reading literature and writing, she says, are nothing less
than crucial to the development of "the whole person." For many interviewees it is clear that works of the imagination or the re-creation of past
historical periods or explorations of other cultures offer models, new
visions for personal exploration. For example, a scholar of ancient Eastern
languages says she was originally drawn to her field by her college work
on the Old Testament; she was greatly moved, she recalls, "by the human-
ity, the gorgeous roundness of the human beings that are in the Old

Testament." A professor of Renaissance literature makes explicit the distinction between fields that are seemingly practical and seemingly impractical in a lament about new trends in women's education. The effort to achieve professional equality for women, she says, has taken the form of pressuring undergraduates to identify themselves as future bankers or doctors or lawyers without exploring their actual individual talents or the terms on which they want to enter the professions. That is, the offer of professional equality was disguising what was really a matter of "pushing women into competing in the male world, at the expense of developing what they were themselves . . . of trying to get out what was inside of them, whatever it was." And this was her goal as a teacher—not to send young women automatically into the "power" fields, but to help them develop whatever they were themselves.

The underlying point is that women jumping into the male-defined practical fields may not gain power but may risk losing the self—a self that, limited for millennia to old norm conceptions of womanliness, has not yet established its wholeness. A broader point is that, for everyone—women and men alike—education should contain interior exploration and growth, the formation of the whole individual, a process that the humanities and the "soft" social sciences advance in ways that the "hard" subjects cannot. That is, women's preponderant choice of humane subjects for graduate study reflects an interest in self-exploration and a concern for women's education but also a broader concern, shared by many women, about the proper focus of undergraduate education for everyone—a concern with focusing the transformational power of learning squarely on the individual.

Another mark of women's work in the academy, a mark less immediately obvious than the choice of "soft" fields, is a characteristic—and maverick—approach to subject matter, regardless of field. To repeat an earlier disclaimer, we do not find a common mark, a common approach to scholarship in the work of *all* women; rather what we report here are commonalities that recur often enough to be notable and that are distinctive in that they tend to remain constant, regardless of prevailing approaches or fashions in the various academic fields.

The most general characteristic of women's intellectual work consists of placing subject matter in a cultural context, in the real and complicated life of the relevant time and place. The point of contextual study is to establish the meaning and the value of the matter under study to a particular group of people by looking closely at its place, use, influence in real lives. This emphasis on the real appears again and again in the use of the term "nitty-gritty" to describe work in a wide variety of subjects. Women studying French social history, early modern family history, Slavic literature, African politics, the English novel, all say they want to get at the "nitty-gritty" of their subject; they want to place it in the patterns of life, or, as some women say, the social matrix, of the people involved. What this often means in academic terms is resistance to scholarship concentrating on the formal characteristics of a subject.

An art historian, tracing a series of changes in her own work, provides a succinct description of the contextual approach. "We think differently about the material now. We are much less inclined to isolate stylistic development, the appearance of the work, from its social context. And I am very excited by a lot of the newer ideas and I am thinking of ways in which I can apply them in the material I am working on. Events that are sometimes hard to connect in the right way, probably do turn out to be connected. . . . Political or religious events that are sometimes referred to as background for art—perhaps this isn't really background, perhaps it is all part of the making of art. . . . [This way of thinking] comes a little out of my own training in archaeology, oddly enough, and anthropology. It's a way of thinking of culture as a whole matrix, rather than isolating out some great works of art or great artists, independent of that matrix. . . . I went through graduate training and latched onto the then very fashionable way of looking at art objects in isolation and learned about style. And I'm not sorry I did that, but I have a rather comfortable feeling of, in some ways, coming back to things that are familiar. . . ."

Another art historian, a specialist in ancient art and archaeology, describes her insistence on doing contextual work from graduate school on, despite the strongly prevailing influence of formalism in her special field. We quote from her interview now at some length to exemplify how contextual study actually operates in a particular subject. "Professor X [her thesis adviser and leading authority in the field] feels very, very strongly that art is something that you can separate out from the rest of a culture, and that it can stand all by itself. I think that's hogwash. . . . He talks about culture a lot, but when it comes down to the actual art object, he uses a kind of formal analysis. By formal analysis, we mean . . . literally the forms of things as opposed to any other aspects, not their iconography, not questions of beauty or aesthetics. It has to do just with what their literal form is, how that fits into the whole body of an art. . . . I always go back to the relationship to the culture."

She then speaks of her doctoral thesis which she did as part of a team working on a major archaeological excavation. She was assigned to study painting and drawing styles, by which her adviser meant studying the form of compositions painted on ceramics or incised on various objects or walls. "However, because of my bent, the way I perceive things, to me there was only one way to approach the problem and that was contextually. [Laughs.] So that if you were going to look at thirty objects in a tomb, or burial place, they had to be understood in their relationship to each other as objects which were painted and made for one person, and part of that person's lifetime. . . . Which was not the way my job was seen by anybody but me! . . . But I feel that the point of being an art historian is to use one's ability to perceive these aesthetic objects as part of the culture; it means that what you're doing is history from a certain angle. It takes a long time. You have to know the whole literature and every object that's ever been excavated like it, and its role in its original site. . . . But it's exciting. I love it. Because it's deeply involving and very satisfying, and because it leads to the most extraordinary insights and reformulations." Still, the prevailing approach in archaeology, she says, is to organize and analyze ancient art objects by their material. "So that you have a chapter on stone objects, you have a chapter on ceramics, and a chapter on this and on that, *destroying* what to me is the most basic significance of them, which is where they were when they were found, and what they were with. . . . Why excavate these objects if you're going to treat them as if they had just dropped from the sky?"

Much the same language applied to a completely different subject appears in comments from a scholar of English literature. She is speaking of qualities that appealed to her in a graduate school professor, himself something of a maverick in his field. "He was extremely informal and direct and you might say connected to history in experience, so that his comments on literature were very directly connected to life and to a social and historical context. But mostly it was the life-connection that I liked. He made more life-connections with literature than a lot of people did. . . ." And in fact this interviewee has made life-connections one of the hallmarks of her own highly regarded interpretations of modern writers.

And a student of Celtic languages explains how the conflict between examining context and form affects her work. A strong emphasis in her graduate department, she says, was on the form of the language—"linguistic theory and analysis." Her own interest was in the substance of Celtic folk texts and then, after taking several folklore courses, in the culture more broadly. "I found my own interest veering much more toward those larger ideas about how societies function, and how literature and culture are shaped and shape the way people live." Her specific interest is in the tradition of lament, the ritualized songs of grief and mourning sung by women at the time of death. Her scholarly aim is to place the lament in a detailed cultural context. "I wanted to put it together for myself as a whole, to be able to look at the tradition of lament, not just to see it in isolation." That is, she wants to contribute, through the evidence of folk ritual, to the imaginative re-creation of the culture as a whole.

Similarly, concentration on culture as a context for significance may produce scholarship eschewing scientific certainty as a mark of excellence in a particular field—refusing, that is, to place the highest value on scholarly work that is provable through either logic or scientific demonstration. By its nature, the culture of any group of human beings is complicated, fluid and endlessly resistant to scientific description whether because of a wealth of information or a dearth of it. Thus scholars who want to understand cultural settings must be willing to accept uncertainty and ambiguity—and the criticism of those who regard such efforts as superficial, fuzzy-headed.

A young musicologist talks, with some dismay, about the increasing domination of her field by a school of thought that concentrates, in studying the history of music, on the precise temporal documentation both of compositions and of the artifacts of musicians' lives. The problem, according to the young woman interviewed, is that scholars quarrel over such factual matters as the dating of watermarks rather than the significance of the dating, and worse, they exclude consideration of anything that cannot be documented—which means excluding the explorations of cultural setting that interest her.

"I think the interest that I have in history has always been in . . . the interesting intrigue of what it might have felt like to be somebody living then. . . . I did a paper on the pitch changes that were added by the performers [of early polyphony]. Nobody really knows exactly how they did it, and part of the way I went about thinking about that . . . was to investigate what the training of musicians was like and to try to re-create, in my own head at any rate, what the circumstances were, who was singing this, and where were they. Can you imagine them in a little cloister someplace in England in the fourteenth century? How many of them were there? Where did they learn to do this? And that seemed like an important part of it to me, to get to what they eventually produced."

But her work was received with tolerance, at best. "It was all right to play around with these things in courses, but when you are doing real serious work like your dissertation, it has to be scientific." She then went on to describe a woman professor she admired who was resisting the scientific trend. "It always seemed to me that one of the primary reasons she had chosen the medieval period, and her particular part of the period, was that there was almost no evidence, which meant that you couldn't be scientific. It was not an option and you had to therefore be speculative and creative about the way you went about doing something. And she did spend a lot of time trying to re-create the music."

Another recurring pattern in women's scholarship is resistance to work that seeks certainty through abstract theory. That is, scholars who make certainty their intellectual goal can achieve it not only through the study of form and the gathering of scientific data, but also through the theoretical ordering of abstract ideas according to principles of logic. The most certain and most elegant theoretical work, the ultimate repository of logic, is mathematics, but the theoretical expression of ideas about any subject is possible—its certainty depending on the precise definition, as well as the logical linking, of premises. And it is virtually a cliché in academe that the great theoreticians in any discipline include few women—the implication being that women do not have the intellectual capacity for theory. Starting from this assumption, critics of women's work do not even consider the possibility that women choose other forms of study for positive reasons. What we find in our stories, in fact, is not an avoidance of theory altogether, but a fascination with subjects combining theory and reality in a variety of ways.

Some women's work focuses on the relation of actual daily experience to larger social or moral patterns. An English scholar explains, for example, that she is particularly interested in William Blake's allegories because they combine an overall moral viewpoint with a "very gripping way of capturing experience, an immediate and concrete sense of things." And a European historian chose to write her dissertation on Jean-Paul Sartre rather than on the German intellectuals her thesis adviser suggested, because Sartre "seems to be more concretely in the world . . . more immediate, personal. . . ." She finds Sartre to be "a link figure" through whom she could work on the relation between philosophy or theory and what she calls "social reality and psychological reality." However, nearing the end of her dissertation, she says that in the future she would like "to do something a little solider . . . than dealing with ideology, . . . something that would deal more with the nitty-gritty."

The work on learning theory of a specialist in art education reflects yet another kind of resistance to abstract theorizing and that is admitting ambiguity in subject matter. Here, the woman in question insists on building theory out of a broadly inclusive range of evidence, even if the resulting complication reduces theoretical certainty. And she describes running into trouble with one of her advisers for this reason.

The young scholar's dissertation was designed to identify stages of sophistication in the viewers' response to art. Her ultimate goal was to heighten and broaden such response, through an understanding of its sources. To this end, she devised her own interview technique, which, simply put, consisted of asking her interview subjects to look at a painting and talk about it, essentially unguided. Then, analyzing the transcripts, she developed her theory of perception out of the patterns that emerged from the responses of many interviewees. She allowed the patterns to surface from the material—much as we did in this book; she did not frame questions to elicit evidence for prior conceptions.

The difficulties with her adviser arose over her insistence on including, in some category or other, everything that her interview subjects said. Her adviser insisted that she should include only those responses that related directly to the art object being viewed—such as its subject, form, or color. Her position was that by predefining what is relevant to the perception of art, you screen out parts of the whole and do not get an accurate picture of the entire process of perception and response. She characterizes this approach as a willingness on her part—and perhaps on the part of women in general—"to accept ambiguity in a situation, . . . to realize that there are some parts that cannot be as articulated as other parts, and not to try to put everything in cubbyholes and exclude that which cannot be clearly articulated."

She goes on: "One of the things that I do when I look at aesthetic responses . . . [is that] I score every statement. I don't throw out anything because it doesn't fit. I score it. I define a category for it. It becomes part of the typologies that I use. *Nothing* do I ever throw out at all—like not throwing away paper bags. Another thing [other scholars] do is to look at responses and say they're not [relevant because they're not] *aesthetic*. . . . I say whatever comes up in an aesthetic response is by definition part of the aesthetic response. If you're looking at an art object and you're talking about it, that's part of how you're perceiving it. You can't just say that's not there. . . . I really felt that set categories, set questions, just gave the interviewers back what they were looking for."

Shulamit Reinharz's study, *On Becoming a Social Scientist*, describes her own departures from the prevailing norms in sociology in terms strikingly similar to those of our interviewees. Her book is both an analysis of the professionalization process and a critique of her particular discipline. Her central argument is that the social sciences in general and sociology in particular are committed to achieving a degree of scientific certainty that they cannot attain and that removes their scholarship from meaningful human experience. Making her claims specific, she sets up dual lists of goals and methods—which we quote in full—one describing the prevailing norms in sociology, the other outlining her alternative approach.

"Mainstream sociology claims to be: Exclusively rational in the conduct of research and the analysis of data / Scientific / Oriented to carefully defined structures / Completely impersonal / Oriented to the prediction and control of events and things / Interested in the validity of research findings for scholars / Objective / Capable of producing generalized principles / Interested in replicable events and procedures / Capable of producing completed analyses of a research problem / Interested in addressing problems with predefined concepts.

"An alternative method would acknowledge that it is: A mix of rational, serendipitous and intuitive phenomena in research and analysis / Accurate but artistic / Oriented to processes / Personal / Oriented to understanding phenomena / Interested in the meaningfulness of research findings to the scholarly and user communities / A mix of objective and subjective orientations / Capable of producing specific explanations / Interested in unique although frequently occurring phenomena / Limited to producing partial discoveries of ongoing events / Interested in generating concepts *in vivo,* in the field itself."

The second list, she remarks, "embodies the rehumanization of sociology to reflect the fact that its researchers are human beings dealing with human problems in humane ways."[9]

Present in all of the projects just reviewed is yet another distinctive feature of women's scholarship—transcending disciplinary boundaries. The women studying art or language or music in the context of a particular time and place combine these subjects variously with anthropology, archaeology, sociology, history. The historian studying Jean-Paul Sartre necessarily combines French intellectual history with philosophy and political theory; the educationist studying how people learn about art combines extensive work in developmental psychology and philosophy (aesthetics) with the subject matter of fine art.

And a random look at projects described by other interviewees reveals the same tendency. A scholar of English Renaissance literature describes her thesis as including work on myth, biblical study, iconography, and art. Another older scholar in the same field wrote her thesis in the 1950s, well before the interdisciplinary boom of the 1960s, on a topic combining literature and religion. This work ultimately entailed taking courses at a divinity school for background that she, and her graduate department, lacked, and adding a divinity school professor to her thesis review committee. A specialist in modern French literature moved through French psychoanalytic theory to feminist theory and beyond that to an examination of European medical history regarding women's diseases.

A number of interviewees have located themselves in new disciplines that are deliberately designed to bridge traditional fields. American studies is one—a field combining subjects traditionally taught as American history and American literature. Such fields also include philosophy of education, history of education, history of science. And most significantly and prolifically, women's studies.

In every field, women scholars have begun to question the treatment (and nontreatment) of women in established scholarship—examining interpretations of women based in the preconceptions of the old norms, making up for the absence of serious interpretations of women's experience, and also adding women's contributions and achievements to the canon of any particular field. A philosopher says that she was well into her career before she began to give serious attention to the issue of women in philosophic thought. Then she was stunned to realize that philosophers, like the authorities in other fields, "based their data on males, and it seems as if women are an anomaly—they either ignore the women, they don't know how to handle women, they distort women's experience, when what they need to be doing is saying, 'Look, the theory is all wrong, the theory has to be changed.' "

In general, women scholars have been writing women into fields of knowledge from which they have effectively been excluded. And such an enterprise is necessarily cross-disciplinary because the causes of exclusion lie scattered in many fields. As one historian says: "I think that working in women's studies, I find we become more interdisciplinary, more cross-cultural in our thinking. I think that is the beauty in what has happened to us as scholars in the women's movement. And I think I might well have gone on and done very much more conventional work than perhaps I'm doing now, had not the women's movement come along."

In pursuing women's studies, women scholars convert their outsider status to a source of strength because their subject is, in fact, the phenomenon of outsiderness. For many, the intellectual excitement, and relief, in this new venture is palpable. A young professor of English literature tells the story of a long bus ride that placed her accidentally in the company of an established woman scholar in her field. "She was trying to elicit what I was doing as a scholar, and I was really kind of nebulous about what I was doing, and I said, 'Well, I'm interested in the sister of such and such a poet, because she keeps popping up everywhere, but there's nothing really about her, and, come to think of it, I'm interested in all these other women writers of that time I keep seeing in the Short Title Catalogue, and nobody has ever said anything about them.' And she said, 'Well, at the very least, you ought to write an anthology, you know.' And then she said, 'Come to think of it, why aren't you doing your scholarship on this? There's a whole field that's untouched.' And by the time I got off that bus, I felt as if I were ten feet in the air. I thought, 'I've just discovered my life's work!' And it was, I just couldn't wait to get started. It was the most exciting day of my life!"

And the scholar of French literature referred to above says she had become bored with her own early work on a notable French writer of the 1930s, then speaks almost fervently about the sense of new life that she felt when she began to focus on the French feminist theory that emerged in the 1970s. "There was a sense of my personal life and my academic life coming together. . . . Suddenly those two linked as a unit instead of being juxtaposed or clashing or something. The way I saw my life, my view of the world suddenly was integrated, and my experience, everything that I was, was relevant to this."

In general, women's outsider status makes them sensitive to the large question of power distribution in the society and its consequences for weaker groups. And here we see another strong commonality in the scholarship of many women, a commonality running through women's studies but also extending beyond it, and that is a strong preoccupation with seeking social change through transformed consciousness.

As we have already discussed in chapter 2, women have a strong commitment to individual transformation through teaching. And we would add here that that interest extends to scholarship on pedagogy. Recall the project described above in art education—the study of viewer response to art. For the scholar in question, the purpose of learning about viewers' responses is to find ways to develop the depth and complexity of their reactions. Her approach assumes that art, if effectively taught, can be widely accessible, not just the purview of the elite. Thus, by refusing to discard any level or type of understanding in her viewers' perceptions, but instead, charting them on a continuum, she provides a base for development. No one, however unsophisticated, is automatically excluded from the enterprise of learning about art—and ultimately, judging it, deciding what has value and what does not. The potential democratization of value making in the world of art would not amount to revolutionary change, but it would entail a shift in social power nonetheless.

Several scholars exhibit interest in change by studying figures whose lives exemplify self-transformation. One woman wrote her dissertation on the British critic John Middleton Murry in part because of her identification with him as someone who came from a lower-class background and literally transformed his life through ideas. "What I saw missing in any [critical] treatment of Murry was the recognition that his life and his ideas were bound up with one another in a way that one couldn't separate. He would say one day, 'Oh, I now have a new truth, I now understand this,' and just completely change his direction. He carried that sort of behavior to the point of real eccentricity. But the point is you couldn't understand any of his attitudes toward literature or anything else without seeing it as part of the matrix of his whole life."

Similarly, an American historian explains her interest in the Greenwich Village radicals of the First World War–era because of her attraction both to their ideals and to their attempts to enact their ideals in their daily lives. They were artists and writers who had "this marvelous vision of a brave new world in which everyone is equal and there are no sexual politics and everybody makes the same amount of money and you can be a laborer and also love Beethoven, and you can be a member of the middle classes and still be accepted by the working classes and somehow you are going to create this perfectly integrated, harmonious, just society where the individual can achieve fulfillment but yet everybody is equal." Their attempts to put their beliefs into practice, she says, "oftentimes almost destroyed their marriages and their lives because they couldn't cope emotionally with their intellectual and political commitments." She has worked to rescue this group from the contempt of "the thirties radicals and the New Left of the '60s" who say only that the artist/radicals did not engage seriously enough in political organization as a means of effecting change, and who failed to see the seriousness of their attempts literally to change themselves. In so doing, however, this scholar opens herself to charges of frivolity for taking seriously people generally condemned as politically naive.

Another way in which women pursue the goal of social change in their scholarship is to study groups of people—sometimes women, sometimes not—who were not the dominant shapers of a dominant culture at a particular time and place—and whose attributes, therefore, have not been regarded as important. For example, a European historian says, "I had done a seminar on the [French] middle class and the thing which fascinated me about them was their life style which seemed to require someone to make life easier, someone to care for them—carrying water and coal and taking care of the children. And so I became more fascinated by the servants they employed, live-in servants, and what I studied was the nineteenth-century pattern of live-in domestic service."

As the historian finds a subordinate class worthy of study, the oral literature scholar, referred to earlier as studying the tradition of women's lament, focuses both on a subordinate culture and specifically on women within that culture. That is, she is concerned not only with understanding whole cultural patterns, as discussed above, but also with identifying the cultural values of a traditional society and recognizing them as such—rather than as deviances in relation to a dominant culture. "Why have all the visitors' accounts from Elizabethan times on talked about these barbaric, antediluvian customs when obviously the two traditions were so totally different? . . . There's a lot of work under way now *on* death and the history of European approaches to death—the restraint, the resignation—whereas traditional societies continued to herald this social transition with violent behavior, tearing clothing, tearing of hair, a peculiar singing and chanting, with certain formulas repeated over and over again. . . . This kind of demonstration of emotion in a ritualized sense was shocking to European visitors." And she wants to replace this shock at particular behavior or the dismissal of such behavior as bizarre and aberrant with an understanding of the values of the whole culture in which these practices were a norm and a source of meaning. And she wants to understand how and why women assumed the role of the lamenter.

We regard such stories as predicated on the need for social change, not because they lay out blueprints for social revolution, but because they direct attention to subordinate groups and—directly or indirectly—question the justice of their subordination. By seeking to understand the values of such groups in their own terms, and not in the terms supplied by the dominant culture, studies of women, servants, minorities, the colonized articulate previously submerged power relations. And to bring these relations into broad social consciousness is a vital step in the process of changing them.

What we see generally in the range of work reviewed above is a strong thread of resistance by women to academic conventions establishing the boundaries of knowledge—from the rules of scientific certainty, the logic of abstract theory, and the division of subject matter into discrete disciplines, to the rules that include or exclude material as relevant to a particular discipline. But, as we have noted, women do not proceed along these lines and pursue such purposes with the applause of established academic authorities. Rather, in flouting these bounds, women call down on themselves, for the most part, the scorn of the academy and end up paying a price for their deviance.

One common form of difficulty women encounter is a by-product of the kind of work discussed above that runs across disciplinary lines. The problem here begins in graduate school where women, following their questions into departments other than their own, do not gain clear-cut interest and backing from authorities in any one field. Thus the art historian/archaeologist quoted earlier encountered animosity between fine arts and anthropology departments based on lack of understanding or interest in each other. She confides: "an interdisciplinary field is between two fields, really. There was no one who was responsible for you. . . ." Sometimes it is difficult for a graduate student doing a crossdisciplinary thesis to find an adviser at all. A historian/educationist recalls with some acerbity: "I did my dissertation really without supervision and it would have been good if I'd had it. . . . My nominal adviser was in the education department, and he told me he would be glad to read the dissertation and approve it and make corrections but he wasn't going to be able to help me with it and so I did it entirely on my own."

Moving across disciplinary lines also makes it difficult to secure pertinent recommendations. As one French scholar who redefined her focus after graduate school phrases it, in response to the question whether she is in a clear relation to senior faculty, "I mean, everyone is delighted to write [recommendations] for me . . . [but] I don't know. I'm in a very anomalous position because . . . what I want to do is something other than I'm trained for. I don't want to be writing French literary criticism. I'm trying to write something in social science. But I have no expertise there, at all. No, that's not true. I have a lot of expertise, but I don't have any paper confirmation."

And the consequences of ignoring established boundaries do not end even when a scholar is tenured and widely recognized for published work, as a philosopher/educationist in this situation relates. "If I try to get a grant from an education agency, they will say this is not educational research, no matter what it's on, no matter how central it is on education, because it's philosophical. But philosophical or humanities-oriented grants-giving places will [also] look upon it askance because it's about education." She sums up: "It was and is a disadvantage. It's an odd specialty within philosophy and on the other hand if you look at it from the standpoint of education, it's an odd specialty within education. . . . Not fitting in . . . that's the story of my life and my research." And a tenured psychologist whose work integrates laboratory and clinical science although her field conventionally keeps them discrete, tells a similar story of continuing disadvantage. "What I'm trying to say is that when I interact with the mainstream I don't have any trouble with them. I just in various ways tend to avoid them and some of it is really not good for me. I won't be a full professor because I do that, or I won't until I do."

Crossing disciplinary lines is only one form of intellectual nonconformity by women scholars and thus only one source of trouble for them. Another kind of choice for which women pay the price of diminished professional standing is their predilection, discussed above, for subjects conventionally regarded as "soft." A tenured historian reports still feeling like an outsider, not taken seriously by students or faculty within her own department, because the invidious "soft" and "hard" labels attach to her specialization in social history. "There are many more women [than men] who do social history. It is a field that tends to [examine] groups like women and/or domestic servants or working people . . . but the department tends to be quite traditional. . . . There is very little social history taught." Thus the woman in question, together with her field, commands less respect because of the prevailing view of what should be relevant in history. And, because her work does center on women, she pays a further price in intellectual segregation. "I'm given books to review in women's history. . . . It really doesn't matter what period it covers, as long as it deals with women. Or I'm not considered to be appropriate for a commentator or as part of a panel on straight history, but rather always get [placed on] panels where the whole group is women even if it is at a European historical conference."

Of course, women's studies itself is the ultimate "soft" subject and endless suspicions attach to it and to the women who persist in studying and teaching it. One problem is getting such courses approved in the first place. A philosopher says: "I had a hard time getting the course 'Philosophy and Women' approved at all. . . . [Even] the students were concerned the course would be frivolous and so I handed them my reading list and I had made it deliberately tough. It was very rigorous. It was thoroughly respectable. The students silently capitulated."

Furthermore, most academic women recognize that the special penalty for adopting a women's studies concentration is even further alienation from the mainstream than interdisciplinary and contextual study have caused. Although, as we have seen earlier in this chapter, women enter the field of women's studies enthusiastic over the opportunity to redress the intellectual record, to include their own heroines, ordinary and extraordinary, and to engage in more vital debate than most academicians in more ivy-covered fields, the potential danger is that by immersing themselves in the study of women, they reinforce their own academic status as outsiders.

In reviewing the price that women pay for intellectual deviance, one complicating point must be made. It might well be assumed that professional success for academic women depends on conventional work and that deflection follows upon unconventionality. But a number of the stories just recounted do involve tenured women, and, indeed, our sample of sixty-two interviewees reveals little variation in the pattern of work between tenured and deflected women. In both groups, the overall rate of non-mainstream scholarship was high—about 70 percent, with roughly half of the women in each engaged in studies focusing on women and another fifth in unconventional studies of subjects other than women. But the success of the tenured women in spite of their departures from the scholarly norm does not undermine the point that unconventional work carries penalties.

For example, as far as women's studies is concerned, it is indeed true that work in this field has become one route to tenure as colleges and universities have added a certain number of women's studies positions to their faculties. The difficulty here is that the number of such positions is extremely limited and can absorb only a small percentage of scholars studying women. Thus the greater number do not receive appointments or promotions beyond the lower ranks because, in the familiar phrase, "We already have someone in women's studies."

As for women doing scholarship that departs from disciplinary norms, but without focusing on women, the picture is yet more problematic. Although the percentage of tenured and deflected interviewees whose work falls into this category is about the same, the stories of the tenured women all include some kind of extenuating circumstance that proved a counterweight to their nonconformity: one started on an unconventional track only to have her subject come into fashion in time for her to benefit from it; another did conventional work until she received tenure, then turned in other directions; several more, although departing from the mainstream, still accorded with strong minority traditions in their fields so that their work had recognizable and acceptable features; still others were tenured at institutions where teaching, not scholarship, was the primary basis for appointment.

The most accurate measure of the difficulties women face due to scholarly unconventionalities of all kinds is still the relatively low percentage of women among those in academe who become tenured at all, and the even lower percentage who become tenured at institutions that are the centers of professional authority.

Here we would add an interesting and complex postscript to the adverse consequences that befall the practitioners of women's work in the academy. Because the position of women inside academe is still so far from the corridors of power, their intellectual labors may include certain moral dilemmas known to every minority struggling for recognition and autonomy. The problem is one of defining limits to gender loyalty. How is the woman scholar to balance the rival strategies of assimilation and group identity? In women's studies, for example, how far is the scholar justified in criticizing a particular line of study if the field as a whole is seen as a hospitable haven for her and others like her? How justified is a woman in devoting her research efforts to a female figure disapproved of by feminists?

One tenured professor testifies that she met lack of interest from other women because of her choice of subject: "This woman [her research focus] was not a feminist, even though she led one of the most independent lives that anyone could imagine and that's one reason she interested me. . . . Many of her friends were feminists but she spent her whole life manipulating and controlling men . . . getting them to create her and make her immortal . . . and that conflict was fascinating to me. . . . Feminist scholars have ignored her, I believe, because she was not a feminist and because they see her as operating in ways they find offensive and antifeminist." Still, as she points out, men don't present the subject of her biography in a fashion that satisfies feminists, either. "They patronize her and present her . . . only as a decoration in male lives." So, until hers, no fair biography of this subject had been written.

The question as to how far intellectual loyalty should be exercised or waived is raised specifically by a critic of French literature. She confesses that, although she finds certain lines of theoretical feminism in her field "sterile," she is reluctant to challenge women scholars writing such theory. She explains, "These are the women who are really making it in modern languages where it's very hard to make it, and here am I saying to these women, 'You will triumph at the expense of selling out.' That's a crummy thing to say. I have not felt good about saying it, haven't said it, of course, in print. My book doesn't go into this question." The conflicts and pulls that women face in the field of women's studies are divisive and difficult, as they are in the settlement of any terra incognita; and there is no reason to assume this field would be exempt from scholarly disputation. But the knowledge that women enter scholarship surrounded by hostility, like most emergent nations, makes them leery of sniping at their own ranks in the approved academic manner.[10]

Given the professional costs and moral dilemmas of pursuing nonconventional work, why do women persist in this effort? The large point is that the established bounds do not admit the questions women want to ask and answer. The old bounds are geared to clarity and certainty, but such standards presuppose values defining what certainty is, and what is worth establishing with certainty. Women, with their long responsibility for human relations and their first-hand knowledge of human intractability, want to gain understanding of a subject by immersing it in, rather than abstracting it from, the untidiness of human activity. Further, out of their increasing consciousness of their own subordination, women are newly examining the allocations of power both in specific social institutions and in the larger society. And, increasingly conscious of the effective denial of their own wholeness—their strength of intellect as well as instinct—they are examining with great intensity the connections between power and truth.[11]

To sum up, a large body of women's work in the academy is marked by common, distinct characteristics: the loyalty to "soft" subjects in the humanities as indispensable to examining human values; the placement of subject matter in a cultural context; the insistence on raising value-related, change-related questions even if their study does not fit conventional definitions and disciplines; the expansion of the canon in all fields by the validation of material previously overlooked or considered irrelevant; a strong emphasis on women's studies.

Overall, women scholars are heavily engaged in integrating knowledge. Their work *combines* disciplines, *combines* theory and reality, *combines* a commitment to change with a commitment to humane study. Its approach to knowledge is inclusive to the point of ambiguity, rather than exclusive to the point of certainty. Its social vision is of an integrated whole with the characteristics and interests of diverse groups honored and supported.

At this point we would repeat that, of course, women are not alone in the intellectual directions they pursue. Men as well as women do integrative scholarship, specializing in humane subjects, crossing disciplinary bounds, seeking social change, and studying women's experience. Furthermore, such approaches sometimes even come into widely followed fashion in particular fields so that their practitioners are insiders rather than outsiders. But generally, the work we have been describing is a minority tradition in most fields, yet it is strongly prevalent, in its various forms, among women—pursued, as noted above, by about 70 percent of our interviewees.

Thus women—again not all, but many—*do* form a distinct intellectual constituency. And doing so, they challenge the established system profoundly with implicit injunctions for change. But for themselves, such innovative scholarship entails serious risks. The lingering association of women with lowly tasks, the ever-ready assumption of the inferiority of women's minds, make it easy to dismiss their unconventional work as unsubstantial, raising yet another obstacle to their achievement of professional authority.

Chapter 6

Life and the Life of the Mind

"Didn't anyone ever tell you it was all right to write?" asked X, years later. Yes, but not to be a writer. Behind me lay the sort of upper middle-class education that encourages writing, painting, music, theater so long as they aren't taken too seriously, so long as they can be set aside once the real business of life begins.

Jane Cooper, *Scaffolding*

An English professor, long tenured at a women's college, sees the central issue of her life summed up in Yeats's poem "The Choice" in which he says that, for the poet, it is necessary to choose between "perfection of the life or of the work." Like most professional women, she has struggled throughout her career with this contention: that serious creative work, including the intellectual work of the academy, requires such concentration that the nonwork life must be sacrificed, or at least put in second place. That is, the claims of family, friendships, civic responsibilities, serious avocations, even recreation, must give way before the claims of "the work." Or vice versa.

Certainly for the women in this study, and we believe for professional women generally, this is an issue that is never fully resolved. Competing claims of the personal and the professional realms loom in prospect for the young woman, take a bewildering variety of shapes while a career is in progress, and finally form a pattern that prods the older woman to ask whether she had made the right choices. From women who feel that they have sacrificed too much either of the work or of the life, we hear the frequent refrain: How could I have done it differently? Or worse: How could I have been so stupid, so naive? Or looking at the lives of women who seem to have achieved a good personal/professional balance: How did they do it? Are they smarter than I? Stronger? Richer?

The initial problem in approaching any of these poignant questions is to work through a snarl of confusion in the underlying issue. Essentially the confusion lies in the fact that the conflict between personal and professional claims sounds as if it is the same for all people in the professions, men as well as women. Our interviewee, after all, cites Yeats as the articulator of her own dilemma. And to a degree, of course, the issues are the same, but to a far greater degree they differ. For women, and not for men, the claims of "the life" include the claims, assigned to women by the old norms of the marriage plot, of primary responsibility for the family. And those claims are so heavy, so long lasting, so fraught with serious consequence if ignored, that they make the choice between personal and professional realms a wholly different matter from the general conflict to which Yeats testified.

For one thing—a point so obvious it is easy to ignore—if women bear primary responsibility for the family, that responsibility is reduced for men, leaving their side of the personal/professional equation relatively manipulable. Men, even if married and with children, can increase or decrease their civic responsibilities, cultural pursuits, even engagement in family affairs, to adjust to demands of "the work." And if they cannot achieve perfection of both life and work, they can seek a fair balance over the long run and, with it, a satisfying expression of various facets of the personality. But the bearer of primary responsibility for family—usually a woman—is far more constrained in seeking such a balance. The needs of children cannot be suspended for several years if work demands become heavy. Thus what is for men a matter of tension between two realms, a conflict requiring shifting emphases and continuing compromise, becomes for women more nearly a choice—either "the life" *or* "the work."

And this is precisely the message of the old norms—that for women it is necessary to choose and that their choice should be for "the life." Here we arrive at the not subtle but central conflict between the marriage and quest plots because, simply put, the marriage plot decrees that women's proper work is responsibility for private needs and relations. If women abdicate this responsibility as their sole task, then the quality of family and community life will decline. The only other alternative, that men share private responsibilities, has as its social cost the loss of men's full energy and creativity in the realm of demanding work. And the assumption implicit in the marriage plot is that most people most of the time cannot do both well, that it *is* necessary to choose. The corollary assumption, of course, is that women's greater gifts lie in domesticity which they *should* therefore choose, whereas men's natural gifts best fit them for larger, creative work.

At the present time, the social norm that enforces the ancient division of labor is no longer a general prohibition against women entering the professional world, but precisely the injunction to choose "the work or the life"—narrowed to mean "the work or the family" and freighted with the threat of losing the option of family if "the life" is not put first.

The message that they should make a choice, to be put into effect when the two options conflict, enters women's lives in a variety of ways. Before the women's movement imposed, to some degree, a rhetoric of equality in professional life, the message was often delivered baldly by a professional mentor. An art historian in graduate school in the early 1960s speaks about an older woman professor who had remained single and was at the top of her profession: "She was very open in sharing personal things with her students and really made [the importance of being single] clear to us—in order to have a career. The inference, of course, being that those of us who were married had doomed ourselves."

More common are reactions and remarks in which the assumption of incompatibility between serious work and family responsibilities for women is implicit. For example, a woman with a recent Ph.D. in ancient languages says: "I remember sitting in class with one of my professors and he was talking about a thesis that was done by a woman student. . . . He was commending the thesis, he was talking very highly about it and then he sort of said, 'But then she got married.' " As if the marriage ceremony transformed the woman's mind to a state of vacuity. An English professor speaks of a similar reaction she encountered in her first regular full-time appointment. "I taught through the fall and then I was expecting a baby between terms and all my officemates got their springtime schedule and only I did not get a schedule. I went to the chairman saying, 'Where is my spring schedule?' And he said, 'You can't teach in the spring, you're going to have a baby.' And I said, 'What do you mean I can't teach in the spring? If I can teach when I am pregnant, surely I can teach when I am not pregnant.' And he said, 'Oh no, no. We know that nobody with a new baby could possibly handle a teaching schedule too.' He was adamant and I was furious." Her response was to go on a crash hunt for other jobs until the chairman, seeing she was determined to teach somewhere, gave her a part-time schedule.

But this is not the end of the story. "In vengeance he appointed me to an

8 A.M. section so that I used to get up at 6:30 and get myself dressed and get the baby dressed and drop the baby at the babysitter and go and teach from 8 to 9, then I came back and picked up the baby, so that I really was not in the department in a visible way." That is, under the old norms, a woman with a child is "seen" as a mother, eclipsed as a professor. Thus, the chairman backed down from refusing to give the woman in question a teaching schedule, but arranged that, as a professor, she would become virtually invisible. Another English professor, visibly pregnant while teaching, reports that, in that situation, she too could be "seen" only as a pregnant woman. "Whenever anyone spoke to me, they brought up my pregnancy. Nothing else ever seemed to come up!"

Another variation of the message that professional work and family responsibilities cannot be combined is the prediction, often casually made to young women, that they will not get far professionally because they are so likely to marry and have children—the implication being, of course, that the one precludes the other. We see the effect of this message, and the degree to which women internalize it, in stories recording the embarrassment women feel when they must announce a pregnancy to their academic departments.

A philosophy professor confides: "I remember when I was pregnant with the second child, I was a teaching fellow and at the beginning—he was born in June—at the beginning of the spring semester I figured I better tell my professor and it was a horrible experience. When I think about that now, it is sort of retroactively shocking because I was very embarrassed to tell him. . . . I mean it was quite legitimate. I was married and there was nothing wrong with being pregnant, but I felt this sense of embarrassment and shame and I think it was partly, clearly the woman thing, that there is this whole kind of admission of yourself as a sexual being that I felt very uncomfortable about." She added, "Everybody was very nice about it, but it's true that it wasn't something that people sort of took as a perfectly normal routine thing to do. . . . It wasn't something that you expected of your male students, and so it was an irregularity. It *was* an irregularity; it wasn't that we just perceived it that way." A biologist tells us of a friend in graduate school who was so embarrassed about breaking the news of her pregnancy to her professor that she insisted our interviewee accompany her to the dreaded interview, and in this case, the professor was a woman. In both cases, the pregnant women anticipated some sort of negative reaction from academic authorities, but the stories also convey a personal sense of worry or discomfort: maybe there *is* something amiss about being pregnant and a philosopher or biologist at the same time.

Another indirect but still highly powerful warning of trouble for women who attempt to combine family life and work emanates from the phrase commonly used to describe that combination—namely, "having it all." This phrase connotes, not a positive balance of life and work, but rather self-concern, even greed. It calls up images of a child hogging all the toys or eating all the ice cream—perhaps a smart trick to pull off, but, clearly, unattractive as well. And its pejorative innuendo is augmented by the fact that the phrase and its connotations are rarely, if ever, applied to men who somehow manage to sustain a rich personal as well as work life. The implication lurking in this distinction is that for a man to achieve such a synthesis is acceptable, even admirable, but for a woman it is in some way questionable. That is, to use the phrase "having it all" is to tell women, however indirectly, that it is selfish to seek demanding public responsibilities—that such a demand disrupts the natural division of labor between men and women and imposes appalling social costs in the process.

But whether conveyed directly or indirectly, the old norms requiring choice between family and work are there to be reckoned with by all women for whom work is too important to be unquestioningly laid aside under exigencies of a personal life. And given the consequences of such a choice, the dilemma is sharp pronged and hard. Here, a historian uses the terminology of a religious vocation—which she briefly considered—to convey the weight of the problem as she has felt it. "My sense of professional life was that it was a kind of choice. There was a choice to be a mother, and a choice to be a professional woman of some kind, and my sense of what I was choosing was limited by that sense, of profession, vocation. Women who are very bright and very interested in having a professional career generally see themselves as somehow then being limited in their choices."

The amazing fact in this case is that the speaker is in her thirties, but still has had to thread her way through the same maze as that faced by the pre–women's-movement generations. She and her peers still must begin their professional lives—as did thousands of women before them—with the question: Must I choose? Is it really impossible to combine a full personal life including marriage and children with a full professional life?

In our interview pool (which of course does not include women who chose marriage and motherhood, eschewing work) only a small minority describe themselves as deliberately choosing "the work" to the exclusion of marriage. Several found the choice easy because they saw marriage, not as fulfilling, but as confining. A historian says she never entertained the possibility of marriage because "I knew all these single women . . . in the movement, that is the civil rights movement, the antiwar movement, and every single woman I knew was living a very fulfilled and marvelous life and the only people I knew who were complaining were married women." Another historian says that her mother's experience of two failed marriages influenced her decision to put work first and to rule out marriage altogether. And she adds: "I grew up in a working-class environment and most women lived with their husbands and husbands seemed to be more of a hindrance in life among most of the women that I saw when I was very young than anything else. So, the advice from my mother from the time I can remember, the earliest years, was, 'You must be able to take care of yourself.' And she was absolutely right."

Others who have chosen to concentrate on "the work" simply say that they knew they could not handle both work and a family. A language scholar, asked if she had had any problems integrating a personal and professional life, said: "Oh, I haven't integrated them. I became a workaholic. But I couldn't, I couldn't really, even if I had wanted to get married, I don't think I could have swung it. I see my friends who are mostly married and bringing up children. I think their lives are a mess. [Laughs.] I couldn't hack that." And another who chose work and excluded marriage says: "I didn't think the two would go too well together, that I couldn't manage both, that I couldn't manage a career and a marriage—just wasn't going to make it. And I was in graduate school and what I was going to do was get my doctorate. . . . I had the conflict of thinking that I had to have either one or the other."

But the willing choice of work alone is not usual in our stories; rather we find that the story of most academic women, in one way or another, is a drama that begins with their *refusing* to choose—or for many, refusing to believe that such a choice is necessary. ("You could call it denial," an English professor remarks.) That is, they refuse to forsake one major part of life, and insist on the possibility—and the rightness—of integrating personal and professional, private and public realms.

Generally, such a refusal is not clear-cut or rationally weighed or even, in many cases, completely conscious. In fact, a chemist tells us that, contemplating the problem of family and career in graduate school, she made a conscious decision to remain unconscious. "I remember very clearly deciding not to think about that because it wasn't very feasible. . . .

Everybody said you couldn't do it, a very uncomfortable thought, so I just decided to worry about it at some later time." Rather than ask, "Can I do it?" or even "How can I do it?" most women simply go ahead and try to do it.

Some follow the course of securing one part of their lives first, in order to feel safer about procuring the other—to nail down, as it were, at least one major constituent of their happiness. Some decide to marry early, without question the riskiest choice if the ultimate goal is integration of life and work. A tenured historian remarks, "I married in my second year of college, at nineteen, because I was a woman and I knew I had to get on with my life." And she eventually established a satisfactory professional life, but it was twenty-five years after leaving college before she completed her first book, now published by a prestigious academic press. Another woman reflects: "The real tension for me has been between the need for affection and the need for interesting ideas. Now there's no question that there were times when I got lost in books, and could see myself forever lost in the world of scholarship, happily wandering. . . . And I think I closed off that prospect a bit . . . by early marriage." In fact, she did not enter graduate school until she was in her forties, and although she completed her Ivy League doctorate, she describes herself, by that time, as "a beggar at a feast" with a university career effectively foreclosed.

Others meet the problem of integrating the life and the work by the reverse tactic—postponing marriage or serious personal commitment while they secure the intellectual life they desire. Thus a woman discusses a relationship in college: "I met him . . . and we became good friends, not boyfriend, girlfriend, but good friends and I saw him all the time . . . It was lonely because it was a superficial relationship . . . but I think one thing I did . . . was not get into very deep relationships with men and I think that's self-protective and I . . . did it subconsciously but knowing I could have, like every one of my sorority sisters, gotten pinned, engaged, and married." Another, making the same choice, follows the same tactic. "I had become good throughout the years at making *friends* out of boys . . . as opposed to a quote girlfriend, boyfriend relationship. And I did a lot of things in a group. I was very active socially, not on an individual basis, but a group."

If some women respond to the tension between the marriage plot and the quest plot by marrying early, and some by marrying late, others find it immobilizing, fearing to set upon either course because of the risk of destroying the other. A professor of philosophy explains how, feeling this hesitancy, she first went into grammar school teaching, then began graduate courses in education before committing herself to study for a doctorate in philosophy. "Most of my classmates [in the graduate school of education] were teachers and married. And I wasn't and I had for years postponed anything permanent, anything. . . . What I remember thinking is that I can't embark on this long-term study because I would stop and get married. It was always just around the corner in what I was thinking. And then at some point I decided it wasn't going to happen or . . . I just got so interested in the philosophy that I thought, 'Well, I've got to take my chances.' . . . But it had been a tremendous issue in my mind. It had kept me from doing things." And because of the delays, her university employment experience was harrowing, although ultimately well resolved, as was her personal life, which includes marriage and children. Others caught in the same bind have not always been so lucky.

But however they proceed, whether boldly or hesitantly or—as is most usual—with small steps rather than a grand stride, these women ground their actions on a stubborn refusal to give up their hopes for integrating a professional and family life. And this refusal stems, of course, from the enormity of what would be given up if a choice were made between the two. What we hear again and again in women's stories is a sense of outrage that they should be asked to forfeit, never to fulfill, one strong and vital part of themselves, whichever way they choose.

A Romance languages scholar who had first postponed any thought of marriage to concentrate on "the work" says that, by the age of thirty, "the big ideas and ideals just didn't say a word to me anymore, and I obviously needed a smaller, personal world." And so she married at that time because, as she insists, "I *wanted* to be married, because I *wanted* a family, because I *wanted* a good relationship with another human being, completely, because I *wanted* a house, because I *wanted* to be domestic." But her remark about ideas and ideals becoming meaningless did not mean that she chose to abandon significant work as an important part of her life. Rather, it did not suffice, by itself. "I didn't want to give that up," she says. "I wanted it all, I wanted all of it." Note that while this woman says she "wanted all of it," thus calling to mind the pejorative "having it all," what she wants is "ideas and ideals" and "a good relationship with another human being"—a far cry from the image of selfishness the old norms cast over such ambitious goals.

Less specifically, but with no less feeling, a professor of English recalls coming to a similar conclusion during an "identity crisis" in graduate school, a conflict between her love of the work she was doing and her recognition of its virtually unlimited demands. "I asked myself, 'Do I want to spend the rest of my life working this hard?' And I said, 'No, I don't.' I was in the library from 8 in the morning until 12 at night. If I went out on a Friday night with a boyfriend to the movies or something, I would be writing a paper in the back of my head. And I just said, 'I don't want to do this. I can't keep it up.' I didn't think I could, simply, physically and psychologically, keep it up. I needed time for my life."

For another teacher of English, now in her early forties, the horrific consequences of relinquishing one major part of a life, and thus a major part of the self, were embodied in two women whose antithetical lives she knew well—her mother and a graduate school professor. Her mother had relinquished "the work" after having made heroic efforts to achieve it, as our interviewee recalls in detail so vivid we reproduce it at length: "My mother was the daughter of . . . a poor farmer [in the West]. . . . I don't think [she] started school till she was nine because she had to be old enough to walk the six miles it would take to get to the school. . . . And, in any case, when she did finish the grade school—she tells this story with great emotion—she says that a neighbor woman had dropped in one day, and said to her, 'Christina, are you going to go to high school?' And she said, 'Well, I can't. You know, how can I go to high school with no high school anywhere?' And the neighbor said, 'Why, lots of girls work for families in town so they can go to school.' That was fifteen miles away. And . . . the neighbor . . . found a place for my mother to work for her board and room with a family, and so she went to high school. And then—this was in 1919—my mother somewhere along the line . . . thought 'Well, I could go to college the same way.' And so she enrolled at the state university in 1919. She was one of thirteen women who were at the university at that time. And she lasted for two years before her gathering of resources just ran out and she was going to work for a year and then go back. My grandfather was not only poor, but also rather mean and certainly stingy. . . . That summer . . . [she] was driving around the countryside with a horse and buggy trying to sell books to get some money together, and my grandfather was charging her a day fee for use of his horse and buggy. But in any case, what happened is that she just didn't get enough money together, and in the meantime, she met my father and ended up being married the following March. So she never got back to school . . . and ended up having five children, and having, really, an unhappy life. . . . I guess the thing that impressed me and that still impresses me is that as I listen, as I have over the years, to her tales of how she went to college in days when no poor farm girl went to college and I look at the person that she was as I knew her—from my earliest memories when she . . . was really downtrodden by years of real base struggle—that there was no connection between the photograph of a pretty young woman at the college, and this depressed, passive, ruined kind of woman."

Avoiding her mother's fate, our narrator put herself through graduate school in spite of considerable personal difficulty, including illness. But still, the life of a professor she encountered there, a woman who chose "the work," seems just as appalling to her. Asked whether she had ever considered her professor—an eminent scholar, married but childless—to be a role model, she responds vehemently: "Oh, god, I would *never* accept that kind of role. . . . She [the professor] made it very clear that she thought it was impossible for a woman to be a scholar . . . and to have children. . . . And I must say, wherever my career is at the moment [part-time, low-level teaching while caring for two small children] and wherever my relation is to English literature [a book recently published by a university press], if there's anything I feel confirmed about, it is that I'm damned glad that I didn't take [Professor X's] kind of life. I say that with total seriousness. It's not, it's not worth it to me." In short, she did not take from her mother's experience the lesson that family life was to be avoided, nor accept from her professor the conclusion that satisfying work should be protected even at the cost of forsaking family life. Rather she learned that she cared passionately about both work and family and would not willingly give up either.

A philosopher speaks explicitly to the issue of refusing to choose between personal and professional lives, notwithstanding her husband's objections that she was putting her work before the marriage. "That certainly is what I was being accused of, but it never felt that way. It always seemed to me that there were a number of things in my life that were important to me and I couldn't rank them. . . . The tradition is that women put their family first and their professional life, if they have one, afterward, and that men allegedly do the reverse and I don't think that was true for me. It also seemed to me that there was no reason why it had to be. It seemed possible that you could have a number of things going in your life and that nobody had a right to demand of me that I should put them in precisely that order and certainly not just because it was the conventional thing to do. And I think that as far as my husband went—and I think this is really true of a lot of men—that it is true that they are programmed to consider their professional life the most important thing. I'm not sure that all of them would want to. I think a lot of them would just as soon subordinate that to their family life, but they don't get any rewards for that either, so in a lot of ways I feel that we were both victimized by patterns that weren't suitable to either one of us and there weren't enough, there weren't any other paradigms to follow, or we lacked the imagination to work them out."

What this woman is suggesting is not only that she *wanted* both personal and professional lives, and that she refused to choose between them, but also that there was no real reason to choose—that she felt it fully possible, indeed, natural, to integrate the two. What stood against this kind of integration was only "tradition" or "convention"—"patterns that weren't suitable." In our terminology, these "patterns" are the old norms of the marriage plot. And the resistance we record here to these norms— the continued, determined efforts of women to integrate two dimensions of life, in the face of warnings that it is impossible—reflects these women's internal conviction, however vaguely formulated, that the old norms are arbitrary and wrong. These rules are not given in the nature of human beings and human relations; they are simply social decrees and they do not fit women's multiple aspirations and multiple talents.

However, neither the family, nor the larger social structure, nor the workplace provides the means for women to effect an integrated life, and it is evident, in the narratives that follow, that changes, both logistical and attitudinal, must take place for this goal to become practical. As a young scholar of English literature says: "I think the root of [the problem] is in the way our society is built now, . . . the kind of institutions we have. Women are going to have to do it, I mean, we're going to have to be the ones who, if we want to do these things, have to suffer, because nobody's going to put out a hand to us, and say, 'Oh, my dear, your lot is so difficult! Let us see if we can make it easier for you!' "

What this means in practice is that women who believe they can opt for an "integrated" life find themselves instead forced to lead two separate, entire lives simultaneously. That is, refusing to lop off either personal or professional dimensions to their lives and yet finding no ready channels for confluence, they end up squeezing two lives into one through super- human effort. And their experience shows that the term "superwoman," often used in praise of such effort, is actually a description of stress and distress.

We hear their voices: "Oh, my God, it was such a bizarre life, it really was . . . it was killing to try to live those two lives, really." And, "You can't do what you did in your early twenties. I find I can't carry that off any longer, multiple things." And, "You become, you know, a split personality, just trying to continually juggle."

One tenured professor works out her double life in staggeringly literal terms. "I learned a trick from my husband when he was an intern. I realized that you don't have to sleep all that much. And I would go for weeks on end on to what I called the 9 to 5 schedule, which was 9:00 A.M. to 5:00 P.M. at the office and 9:00 P.M. to 5:00 A.M. in the study downstairs, which is how I did my writing. I'd come home, and cook a meal, and take a nap, set the alarm to get up at 9:00 P.M. to write. . . ." If this example seems hyperbolic, another tenured woman sums up her day—which sometimes ends at a twenty-four-hour supermarket at midnight—with the remark, "It's a two-day day!"

But they do it, the impossible task, and pay later. Here is further commentary from the young woman who remarked above that no one was likely to lend a helping hand to such efforts. "I turned up . . . a job, and it was a very good job, full-time. It was a replacement position, a one-year contract, but the courses were yummy. I mean . . . I really needed it, because I'd had a kind of desert period . . . [at home with infant and no work]. So I went back in September when the baby was nine months old. And that year nearly killed me actually, because I was still breast-feeding. I was staying up till one o'clock in the morning trying to get all my courses ready. I was teaching three courses each semester. And my husband took a picture of me, and I'm glad he did because I mean, it shocked me so much to see what I looked like in this photograph. I'd been living on coffee and chocolate bars sort of thing. And I said, 'Oh my God, what have I done to myself?' But it was a wonderful year teaching. But the expense was enormous."

Taking on the burdens of two lives, women are often blinded to difficulties by their firmest beliefs in the integrative impulse, which we found so many women implemented in their research foci as well. ("I really thought I could do anything!") What they actually experience, however, is rarely the joy of integration, but rather the hardship this goal imposes, given prevailing norms and institutions. And they are the less prepared to meet such hardship because they do not acknowledge its full depth and scale. "Romantic unreality. . . . I really did have this sort of notion that I was going to rock the cradle with one foot and type my dissertation, and you know, I was sort of going to integrate all of this stuff. One thing that happens is your energy level doesn't [remain] and I find I can't carry that off any longer, nor could I a few years ago when the children were younger."

One source of constant worry and strain is the experience of traveling between two domains—even figuratively. "I knew what the trap in being a superwoman was. I had told myself I wasn't going to do that. But what choice do you have, when you know you have to be somewhere to pick up the kid? I used to have the only calm moment of the day after I dropped the baby at her day care, and I had a fifteen-minute drive to school. I taught Milton a good part of the year first thing in the morning, and I would try to settle my brain and forget about diapers and everything, and try to think about Eve . . . and the angel Raphael."

Then there are the strains of literal travel. One untenured woman, desperately eager to return to full-time teaching after her third child entered nursery school, undertakes to commute to an institution three hours away from her home, dividing her week between her family and her work. "I was commuting, I was living there between Tuesday and Thursday, and sometimes through Friday if I had another faculty meeting on Friday. I found that the kids could bear my absence for three days, that by the time you got to the fourth day, both the two-year-old and the five-year-old were running a bit thin with their endurance. I think it would have been absolutely impossible if my teaching schedule was a five-day schedule. For the short run, even despite the schedule, it is possible to do the work necessary to run a household, which is food shopping and meal preparation on the weekends, and then run off to your job in the middle of the week. You can do that for a semester, but I don't see how you can do it much longer than that. I . . . I felt very split. When I was at the college, I was trying to get the maximum amount of work possible to keep the courses going, and when I got back home, I was annoyed. It was almost impossible to do class preparation for the Tuesday classes, to make my presence in the family known and loved, and to do the grocery shopping." The price seems enormous, even prohibitive. But her professional reentry was at stake; she had already taken time off to have a family, and was eager to resume work; but she couldn't postpone her family responsibilities, either. As we see from her account, her attempted integration was effectually a division.

Another weak point in such attempts at wholeness is the widespread practice among women of keeping problems underground. Already suspect in the academy, their seriousness questioned, women feel compelled to exclude reference to their personal lives in the workplace. Thus one woman who engaged in a difficult commute seeks work closer to her husband's but finds it awkward to explain to prospective employers why she wants a new position. "[I] always felt that somehow, in the application letter, I had to explain why, with a perfectly good job, I was trying to get out of it, and . . . I always felt that putting in the business about not wanting to commute ninety miles anymore was somehow one of those female reasons for wanting to do things . . . to live with your husband, trying to integrate [both] lives." Her reason for wanting to change institutions—to live normally with her husband—wasn't a professional reason! And then when the baby came, the commuting became impossible. "What was I going to do, drop it halfway . . . ?"

An older woman, a tenured historian, reflects on the same point. "I think the one place [in my work life] where I have been conscious of being a woman is to be very careful to keep my personal life out of the department. Whereas my male colleagues will bring their children in to be babysat by the secretary over spring vacation, I wouldn't have thought of doing that. . . . And in terms of my divorce, I probably walked very carefully, to be certain they didn't feel that it was interfering in any way." But if acknowledgment of the importance of relationships outside the workplace is unacceptable within it, how are women, or men either, for that matter, ever going to achieve integrated lives? The issues are tabled.

If integrating a work life and a family life are difficult for married women, there are particular difficulties in balancing life and work while single. A number of stories attest to the special problem for single women of trying to establish a marriage and family while also devoting time and energy to their own support. Of course, single men also face this difficulty, but with a key distinction: men can defer marriage and children without losing them irrevocably, whereas women direct their lives in the knowledge of their child-bearing span. A single historian, facing the stupendous debt of $17,000 in tuition and living expenses during graduate school, describes the cleft stick she is in. "You know, I've been in this so long, I'm in such a rotten financial position, and I want to get going, get real, get, you know. . . . I'm thirty-seven, got a couple of years, maybe, if I'm lucky, for the issues of kids and man . . . at least the kids part. . . . And I don't know how it's going to work out, but I don't think sitting here working on my dissertation is a very good way of resolving the issue of man and children." And another single woman who supported herself through graduate school for ten years in three institutions ("To some extent, I went where the fellowships were") speaks of her desire to have children, thwarted by the fact that study and earning money for study have left her with her "biological clock running out."

A third woman speaks poignantly about the emotional strain attendant on this form of personal/professional conflict. "I feel . . . if only I could get my private life straightened out and I wasn't devoting such enormous amounts of energy and pain and strain and running to therapists . . .

trying to get myself married, then I would have the mental space to really move ahead in all the areas that interest me. . . . I guess what I feel about my whole adult career is that the energy that I've been able to put into any intellectual and social function . . . has been at every turn undermined by the amount of energy that has been drained off worrying about my single situation. . . . Some people say, 'I couldn't do it because I had three small children and a husband and I had to make dinner every night.' I feel that people think, 'What was your problem? You didn't have all those responsibilities.' It's hard for people to understand that not having those other things can be just as exhausting as having them."

In all of these stories, time is the despot. As one young woman exclaims, "Now if only my day were two hours longer! [My only problem is] not really having enough time for the baby, having enough time for my husband, having enough time for me. Because there's really nothing left for human relations." Her real dilemma is how she can allot the proper time for everything, without neglecting either of two different worlds, each claiming from her primary importance. And, under the remaining influence of the old norms, which assign responsibility for "human relations" to women, devising solutions is up to her. The crucial fact that something very large has changed in the personal/professional equation, that women are claiming equal professional opportunity with men, has not yet been translated into a correspondingly large change in the allocation of private responsibilities.

Given the relentless pressure of time, the necessity to compress two days, two lives into one, the most serious threat to women's superhuman effort at integration is encountering unforeseen trouble—sickness, financial reverses, unexpected family responsibility. The point is that women have so little margin, they operate so close to the bone, that it just takes that extra burden to break the personal/professional synthesis to pieces.

A well-known critic, a woman with a successful career and a family, totes up the sad arithmetic—how many conditions must coincide for a professional woman to integrate two lives. "I think physical stamina is so important it can't be described. I would say that the difference between the women in my generation who stayed in the profession—also luck—and who dropped out, was simply that . . . just the plain energy level one has. I have a lot more energy, I discovered over the years, than most people. . . . I was lucky enough to have only one child, but some of my friends went ahead (as I would have done, had my husband not been opposed to it) and had two. And I think two children is four times as much work as one. . . . So that I think I benefited from the combination of the single child and the physical stamina. . . . I knew brilliant people, committed to the idea of being writers and teachers, who couldn't stay the course and it was mostly because of more children, some sort of marital distraction, personal illness, illness in the child, and they just couldn't do all those things at once. . . . I had a very healthy child, he was never sick. . . . The real problem I think is that the responsibility for the house and the child still lies with the woman. You can't do everything. And if something goes wrong there, you usually end up feeling your responsibility to the child outweighs the responsibility to Freshman English, naturally, if you are a human being, and that therefore something happens [the unforeseen trouble] and you drop out and you think you'll go back, but you don't, or you go part-time or you take an adjunct position, or something like that."

In this description of the hazards professional women face, perhaps the most important is the speaker's realization, put into words, that one strike against you is sufficient; you're out, if you are a woman. Every factor—personal relationships, health, endurance—must combine to foster a whole life for women, because the human responsibility, the life, and not just the life of the mind, is theirs to maintain for the common weal.

Our stories document unforeseen trouble in many forms.

Divorce is one. A graduate student reports, "The divorce stuff has been dragging on for five years, and it was sapping my strength."

A sick baby causes immense strain, as is clear in the story of a young tenured professor whose baby was born with an abnormality that necessitated major surgery at four and a half months. The mother speaks of her trauma, which, though it finally had a successful outcome, revealed that there was no room in the mechanism of her department for trouble. "My baby was operated on in December, an emotionally traumatic and physically grueling situation for parents who stay in the hospital during this time. I was still breast-feeding. My professional life was very demanding. I am chairman of a large department in which many senior faculty are in conflict with each other and the junior faculty. I was serving on the university-wide educational policy committee which meets for several hours each week. I was headmaster of a residential college . . . and although I did not teach that first semester—given my administrative duties I was only slated to teach one course—all the other tasks continued. No one tried to help make any accommodations during those excruciating first six months of my child's life. I would be observing classes to evaluate faculty and thinking about taking my child to the hospital. Our babysitter was so frightened that immediately after our child's operation, she left.

The baby is fine now, she's great, but people's expectations of me did not change. They refused to acknowledge that anything in my life had changed and demanded the same amount of attention as they had had previously."

For another woman—in this case, not tenured when calamity struck—the crushing blow was not a child's illness, but her husband's. She, too, experienced official lack of comprehension, particularly on the part of her department chairman, but here the official attitude was directly dangerous and not simply a burden, because it contributed to the eventual deflection of a highly promising career. "He [the chairman] is a terrific scholar, a master in the field, a slew of books, but he also had a wife at home full time. I was working my ass off that year. I mean, I was teaching all those wretched [introductory] courses, I was commuting to and fro, I was doing all the housework when I came home, was trying to support my husband who had just had heart surgery, and was looking after two small children. I mean . . . ! You know, this was nothing, okay? Where are the articles? Where are the books?" We add as a postscript that this woman subsequently published a substantial book begun during the period described, but, irrevocably off tenure track by the time of its publication, she left the profession entirely, rejecting the prospect of peripheral positions, introductory courses, and low salaries which was her likely academic option.

Another shape that trouble can assume is care of an elderly parent. Whatever the individual circumstances, the burden is not decided individually. Care of the elderly, as of the sick, is automatically seen as the woman's obligation, the man having more "serious" occupations. One interviewee, married, with children, working full-time, and writing a scholarly book, speaks of the assumption within her family that she, and not her brother, held responsibility for their elderly mother. "When my mother became senile, I was determined that my brother, who lives in the area, was going to help out too. . . . And I had an extended argument with him because his wife didn't want to help out. So I finally laid it on the line, and I said you're going to have to take responsibility, and take her on some weekends, just like I have to."

And trouble may not even be a grave event. It may just be more than a career can contain. Says one scholar of English literature, "So, finally, then, I was to take the comprehensives and I took them—three writtens in twenty-four hours, and a couple of weeks later the oral was scheduled, and I took the oral, and the day after the oral exam I had an appointment with my obstetrician who said, 'I think you're having twins!' And what really happened to life for the next several years was that I really couldn't lift my head above diapers."

A common problem that arises for the professional woman is that her husband is usually becoming established in his own work at the same time that her career is getting under way, and so her balancing act must include accommodating two careers. And such accommodation often has unforeseen—and disastrous—effects for the woman, because the weight of opinion says, the husband's career comes first. For example, a married graduate student, writing her dissertation, went with her husband to a rural area where he had obtained a teaching position. "I was in the house, there was no one at the school particularly able to talk to me. I was seen as an anomaly. We had no children, which is the way the other women [faculty wives] spent their time, raising their children, and taking care of them and there was just really no place for me. I mean it was very isolated. It was frightening. We were living in a tiny little old schoolhouse on the other side of town in the bush. So I was there all day supposedly working on my thesis, feeling as if I were in solitary confinement." Part of neither world, away from her dissertation adviser, her peers, any structure at all, away from a large university library, this scholar could not work and her thesis was postponed indefinitely.

Another narrative is a variation on the same theme. "We decided we'd rather be together, and so I gave up going to Yale graduate school, which was considered to be one of the best in my field at that time, and went to Brown, because my husband was working near Providence."

The family follows the man because traditional mores dictate that he is the principal wage earner. But, in circular fashion, the woman cannot be a substantial wage earner if her career advancement is repeatedly sacrificed. The constant principle of putting the husband's career first within a dual-career marriage plays havoc with women rising in any profession, because they are, of course, competing with men who are free to relocate wherever their advantage lies. "I was offered a full-time professorship at X University [in the Southwest], and I obviously had to say no. Then they asked me if I could come for a semester, and I said no several times, and then I said yes. And did it. That was a real, legitimate job. If there hadn't been a conflict with my husband's career. . . . I would have taken it. If I were all alone, I probably would have taken it. I liked it. I liked the department." This woman never again had such an option. At the time of the interview, she was pursuing her own research and writing, as well as serving on national committees in her field, but she did not have a teaching appointment.

Other women follow their husbands' moves: "Well, we got married. He got his degree a year after I did, and he got a job at the University of X in the West, and I left [the college in the East] where I'd been teaching . . . and went . . . and never thought about it. When we knew he had a job there, I wrote to see about getting a job there too and I got a letter back from [a different, less prestigious university than her husband's] and I got part-time there. Then we were there three years and we came back here because my husband got a job, a position at a university in the Boston area. So then I started looking for a job again. . . ."

The reverse, however, i.e., a husband's following his wife's rise, rarely occurs (although, as we will see shortly, this is an inversion of roles that has worked in some marriages). Thus an anthropologist observes, "I don't think my husband would be ready to relocate. He feels even less flexible in the job market than I do. There were points when he was forced to consider relocating [for his own career future] and I had to face the question of what I'd do." But, she says, she doesn't entertain the idea of moving to advance her career because she is sure her husband would not accommodate. To preserve the marriage, she has also resisted the natural step of doing field work in Africa, her field of concentration. Similarly, a woman now teaching part-time in the Boston area evaluates her chances in an extremely tight job market. "Some of them [graduate school peers in far-flung areas of the country] are in one-year slots, as assistant pro-fessors . . . not necessarily tenure track. But some of them who had that kind of position last year have moved on to tenure track and I've really published more than any of them. I've had more fellowships. I've been told that I would have gotten them, but I've not applied, so I have lost out, on the basis of staying where the husband is . . . because he is really not anxious to move, to find another job."

What happens to our superwoman when she cannot follow her best career opportunities? Or when she is forced to leave her position because of her husband's change of employment? What happens to her when she is worn down physically and psychologically by her attempt to integrate two lives connected only through her? What happens to superwoman when an unexpected area of trouble tips the delicate balancing act she must perform between the life and the work?

The consequences are enough to strain and sometimes topple a mar-riage for some, but a larger proportion lose the work. Describing a fellow student in graduate school at a large midwestern university, a philosopher recalls, "There was one who was really my pathetic model; she was brilliant, she was brighter than any of the other graduate students. She had been married once before and while we were graduate students she got married again and I think she even got pregnant and she dropped out. . . . So when I asked her why she was dropping out, she said simply, 'I can't afford to risk another marriage.' I mean it was very straightforward, that was it. That was very sobering. . . ."

For most, the loss of work is not so clear-cut. Rather it consists of scaling down the work, reducing its demands, usually by taking part-time positions and usually without full recognition by the woman doing it of the degree of professional loss she is likely to sustain. Many simply are unaware that no amount of part-time work aggregates into tenure-track eligibility; rather they see part-time teaching as a welcome way of holding on to both the life and the work—as we hear in the following story from an Americanist, now in her fifties, the author of two books and numerous articles, and a veteran of years of teaching, but never on tenure track. "I didn't even think about tenure track because I was teaching in this lively adult program. I felt happy to be there and considered myself the luckiest person in the world to have such a part-time job. I can't believe how stupid I was. . . . my job seemed great because the students were very good, and the campus was only ten minutes away from my home so that when my children needed me—and sometimes they did—I could be there in five minutes. And the fact that the job wasn't tenure track, that it had no fringe benefits, that it provided no intellectual community, all those things seemed irrelevant to me at the time. When I finally went back to graduate school, I realized what I had missed, and that I had been, in a sense, exploited."

Another compromise is to accept some form of less demanding work. That is, we and our interviewees have been using the words "job" and "professional career" interchangeably, but they are not synonymous; indeed the difference between them is highly important to mark. Women who lose either the work or the marriage most probably would not have placed either at risk if they had less ambitious stakes. It is the extra measure of commitment, of devotion to carefully chosen and highly demanding work, coupled with the length and high financial cost of the training period, that differentiate a professional career from a job. And it is the investment in career that is particularly threatening, both logistically and psychologically, to the partner in a relationship.

"He [her academic husband] jokes," one interviewee discloses, "about the fact that his support hasn't always been totally nonambivalent, and I think it still is not always. It's tough to have a wife who is as wrapped up in her work as I am." This woman did not refer to difficulties about arrangements (her children were nearly grown when she returned to academe) but about attitudinal difficulties; her work threatened her husband because of the measure of her involvement, because their marriage was not her only intense engagement. Another scholar, faced with the same issue, incorrectly assumed tensions would have been eased if her husband had been an academic himself, that then he would understand the excitement of her intellectual pursuit. She elaborates, "Well, the big push . . . my poor husband, in all fairness to him, he's not lived in an academic . . . I mean, he's not an academic. So that the tremendous spurt of energy that I put on to finish the dissertation really terrified him. . . . I mean, it's been very hard all along for him to see it, and he had . . . he was not . . . or to see it as something natural, . . . I mean I've discussed this with other men and they, I can't tell you how many men have said to me, 'We really expect you to revolve around us.' An academic said that to me at the MLA meetings last year . . . I mentioned to him that whenever I was going great guns . . . whenever my work was going well, my husband was threatened, and he said, 'Well, what do you expect?' "

Another interviewee, now divorced, contributes her understanding of the same problem: "Looking back somewhat more sympathetically now, on what was happening to him it would have been pretty bewildering if you were an intelligent but conventional male, that here you are really wanting a family-centered situation which you can't create and this other person who is supposed to be responsible for creating it is off doing other things that are also threatening to what he is doing [rivalry in the same field] so it's an unfortunate situation to be in. . . . The way of history was with him, so that, you know, I'm not saying he couldn't have behaved better, but he didn't, and in a way I can understand that because there wasn't a lot of encouragement for men to behave better."

In all of these examples, there is a demand to establish priorities that would subordinate the work. An interviewee who has resisted this choice reviews the issue as it presented itself for her, commenting about being a faculty member at a major university. "I feel that, in whatever profession, there is a slow track and a fast track and I like the purposes of being in a fast track and I like being with people who are alive in their fields, doing things. It's not the power, but not being in some backwater, you know, people who haven't made anything in twenty years. . . ."

But most academic women, as the statistics clearly show, find themselves—whether or not through a process of conscious choice—on one or another of the slower tracks where claims of the work are less demanding. This may mean part-time teaching or work in a college or university where the emphasis is not on authoritative research but on teaching—work that is highly valuable but not so highly regarded or highly rewarded as that of the fast track. That is, the old norms set up pressures for professional women, the result of which is that, often, the most reasonable choice they can make, as they try to balance the work and the life, necessarily puts them outside the authoritative precincts of the profession.[1]

Then, beyond the slow track, there is the choice, for academic women, to leave the profession altogether, or at least to take work other than the usual professional combination of teaching and scholarship. Of the thirty-seven interviewees deflected from the normal tenure track, thirteen were in college teaching part-time or off tenure track, nine were in academic or education-related administration (none in positions of substantial responsibility for academic policy), seven were doing consulting, editing, paid research, or commercial writing, three were writing full-time, and five were in business full-time.

Clearly, there is less conflict over work for women in job markets outside the male-dominated professions, in work that does not claim a high degree of social authority and thus does not challenge the old norms in their allocation of authority to men. Directly addressing this issue, an English professor, divorced and remarried, describes her former husband: "He is now, happily, well married to a woman who will never have either children or a profession. She teaches in a high school, but it's not the kind of thing that. . . . It's a good job and she cares about it, but she is not ever going to compete with his job. She will always be in a subordinate position and that is a supportive position, I should say. And that is something that both of them have accepted and acknowledged and I think it is absolutely necessary to his happiness and his ability to sustain the relationship."

If, as young women enter the professions, they are not to be deflected by marriage and a family from the continuing, active practice of their chosen career, nor be forced to the extremity of choosing to remain single and without family as a career strategy and not by personal choice; if a unified, integrated life is seen as a positive goal for both men and women; then it is manifestly clear that major changes must be made in both the structure of the workplace and the functioning of the family unit.

The consequences that we have been examining in the body of this chapter, consequences of the refusal to choose between life and the life of the mind, themselves indicate where the trouble spots are. Contrariwise, by examining the cases in which women have succeeded in integrating the life and the work, we can outline the conditions that seem to be present in such cases.

The stories we have heard from our interviewees show that where a woman has succeeded in combining successfully a personal and professional life, some extra measure has intervened—extra financial resources or human resources, including a husband whose stance in the marriage resembles more closely that traditionally taken by the woman, e.g., he has flexible hours, a willingness to travel, a willingness to assume domestic responsibility. Some women mention help from other family members, a mother or mother-in-law. Another source of extra support may come from professional colleagues, departments that acknowledge a personal existence that cannot or should not always be divorced from work. And— a crucial condition in all the successful "wholes"—no disaster or special trouble stories were present.

When it works, this is what we hear about financial resources: "I didn't have children until I had the degree; I was making a salary so that when we started, we decided this wasn't something we were going to save on. It was just the combination of my having the salary, and being willing to spend it, and living where there were wives of foreign graduate students looking for jobs. . . ." Or from another woman earning a good salary and expending much of it on household help: "I think women nowadays are stuck with two jobs [referring to the difficulty of finding help]. I didn't have to do that. I haven't vacuumed in years. I don't miss it one little bit. I'm very, very fortunate."

For others, at points when the joint family salary is low, family help may be crucial. Here a young English scholar speaks of her intern-husband's contribution to her work: "He is sole guardian of our daughter on weekends, so I can have the whole weekend to write and finish the book. We couldn't afford to have nannies. . . . Without his kind of support, I wouldn't have been able to keep on. Just knowing he was involved at some level was terrifically helpful. . . ." In fact, a number of our older interviewees expressed regret that the new mode of sharing tasks had not come early enough to afford them time for their work when they were young enough to get established.

Some, of course, receive help from more traditional family sources. A tenured historian says, "My mother-in-law ran these camps the family had and that began a succession of five summers when I went off . . . to do archival research. The children were comfortable being there those summers." And another tenured historian recalls her resumption of child-interrupted scholarship, aided by her mother who came from Europe to assist her.

Support may also come in the form of an understanding department. "My second baby came to work with me for the first semester of the next year and I brought babysitters to my office so I could see him in between classes and at lunch." And the rare academic employer who doesn't equate part-time with second-string: "He's just an extraordinary person, and I worked [in his lab] for seven years, three days a week, which meant I was in there three days a week, but the other two days I would calculate stuff at home, read journal articles, and so forth."

This tenured interviewee's years spent in part-time work did help advance her career. She is the exception, but there is no reason inherent in the academic workplace that such experience *should* be exceptional. Part-time work is now treated as inherently inferior, not counted as a serious career step, because to rate it thus serves the budgetary interests of the academy. Furthermore, the old norms decree that the second echelon, the supportive ranks, are a proper and fitting place for women. Thus it is easy to operate such a system without moral discomfort, especially when, as discussed above, part-time work can seem to be a godsend to women caught in a difficult conflict between family and work responsibilities.

But the workplace is only part of the problem. One of the indispensable conditions for unifying a personal and professional life is a restructuring not only of the duties but also of the conventions of a marital or other intimate ongoing relationship. Several interviewees cite a virtual inversion of traditional roles as the key factor in their ability to combine family lives with demanding professional work.

In one case, for example, the husband works at home: "Mostly it was he doesn't like working for anybody but himself," says a tenured professor of literature. "And he wanted that. I didn't push one way or the other on it. It turned out to be terrific for our daughter because she had me around most of the time in the first few years of her life, because my husband always supported us. He worked a five-day week. And then when she was five I went off to work full time here, and he was home and it was great because he was the only male in the entire town who was home and who was a house-husband. Her friends would come in and they would say, 'What are you doing?' and she would say, 'Oh, my Dad and I are baking a pie,' and her friends would say, 'Daddies don't bake pies.' It was one of those classic free to be you and me scenes. 'My father bakes pies, he cooks. . . . ' He doesn't have any trouble with it. . . . He had waited to leave his job, because he had tenure at X University in this city, until I had a full-time job, because we couldn't have swung it financially and it's still very tough financially because his business is really on the thin edge of making it or not making it. We're never quite sure, but he loves the independence and freedom of being his own person and being at home. And I don't know how, given as much energy as I put into my work, I could have done it without him being home to do half the cooking and half the housekeeping and more than half the childrearing."

In another story, a woman, now tenured in the Boston area, tells of geographic conflicts between her husband's and her employment and the nontraditional resolution of the conflict through her husband's work changes. "We have had a peripatetic career. My husband, when we came here—we got married right after I left X University and had the job here—we had the choice of either getting married and his coming with me and getting a job here, or of not getting married or breaking up, whatever. We decided to go ahead and get married. He was ready to look for a change. He was teaching in a private secondary school. . . . What we didn't count on was that that was just the time when secondary education was . . . retrenching. There were people losing jobs all over the place and he had a great deal of difficulty finding a job in his field. The first year we were here he had a part-time job and I had this one. The next year he got a full-time job but unfortunately it was in the New York area, so he went there and I worked here and I commuted on weekends because I could get a Tuesday-Thursday teaching schedule and those were long weekends. That was when I was pregnant with the first child. That was an unbearable system, and we decided that Boston was a better place and I liked my job better than he liked his new job, so we came back here and he went for some advanced graduate work for a year and worked part-time. Then he got a full-time job, an ideal full-time job in New Hampshire, which was closer, but not close enough—it was two hours away. So he worked there and we had a house up there that we rented and again I commuted weekends with one child and again pregnant at this point. So we were moving all the time. At that point, he gave up that one, though he really liked it . . . and came back to Boston, worked part-time again . . . and kept that up for a while, then got a job full-time in southeastern Massachusetts. . . . We lived there for two years and I commuted up here which was an hour and a half commute. And then he quit that to come up here. We moved up and he quit the educational field for good. He's now in high tech, and he works in Boston so that he's around for the kids. . . . And in all of this, my job has been the stable thing, but largely because he keeps deciding it's not worth the dislocation. He wants to be around the kids. He's very close to the kids and can't take the separation."

The woman speaking is in her late thirties and thus part of a generation more open than earlier ones to flexible marriage arrangements, but a woman in her fifties relates a similar story of her eventual happy, second marriage: "We both commuted for several years. . . . We were both willing to let the relationship absorb the blow and we were both willing to do whatever we had to do. He was willing to move here for me. He's not in my field. Happily, he has found a wonderful niche for himself at X University here. It's just exactly the kind of work he loves to do, but it was a tremendous risk he took in coming to follow the woman. And he had the courage and strength to do that. And again not many men of our generation would have done it."[2]

Still, on observing the benefits to professional women of flexible marriages, of men and women placing equal value on one another's careers, we must note also that such egalitarianism has its costs. Most obviously, as the result of a man's support for a woman's work, he will often slow his own pace in relation to his peers. If he is taking care of the children on the weekends, he is not writing the briefs that will win him an early law partnership, or articles for the *New England Journal of Medicine* that will clinch tenure at a major medical school. In short, he may have to step off the fast track himself—as most of the men in our stories of professional equality clearly have done.

Of course, in these stories, the men involved have engaged in their role reversal willingly. Most are men whose highest priority is not conventional professional achievement. But even couples who are clear about their priorities may have to pay an indirect social cost for inverting the normal marriage relation. That is, an egalitarian marriage flouts societal norms as to what is sexually appropriate and attractive, specifically the hallowed expectation that a woman will marry a man who is smarter and more successful than she. Thus the professional woman who does not subordinate herself not only lives with doubts that she is a "real woman" despite the fact that she acts "like a man" (as discussed in chap. 1), but also with the suspicion that she is not married to a "real man" because her husband does not act in the way society expects of "real men." Rationally, she knows that men who can live in fifty-fifty marriages *are* strong and masculine, so much so that their sense of masculinity can withstand being married to women who do not fawn on them and who have another powerful passion (i.e., their work). But, under the pressure of contrary social rules, neither she nor her husband may always *feel* this way, day-in and day-out; rather, they may be assailed by serious doubt, sometimes acute pain.

In sum, we can conclude that egalitarian marriage is right, that it gives witness to the possibility for an integrated life for men and women alike, and that such witness matters to both the present and the future. But we must acknowledge that when women flout the marriage plot, in this as in other ways, society exacts its price.

At this point in our review of career/family strategies, it must be patently clear that the conditions necessary for even reasonable balance—the presence of substantial support and the absence of heavy burden—are conditions so rarely combined that, statistically, the number of women who can integrate their private and work lives well is miniscule. Nevertheless, we find that professional women seeking integrated lives either are unaware that the probabilities are against them, or fail to internalize that fact. Rather they blame themselves for falling short. Their vision of a whole integrated life, after all, is a humane goal that seems worth pursuing and thus the failure to achieve it is profoundly confusing. If there is nothing wrong with the goal, then, women think, there must be something wrong with themselves—somehow, in some way, with more skill, creativity, effort, canniness, whatever, they might have succeeded. But in blaming themselves, women fall into the trap of blaming the victim, because the chances of achieving the integration they seek are so small under existing conditions. They are not supposed to want professional attainment integrated with a rich domestic life, not supposed to "want it all," so society is not constructed to aid their purpose.

In the following passage, excerpted at some length, we hear a vivid expression of this complicated experience. Earlier in this chapter, we quoted much of this same excerpt, but listen to it here in its larger context as the woman speaking, now in her late forties, justifies her desire for integration and traces the confusion and self-doubt that attend her failed expectations.

"I hadn't organized my life cleverly enough to know where to put my energy, partly from a lack of belief in myself, partly from poor preparation, partly from the picaresque quality of the years. . . . It wasn't the kosher and orthodox route. . . . The whole time I was teaching, the whole time I was doing my doctoral work, I refused to sacrifice any of my family life. That, you know, I really did all of that with a part-time mentality, and really did not stint on the kids or my role as mother and wife. . . . And I have to say that that was because I willed it that way . . . because it was extremely important to me. . . . I attribute the whole thing to enormous naïveté. I think there was a basic misunderstanding on my part . . . because I *wanted* to be married, I *wanted* a family, because I *wanted* a good relationship with another human being, completely, because I *wanted* a house, because I *wanted* to be domestic. I had been for ten years not [any of those things]. I had traveled. I had lived another life. I had been another kind of person. And I didn't want to give that up. *I wanted it all, I wanted all of it.* And it doesn't work. And I think I've been very good with the children. . . . I never abused babysitting time. I was always there. And you can't do it that way. Either you have to be serious about one thing or the other. And I feel as though I've cut corners on all the lives I'm leading, through naïveté, lack of preparation, basic subversion on my part." This apologia pro vita sua is the painful formulation of what "wanting it all" feels like in a society still dominated by norms that deny wholeness to women.[3]

If women are brought up short trying to integrate what are now two distinct lives, trying to be superwomen, is there another interpretation of their roles that will serve them better? We have no panacea; a major restructuring of the workplace and of marriage roles is required, and will not be achieved until the attitudes that they presently reflect have also changed. Certainly, a straitened job market will defeat any strategy. But we do see here one way—and this arises from our consideration of the pervasiveness of self-blame—in which women themselves can affect their situation.

The clue is embedded in the speech of the chemist quoted earlier in this chapter, who was pleased to forego vacuuming. The end of that speech was, "I'm not a superwoman; I'm just doing a man's job." This academic woman has managed to liberate herself from the burden of guilt to which so many interviewees attest. In fact, in a follow-up letter to her interviewer, she announces, "I had not really thought it out before—obviously, or I would have mentioned it. Unlike you, I did not always put the needs of others first. I was (am) selfish, and that has been very important. Perhaps you'll ask other women the same question—it might be very interesting. Do consider this paragraph as part of the oral history!"

Are we, then, advocating selfishness? Are we helping to bring down the temple of virtuous women? What we are doing—perhaps clear enough by now—is rejecting the old norm *definition* of selfishness in women, which, we suggest, is what the woman just quoted is also doing implicitly. When she asserts that she is "selfish," that she does not "put the needs of others first," she is not really being self-condemnatory. She is saying, perhaps with a touch of asperity, that it should be possible to reassign domestic responsibilities—both petty chores and serious caretaking—in such a way that they are not unfailingly the woman's portion.

She understands that to put the needs of others first, as a reflexive feminine response, is necessarily to put one's professional needs second, which is to risk giving them up and thus to risk losing a vital part of the self—to act as if one had no right to claim that part of the self. And this is to accede to the old norms that decree that indeed women's nature does not include capacities for highly disciplined and creative intellectual work and that their proper role does not extend to the most responsible levels of the professions. In claiming to be "selfish," the chemist quoted is asserting a dimension of self that exceeds the old norms and her claims do not fit well in the world the old norms shaped. What they do fit is her inner knowledge of who and what she is. And this assertion is a step women themselves *can* take. It is a step from the marriage plot to the quest plot, and it is the beginning of change.[4]

Chapter 7

Countervalues and Change

Women's aspirations, transformations, perceptions, values, conflicts, achievements, losses—in the face of all of this, Freud's question remains to be addressed: What do women want? Or more specifically for us, on what terms do women want to enter professional life? What terms would allow them—and their male colleagues—to integrate the full expression of their intellectual and creative capacities with a fully satisfying personal life, the full expression of feeling and sexuality? The countervalues expressed in various forms by our interviewees suggest that what women want is a radically different system of professional organization—indeed of social organization—from the one that prevails. Most, of course, do not cast their opinions or actions in such grandiose terms. Rather, far-reaching systemic change is implied in the countervalues we have identified, in the way individual women articulate their purposes and seek to practice their profession.

To put it most generally, the countervalues add up to a countersystem of social order, one that opposes excessive hierarchy and exclusivity in the holding of authority, one that incorporates diversity, spreads authority through processes of cooperation, resists centrality both in the holding of political and intellectual authority and in the defining of truth and value, and protects individuality through the legitimizing of a personal component in professional life, a personal component to a professional voice.

The key to women's interest in radical change is the transformational process, because it is itself, enacted in the life of an individual, a process of radical change in identity. Through learning, a woman whose social identity is essentially sexual, and whose social role is essentially supportive, develops another dimension of personhood. Her intellectual abilities grow and she acquires methodological tools for acquiring further knowledge and assessing it, for creating inquiries of her own, for offering new findings and interpretations to colleagues and to the public. She gains the power of initiation and the authority, the inner authority, that is, to speak definitively about what she knows. An active self, an intellectual self, extends the sexual and relational self already fostered by social encouragement, and the result is the exhilarating sense of wholeness, of new life that many interviewees express.

This personal coming-to-life instills in many a strong interest in replicating that experience in others through teaching and seeking institutional change that would allow the transformed individual social room in which to practice new-found strengths. And this, of course, is the point at which the prevailing social and professional order impinges on the transformational agenda. Women and other groups historically excluded from the exercise of social authority still encounter the exclusionary force of the old norms as they are given form in institutional organization.

In the professions, overly rigid hierarchies narrow the number of authorities and foster competition among individuals and small groups for the capture of authoritative positions. Under competitive pressures, authority holders tend to buttress their positions by co-opting into the power procession others like themselves. This tendency reinforces the continued exclusion of groups already excluded—groups made up of people unlike the authority holders. And professional authorities justify, to themselves and others, practices that are, in effect, exclusionary by finding members of the excluded groups in some sense inadequate—for example, women aren't serious; women aren't tough; women focus on irrelevancies; women don't want to put in the hours.

In one way or another, women's countervalues resist the tendency of closed hierarchies to place limits on the numbers of possible rule makers and on the pool from which rule makers are drawn. Princeton professor Natalie Zemon Davis, discussing her prospective presidency of the American Historical Association, describes this resistance as a key principle in her professional life. "In my past service on AHA and university committees, I have tried to combine commitment to shared institutional values with loyalty to the critical experience and memories of an outsider. This is the perspective I would bring to the presidency of the AHA and would hope, in so doing, to help other outsiders increase their impact on the profession: minorities, women, teachers at non-elite institutions, and non-academics."[1]

And recall the various forms of resistance to hierarchical practice that appear in our stories. In dealing with the rules of the game, women tend to shun academic politics and place their faith in a merit system, a practice that is at once an expression of naïveté and of commitment to a principle that would make the fullest possible room for individual energies and contributions. They also seek to decentralize decision making, as we have seen in the stories of department heads and administrators who tend to use councils and committees, negotiation and persuasion, as far as possible in setting policy.

In exercising their professional voice—in the classroom, in public speech, even in writing—women frequently rely on techniques of suggestion, questioning, engagement, discussion, demystification rather than on the delivery of their findings in tones that brook no disagreement. The effect of this latter, handing-down technique is to narrow the band of those who define truth and value. The effect of demystification and open discussion is to widen it.

And similarly in their scholarship, women practice—in their choice of subject matter and methodologies—an inclusiveness that strikes indirectly at habits and practices of social exclusion. Most obviously, there is the insistent interest in the history, nature, philosophy, art, biology, and other attributes and practices of the excluded groups themselves—including women. Less obvious is the refusal to follow methodological rules that define importance and relevance in narrow and inelastic terms. The practices reviewed in chapter 5—placing subject matter in a cultural context, eschewing scientific certainty, combining theory and practice, admitting ambiguity, transcending disciplinary boundaries—all operate against a predefinition of matter worth knowing. If you may pursue only questions defined as important by disciplinary authorities, only questions the answers to which can be established with scientific certainty or accord with a system of theoretical logic, it is obvious that many questions are excluded. And although the justification for such exclusion is the maintenance of intellectual rigor through the application of objectively sound principles of inquiry, the actual effect is to enthrone the interests and perspectives of those defining the principles.

The final piece of women's professional countersystem, the piece that moves the question of inclusiveness to the level of wider social rearrangement, is the insistent impulse to integrate a work life and a personal life. And to do so not as an exceptional, isolating—even selfish—feat, but as a wholly natural way to live. As things stand now, women must take primary responsibility for shared living arrangements, whether in a marriage or other relation, if they want to have close, intimate bonds as important parts of their lives. And if they also want to engage in a demanding professional life, the usual understanding is that it is up to them to make the ambitious scheme work *without* jeopardizing the private arrangements for which they are responsible. As we saw in chapter 6, most women struggling to lead this double life end up compromising their work lives in some way. In other words, the allocation to women of primary responsibility for the private sphere effectively excludes them from full participation in the public sphere. For women to have full professional work fully open to them, or as open as it is to men, men would have to share fully in private responsibilities.

All of this is what we mean by the radical nature of women's counter-values. One can scarcely imagine a more radical shift in power, in the placement of social authority, than the actual inclusion of women in professional life in numbers and on terms equal to those of men. It would not be a matter of retaining the status quo with fuller lives for women *added on.* Inevitably it would mean a gain in rule-making authority for women entering the professions, which in turn would entail a gain in control over the capital organized and managed by the professions, as well as some control over the entry of other women into places of authority. And for men shifting part of their time into the private sphere, it would mean a corresponding loss of social authority and control over capital. Of course the argument is often made, and we endorse it, that such a shift would produce more humane conditions of living for men and women, but there is no getting around the fact that it would mean, for men, a significant loss of power.

As Carol Bellamy, former New York City Council president, remarked of the problems of women in authority: "I'm telling you, it frightens people. I don't care whether it's labor institutions or corporate institutions or media institutions or political institutions. They're scared silly that all of a sudden women are going to take positions of power."[2]

And yet the impulses toward inclusion in the professions of previously excluded groups, toward the decentralization of rule making, toward the integration of life and work, mean nothing less than this. However softly stated or quietly enacted, they imply radical changes in the prevailing social order, and they challenge squarely the stereotype of women as social conservators. As a women's college president (not among our interviewees) remarked to us, "To educate women to take themselves seriously at all is, in itself, a subversive act."

The obverse of women's desire for change, of course, is the impress of the social norms that require women's subordination. That is, integrating intellectual and sexual dimensions of personhood, professional and personal responsibilities, would not be a radical agenda if it did not run strongly counter to a deeply entrenched social system. The system, as we have noted throughout this study, is changing, but there are still strong forces resistant to serious rearrangement.

One so obvious that it is easy to underestimate it is the clear-cut economic interest of men who benefit from the present division of labor by gender. For many men the implications of professional equality for women are indeed revolutionary because their professional productivity most commonly depends upon a private support group, which may include wife, secretary, housekeeper, researcher, junior female staff, many of them women who, under a changed system, would no longer be available for such support roles. In her book *Does Khaki Become You?*,[3] an analysis of the role of women in the military, political scientist Cynthia Enloe describes this as a teeth-to-tail model of organization: women are the tail—supply workers, office workers, elaborate communications technicians—literally the back-up that enables the teeth to bite.

In the academy, as increasing numbers of women enter the professional ranks as faculty, the gender-based division of labor is taking the form of a permanent underclass of heavily female faculty—women who hold terminal contracts, teach part-time and in other non-tenure-track positions, teach remedial courses and English as a second language, fill temporary replacement positions.

To change the social order so that women pursue careers that carry them beyond service or supportive relations would be to call the entire professional structure into question. It would be to alter the existing distribution of economic power between the sexes. And, we must add, it would also be to disturb the positions of many women who have found, if not autonomy, then a certain measure of security in well-defined supportive roles. Thus both men and women who benefit from the present system naturally resist its radical alteration.

Then, in addition to interest, and inextricably combined with it in support of the prevailing order, is the old-norm conception of women's nature making them unfit for responsible public roles; this, in turn, justifies a division of labor along lines of complementarity, not equality. Even the early feminist Margaret Fuller put it in these terms: women are "harmony, beauty, love"; men are "energy, intellect, power." And in this rendering, the two sets of attributes suggest not sameness, but equality—

equal dignity, perhaps even equal power. But in fact, complementarity does not signify two equal halves joined in a whole; rather it has always resulted in social forms, private and public, in which men have final power, in which men define the rules.

Specifically, the male-female complementarity of the old norms allocates to men, in a way it does not to women, the active properties of individuality. A man may be strong or wise or intuitive, charismatic, inspired, demonic, or humble. And the ideal for men, since it was defined in the Renaissance, is precisely the broadest development of individual powers. If our present times flatten that ideal with pressure toward specialization and fragmentation, the image of the whole man remains as a measure of what has been lost and may be regained. But women are not seen first as individuals with particular characteristics and potential strengths; they are seen first as women, defined most importantly by the supposed properties of their gender. As Constance Bennett, women's studies director at Harvard Divinity School, reminds us, "the *whole* man" of the Renaissance referred strictly to "the whole *man*." Therefore, we do not so clearly visualize "the whole woman" and have difficulty seeing women as broad enough, fair-minded or disinterested enough to carry high responsibility for public affairs.[4]

Another related distinction carried in the concept of complementarity is that by nature men are tough and women are soft. And this distinction also relegates women to subordinate roles because authoritative roles are assumed to require toughness, the exertion of power, as part of their necessary functioning. Women cannot be trusted with high responsibility, it is commonly urged, because they may not be forceful enough in harsh situations. They may do damage to their university or corporation or hospital or even the nation by knuckling under to whomever the putative enemy is. This fear was classically expressed in the challenge put to Geraldine Ferraro during her 1984 campaign for the vice presidency: "Could you push the button?"[5]

On the one hand, that is, women are accused of being too "soft" to fulfill the authoritative, dominant role of high public office. Curiously, however, at the same time the opposite charge is leveled against them—look at how hawkish Indira Ghandi, Golda Meir, Margaret Thatcher became in their positions of leadership! What has happened to the differences? Where are the humane values? As things stand now, with so few women holding public power, women must "act tough" to achieve credibility, must behave in a way easily recognized as belonging to leadership. They must be "like men." But being tough in the exercise of power, moral questions aside, is not always a winning professional strategy, because the belief is not only that women cannot be tough, but that they should not be, that, though natural to men, it is a perversion of women's nature.

This ambivalence toward the conjunction of women and power surfaces in current dress codes for professional women. In a Jos. Bank (a national clothing chain) advertisement in the *New Yorker* magazine, a woman executive pictured with two male colleagues is dressed in a tailored (Banks) suit because, the advertisement warns, "women know it's just a little harder to be taken seriously." But there is the reassurance of lurking femininity in the addition of a floppy bow tie which (uniformly) accompanies this adaptation of male attire. In the need for the floppy bow, we see that even if a woman seeks to behave "like a man," she meets a profound, generalized distrust of tough women who are seen as becoming "rogue," i.e., unpredictable, even dangerous.

In short, because our institutional structures function through manipulations of power, and because complementarity assigns the attribute of toughness in the use of power to men, it follows that men must hold primary authority in those institutions. It is the part of women in this scheme to supply the softness the society needs in their private and other supportive roles.

Given the invisible barriers raised by the old norms against women's pursuit of wholeness, of autonomy and authority open to them as the new norm and not the exception, what is to be done to bring about change?

As a general strategy, we would emphasize the importance of women's continuing to press for positions in the professions as if their holding public authority *were* the norm, continuing to claim authority as rightfully theirs. And we urge this even against the objection that women risk losing their particular perspectives and values if they commit themselves to a work life structured by male-defined institutions.

The objection is a serious one. It raises the truly difficult problem of co-optation—the queen-bee syndrome, the loss of gender loyalty, the adoption of institutional habits of mind and methods of operation. It raises the question whether women must effectively renounce their countervalues if they want to practice a profession as that profession is normally organized—whether women must remain outside the institutions in order to remain true to their own convictions and knowledge.

Responses to these questions vary within the women's movement, but they include a strong strain of suspicion directed at the woman who seeks a mainline career in professions established and run by men. The suspicion is that such women must either be unconscious of the implications of their acts or be concerned with nothing higher than their own self-gratification—and that they must be willing to suppress any inklings of gender loyalty or sympathy for other powerless groups to gain personal ends.[6]

This is, we believe, an unfair and highly dangerous attitude for women to harbor. No doubt it is true that many women as well as men enter the professions primarily for personal aggrandizement of some kind, with little social consciousness or commitment. But an examination of motives, person by person, is beside the point. The larger point is that the professions, including the places of highest authority in the professions, should be open to women as the norm, not the exception. And this is important because without the possibility of functioning as professionals, women effectively lose the possibility of expressing fully those parts of themselves—social commitment, creativity in philosophic or social realms, intellectual or scientific creativity—that have their greatest effect in professional practice. They lose an effective outlet for the expression of wholeness that *all* women seek.

Of course, women may opt for practicing their professions outside the mainline institutions—as many women are forced to do in any case—but this is a position fraught with difficulty. With respect to academe, it is extraordinarily difficult to carry on an enterprise of serious research and writing without access to the universities' stock of libraries, laboratories, funds for research trips, general research grants, office machines, and office space. The plain fact is that most of the capital the society allocates to the support of intellectual inquiry and writing is allocated to the academy. The sources of support for outsider work are negligible, which means that the outsider's impact on the thought of the society is negligible.

There are the glorious exceptions, of course, like Rachel Carson or Barbara McClintock, but we would not advocate a route depending on this kind of exceptionalism for its effectiveness. Exceptionalism condemns the voices of most women to silence. And if not heard, women cannot affect the way the professions function. They lose the possibility of rewriting professional rules—and the society loses the labor and the particular visions of their fields women are able to contribute.

Finally, the reason we are confident that women *can* stake out a professional place for themselves without wholly adopting the mind-set and practices prevailing in professional institutions is that the stories of our tenured interviewees indicate that this is precisely what they *are* doing. They may be cautious. They may adopt some kind of protective coloration in their professional dealings—whether in mode of speech or dress or other conventional practice. They may not declare themselves, or even see themselves, as revolutionaries seeking to overthrow the present system of social organization and to replace it with one based on women's counter-values.

But still their stories are full of enactments of values at odds with those that prevail. Recall: the department chair who quietly resisted the tradition in her university of decision making from on high and worked cooperatively by preference; the philosopher who introduced a course on women in philosophy in what had recently been an all-male Catholic college where such an inquiry was unheard of; the many instances of scholarship placed in the untidy context of human culture as opposed to a predefined context of logic or abstract theory; the impulse to demystify subject matter, to "translate" it into words and ideas that are widely accessible; the commitment to transformational teaching. The women engaged in these activities did not relinquish their view of the world, their individual reactions to their own experience, on entering the academy. They probably could not; they are too deeply engrained. And that experience—essentially one of outsiderness, whether or not women fully perceive it that way—necessarily informs their judgments and actions. Thus women in professional institutions do have their effect, and more women will have more effect, which makes it self-defeating and dangerous for women to stigmatize those entering mainline institutions as somehow selling out.[7]

If, then, women *should* continue to enter professional institutions as a matter of right, how, specifically, can they do it? How can they cope with the problem of achieving the professional security that will give scope to their creativity and a voice in rule making, in the face of continued resistance to these efforts? What are their best career strategies?

Much of the advice that is marketed to women in aid of their professional advancement is actually dangerous because it is based on the unspoken premise that what women want is achievable *as things stand*. The implication, then, is that if women do not achieve what they want, it is their own fault; they have done things wrong. And doing things right, in this view, consists of learning exactly how the present system works and of following its strictures and mores exactly—or as exactly as is possible for women. According to these lights, though women may not be able to wear three-piece suits, size 42, they can dress for success in adaptations of the conservative male suit. And they can learn to speak as their male colleagues do, develop and use networks of useful connections, never betray emotion or speak at work about problems at home, and so forth.

Our point is not that such advice is wrong or useless in its particulars. Rather it is wrong in its implication that following these right rules will produce a happy ending—a full professional life *and* a full personal life. And it is dangerous because by not warning women of the enormous blockages placed in their way by the old norms, blockages added on to the blocks and frustrations they share with men, such advice leaves women defenseless before the most serious threats to their professional lives.

Sound advice must begin with the right questions. And the right questions are those that acknowledge the necessity for serious compromise— that recognize the power of forces militating against women's attainment of significant authority and against the successful integration of professional and personal lives. The right questions include, for example: Do we play by rules we seriously dislike? For academic women: Do we deliberately produce self-promoting scholarship on limited, do-able topics even if it means putting aside a long, serious exploration that intrigues us? Do we seek positions on the academic periphery where women are relatively acceptable, or strike for the centers of authority where they are not? Do we avoid marriage, or having children, knowing that serious personal commitments will compromise our professional lives?

Always remembering that no advice can remove the extraordinary obstacles to women's professional and personal fulfillment, we offer the following thoughts as the best general rules that emerge from the stories we have seen:

(1) Read, study, talk about the place of women in the professions, the relation of women to social authority generally, in order to choose knowingly in a situation of necessary compromise. Academic women in particular must resist the temptation to regard the academy as set apart from the other professions, a sanctuary from the exercises of power that organize the commercial world. The academic commitment to truth seeking may set it apart in some ways from the ethos of the more commercial professions, but the societywide conception of women as properly subordinate, and the societywide hierarchical organization of institutional life prevail in the academy as elsewhere, and operate against the advancement of women there as elsewhere.

(2) Join or organize women's groups appropriate to your particular study or place or activity. Repeatedly, the stories show that on-going

contacts with other women—mentors or peers—provide the necessary medium for recognizing the play of gender in problems that seem to be only personal. An ongoing reminder of the importance of gender in women's experience is particularly necessary for professionally trained women because professionals are strongly inclined by their training, the sharpening of their intellectual powers, the growth of their knowledge and experience to approach problems autonomously, to assume that their responses should be self-generated. Their training produces a highly individuated person, and it is difficult for such a person to maintain a simultaneous self-conception as an undifferentiated member of a group—especially a group as large as "women." And yet it is essential because the old norms define any woman, highly trained or not, as part of the group "women," and much of women's experience flows from this identification. Women's groups define and reinforce that knowledge. And the bonding of women is important too for joint action on behalf of women within particular institutions.

(3) Perhaps the most important specific rule is to plan strategically for a career, to make five-year plans and ten-year plans as part of a process of conscious decision making. As we noted in chapter 3, "Rules of the Game," women tend to hold general long-term goals or aspirations; academic women want to teach and write and, usually, to establish a family or some other relation of personal commitment. But they approach this goal, often, through ad hoc, reactive maneuvers, almost on a day-to-day basis, trying to hold all the pieces of their complicated package together. What is crucial is the middle-range planning, the projections of ends and means for several years ahead. Such planning forces a confrontation with the conflicts that beset professional women's lives and induces, or should, recognition of the necessity to make hard choices, to set priorities.

So, the third rule is *plan ahead*, and, as you do five- and ten-year planning, involve your partner, if you have one. If you are married, such planning must obviously be joint. If you are in a relationship but not as yet fully committed and your partner does not understand or sympathize with your goals, consider ending your involvement, as people do not change much.

What most of our stories reveal is that their protagonists, caught in conflicts they could not resolve, ended up with whatever it was they valued most. If the conflict was between family and work, and the end result was family and seriously compromised work, it was because the woman placed her highest value on family. But generally she did this without knowing, or believing, the full odds against the eventual *satisfactory* integration of her two goals. This is not to say that we advocate choosing one and giving up the other, but rather urge that women recognize the difficulties implicit in their integrative enterprise, count the costs of different alternatives, and make *conscious* choices about how to proceed. The conscious facing of risks and costs should make it possible for women to proceed more self-protectively, with a greater margin of safety for their goals than is otherwise likely.

From what we have seen of young women now in graduate school (a group not interviewed but encountered in various ways), the block to full recognition of the difficulties before them is not lack of knowledge—the women's movement has produced a large cautionary literature—but a refusal to believe what, in some sense, they know. It is difficult to believe that goals that are good in themselves should be extremely difficult or impossible to achieve. And it is easy for young women to assume that the doleful warnings from their elders reflect the experience of prior generations encountering barriers that have now been removed, or perhaps the experience of women who were not sufficiently serious about their goals, or not sufficiently competent, to achieve them.

Such attitudes are, in a way, healthy. In themselves, they reflect the powerful impulse in the young to become whole persons, to allow all parts of themselves to be developed and expressed, not to allow themselves to be forced into the shapes and spaces defined by the old norms. Rejoicing in the appearance and reappearance of this powerful, healthy impulse in women, we want only to say to new generations of women professionals: Do not let your goals be defeated by underestimating the opposition to them of powerful social norms. And be aware that we all carry those norms, women as well as men, and that it is easy to be confused by them.

(4) For academic women, including those in graduate school, a highly specific word of crucial advice: Publish. One strategy, certainly necessary for a fast-track career, is to plan a dissertation that can be converted to a book within two or three years after receiving the Ph.D. But respectable careers can also be built on early, good articles, and it may be wasteful of time and energy to seek a publishable thesis topic rather than one that is limited and do-able in a relatively short period of time. In either case, it is wise to publish articles regularly and to present papers at professional

meetings. And it is wise to remember that although such professional activity will not guarantee a successful march to tenure, lack of it will almost surely preclude its achievement.

(5) Participate actively in the professional life of your institution, but do not allow your time to be consumed meaninglessly. For example, graduate students might serve on their graduate council, and junior faculty on not overly time-consuming faculty committees. The point is to counteract the given condition of outsiderness, to establish a network of possibly helpful acquaintances, to make your skills known, and also to put yourself in the way of useful information.

(6) Join your professional association, either regional or national, and attend its meetings. You may despise the game playing, but you may also find out what is going on, meet people who will be helpful to you, and (in the best of circumstances) stimulate your mind. The professional establishments are bastions of largely male power, but that is giving way somewhat, and in any event there is nothing wrong in using such associations and meetings to establish networks and to develop and test ideas.

(7) Both in graduate school and later, find a mentor, male or female. Realize that people like to help others. It makes them feel useful and influential. Anyone in a position to help or guide you has been helped or guided by others, and in addition to aiding you is paying back a general professional debt. Accept such help freely, gladly, and graciously, and extend it in turn to someone in the future.

(8) Develop the habit of persistence in seeking what you want and what you need. Do not allow yourself to be defeated by criticism or indifference or, as discussed in chapter 2, by rejection of work that is, in effect, a love child. And do not fall into the trap of self-blame, self-doubt, excessive apology. Remember Emily Vermeule's words to the Harvard women graduates of 1985, "Do not accept that discourtesy which denies your talents to you. Never believe it."

(9) In following these or any other rules, especially those you dislike, remember that there are various phases to a career. Many academic women have gained what they wanted, or at least some of what they wanted, by following established professional rules and mores until they won tenure, at which point they began to follow their own rules. Conversely, it is not all over if you do not follow a traditional career path, although it is a lot harder. If you want to go for a Ph.D. at age thirty-five or reenter the profession after a hiatus, do so, but double your efforts to follow the rules about becoming known, networking, finding a mentor, and publishing (also, see the twelfth rule).[8]

(10) On the question of marriage, the stories are startlingly clear. Women have the best chance of integrating rich personal and professional lives that include marriage if they marry a man willing and able, in advance of any general societal restructuring, to restructure the traditional marriage relation. And this will be most possible for men whose own work falls into flexible patterns—entrepreneurs, consultants, writers, sometimes academics. But here a word of caution must be added. Because the work life of academe is, by its nature, flexibly scheduled, it appears to many that the profession does indeed allow the flexibility that is obviously necessary in a dual-career marriage. But this is by no means automatically the case. Although there is no fixed workday except a class schedule for professors, the sheer amount of work that academics must do during graduate school and pretenure years is staggering, and it is work requiring an enormous interior pull, an inward concentration at odds with the external demands of complicated family logistics. If both marriage partners are in the same phase of their careers at the same time, the stresses in an academic marriage will be just as great as in any other professional pairing. Conscious planning and choices may alleviate the worst of them, but the flexibilities offered by academic life are more apparent than real.

The larger point is that a marriage in which the husband's work makes inflexible demands and is, at the same time, regarded by both partners as the first priority on their joint time, is a marriage likely to defeat the possibility of demanding professional work on the part of the woman. This is true for the obvious reason that she will almost certainly assume primary responsibility for their private life and thus bear the brunt of family-work conflicts in the various ways told in our stories.

Which brings us to the problem of guilt. If you are married to another professional, the two of you are performing three demanding jobs: yours, his, and running the household. Two people cannot do three jobs adequately. What matters in family life is that you spend time with and enjoy your children, your spouse, and your friends. What matters professionally is that you find and perform satisfying work. What does not matter is that meals be cooked by you, that your children's Halloween costumes be homemade, and that your house be neat. The norms of the marriage plot generate constant guilt for women about household tasks—fight it, and help other women to fight it.[9]

(11) Part of the process of personal self-protection should include efforts for the protection of women's interests generally within the professional sphere. And the major need, beyond women's own greater consciousness of their complicated social position, is to produce greater con-

sciousness of this complication on the part of male authorities. Women should do what they can, given their circumstances, to make their male colleagues aware of the extra social baggage carried by women on their professional quests, and the costs of that extra burden.

In our experience, well-meaning men, faced with a personnel decision concerning a woman, appeal to women friends with plaintive questions, such as: "How can we reappoint her when she hasn't finished her thesis?" or "She seems really bright and energetic but she just hasn't written as much as the male candidate—what can we do?" The answer to such questions should be an exercise in consciousness-raising. In both cases, what looks like a deficiency in a woman's record betokening lesser academic talent or commitment than that of male peers may very well be the result of pressure imposed by the old norms on a woman whose talent and commitment are fully the equal of any peers.

As for the thesis-writing process, the old norms may have a confusing effect in several different ways. A woman may choose a thesis topic because it lies within the current focus of her field and then find she has little personal interest in it. It does not allow her to explore questions that are actually on her mind—questions stemming in some way from her particular experience and intellectual slants, but departing from the norms of her discipline—and the work lags. Or, at the other extreme, she may choose precisely to explore her own questions, move across disciplines to find answers, take the time to learn material in several fields beyond her supposed base, lose touch with her thesis adviser, and find it extraordinarily difficult to pull the resulting mass of material together on her own. In either case, she may have left her graduate university at the thesis-writing stage to follow her husband to another locale, and found herself working in intellectual isolation and without a convenient or adequate library.

The well-meaning male friend or colleague, having been instructed in these complexities, should be urged to find out exactly what is going on with the stalled thesis, to try to decide whether the problem is indeed incompetence or whether a serious intellectual issue is in the way. And if it is the latter, he should be urged to do what he can to slow the personnel clock in order to allow the woman time to resolve her dilemma.

And the same applies to the plaint concerning the shorter publication list. The decision-making male should find out why the woman in question has not published more. What has she been doing with her time? Eating chocolates? Playing pool? More likely she has taken time from her professional work to carry out private responsibilities. The point is it should be made as difficult as possible for professional authorities to regard such a scenario as evidence of lack of professional ability or seriousness, a predictive base for lesser professional attainment in the future. It is not, or need not be.

Of course, the objection to this kind of specialized review for women is that it employs a double standard, that it departs from the central principle of professionalism which is objectivity in the rendering of judgments. To be fair, the objection goes, personal burdens would have to be taken into account in making judgments about men too, with everyone, then, being given points for hardship rather than accomplishment. The answer, again, is that women encounter the same run of personal hardships that men do, and where their burdens are similar, women cannot ask for any greater indulgence in professional judgment than that accorded men. But in addition, women encounter the force of the old norms that define women's public place as subordinate to that of men. That is, women enter the professions fighting a preexisting double standard. And that struggle takes time and energy.

If the professions are to operate fairly with respect to women—if professional authorities really seek to further women's professional development—then the time and energy claimed from women by the old norms must be taken into account in judgments of women's competence. Review committees should look at what she has done professionally with the time left her after the society has claimed the time needed from her for private lives to be sustained. And they should discount also for the time it takes her to resolve intellectual and personal dilemmas imposed by the old norms in ways that her male peers are spared.

As a general rule, women should be allowed more chronological time to demonstrate their professional competence than that usually allowed to men. And women must make this necessity plain. Natalie Davis discussed this point also in the remarks noted above on her prospective work as president of the American Historical Association. "Data are now available on the relationship of different life cycles to rhythms of scholarly productivity," she said, and "this should be made known to the profession."[10]

Women now have an excellent model for this argument in Barbara A. Black, appointed dean of the Columbia Law School in 1986 after a career that included ten years spent out of academe raising a family of three children. "The message," Dean Black says, "is not merely that a woman was appointed dean at Columbia Law School, but a woman who did what I did: who took on the traditional duties and obligations and joys of the woman's role, who traveled a terribly circuitous path back to the job that she had always wanted, whose work was not of the quantity that the more direct male path would have produced. What it suggests is that this kind of life experience is relevant to the professional world, perhaps even important, perhaps even critical."[11]

(12) This book is focused on the snares that the marriage plot puts in the way of women undertaking professional careers. It has shown how academic women need to focus on *careers* rather than *jobs*, which means focusing, in most cases, on gaining tenured positions. But the larger point is that many women become sidetracked into seriously compromised careers *unconsciously*. They become deflected from their work by traditional societal expectations of men's and women's roles rather than by their own choices.

Our interviews have shown the extraordinary difficulty of combining the marriage plot and the quest plot, and readers should not think there is a single solution better than all the others. Part-time work is not always a bad thing although its disadvantages—little status, low salary, no benefits, no tenure—are serious. Similarly, teaching at a community college may not fulfill a woman's highest aspirations for herself, but it may in some cases provide the best solution to the complex problem of combining a professional and a private life.

The fact is that as society is presently structured, most people cannot satisfy their desire for a rich work and home life. The point, then, facing bad odds, is to make your choices consciously and, for married women, from a position of equality with your spouse, not to drift into choices because of societal expectations, outmoded sex roles, and deference to male power. If you can do that, you will have done all you can to achieve the good life for yourself and to shape a better future.

Once women have secured some piece of professional ground and are able to speak with some degree of authority, not only about their fields but about their experience as professional women, it becomes important to ask: What should they say? How can their voices advance the cause of change beneficial to women?

We do not offer a single script, a party line. Rather, we urge that the insider woman should use, and not suppress in herself, the perspective she gains from her societal position of relative powerlessness. That is, as we have argued above, the woman who enters an established profession does not automatically acquire an establishment outlook. To do so she must actively suppress that part of her experience that differs from that of men and that places her, to some degree, in a position of intellectual detachment from institutional norms. What we urge is that she use her detachment, and the critical point of view it engenders, as a tool for understanding professional functions and carrying them out herself— although we do not underestimate the difficulty of this prescription.

Women academics, for example, can subject the canon in their fields to their own questions, to their own rules of relevance, and to their own values. The difficulty comes in believing in their own findings when these differ markedly from the landmark works in their fields. Not only do women in such circumstances fear that their work will not be taken seriously by professional authorities, they also have difficulty taking it seriously themselves. Again, this is a point where discussion with other women who have encountered similar dilemmas would be helpful. They can provide a context within which individual self-suspicion may be allayed.

In addition to using, not displacing, the outsider's voice, women should also use whatever positions in the profession they are able to secure as a ground for change. It is clear that, as things stand now, these will be predominantly positions on the periphery—for academic women, positions in women's colleges, religious institutions, community colleges, rather than at research universities. However, and this is an important point, a position on the periphery does not preclude the opportunity to exert influence.

The evidence of the interviews is that women establish their own countersystems, are able to enact their own countervalues, wherever they land, and if such systems or classroom styles or foci of scholarship become widely enough established, even outside the corridors of power, they will exert an influence. Just as the speech of blacks in America has changed the spoken and written language of the dominant whites, women's influence is felt in the academy, expanding the canon (e.g., the examination of women's diaries, journals, the extraordinary surge of biographies of women), altering the foci of scholarship and classroom pedagogy, offering revisionist interpretations of texts from the Bible through Joyce's *Finnegan's Wake*, adducing theories of neurobiology and psychology that reveal differences in gender development. Of course, the most direct influence women faculty have is through women's studies, a field that did not even exist as a pocket of influence twenty-five years ago.

Furthermore, the influence of women, present and accounting for themselves in the academy, is of inestimable value to their women students, who both see older women deploying themselves in a professional role that then becomes credible, and are guided through the shoals of graduate school to a professional passage. In sum, we are not temporizing when we point out that although the position of women in the academic professions is peripheral, these women possess influence, and should use it as fully as possible.

And women on graduate faculties should, of course, make every effort to acquaint their women students—and their male colleagues—with the common problems women confront. Forewarned and forearmed as graduate students, women have a better chance of forestalling the trouble they face, if not avoiding it altogether.

In all the professions, it is absolutely clear that advocacy of substantial change in the structure of the workplace and of family responsibilities is an important strategy for women seeking full professional and personal lives. And the obduracy of the old norms against such change is distressingly evident in recent retrenchments in government funding for day-care centers, care of the elderly, and health-related issues in general. Reduced social support for such problems militates against a widened work life for women because care of the sick, the elderly, and the very young is still primarily women's responsibility. To the extent that such care must be privately provided, it is generally women's time that is claimed for it. Also, women as the second tier in the workplace are more poorly recompensed than men and yet comprise most of the single-parent families, so reduction of human services can have a crippling effect on their work lives.

Most significantly, however, the problems of child care and health care are commonly and erroneously seen as "women's issues" when, as Representative Patricia Schroeder (D-Colorado) declares repeatedly, "It's a family issue, a human issue, a quality of life issue." But as long as family welfare is seen as a women's issue, women will be vulnerable to the charge, intensely pressed by fundamentalist groups, that women's neglect of the family is eroding the mental and moral health of the society. And the fundamentalist prescription, predictably, is for women to solve the problem by returning to the private domain, as if women at work were at odds with family health. Yet, as we have seen in our stories, even those women who fled from bastions of fundamentalism—small midwestern towns, conservative Jewish or Catholic communities—to find room for intellect and creativity, were not fleeing the value of the family as such. On the contrary, their consistent struggle is to *integrate* work and family life, not to give up one for the other.

It is not women working but the resistance of the old norms to the new reality of women working that hurts the health of families—resistance that results in the failure of the society to support women's new roles with redistribution of family responsibility. And evidence is mounting that the family as a whole would benefit from such distribution. Concerned with the increasing compartmentalization of professional and personal lives, Dr. Abraham Zaleznik, a professor at the Harvard Business School, teaches a course probing the relation between the two. He refutes the idea "that there is an inherent contradiction between the intimacy of family life and being a high-powered executive." According to his research findings, "Not only is there a direct connection between the capacity to give and personal satisfaction, but also it seems to release more creativity [in management roles]."[12]

Certainly, if the best interests of all are to be served, the problem of combining work and family cannot continue to be regarded as only a woman's issue. And, as Betty Friedan urges in *The Second Stage*,[13] professional women must continue to use their voices clearly and persistently to redefine the terms of this debate.

Finally, professional women must use their voices to confront and define and raise to a level of general discourse the linkage in the professions among overly rigid hierarchies, an overemphasis on power, and the exclusion of most women from places of central authority. Hierarchical organization and exertions of institutional power are necessary to some degree, of course, for efficiency and order. But such instruments, if not energetically examined and monitored, can easily be employed self-interestedly by the people holding them—which means excluding any challenger to their power. And when women are the challengers to male authority, the exclusion of women is justified, as discussed earlier, by the professional's need to exercise power and the supposed inability of women to do so. It is this self-serving knot of assumptions that women must constantly refute. Geraldine Ferraro, for example, in answering the question "Could you push the button?" said flatly, "Yes," but then went on to say that the ability to push the nuclear button was not the most important attribute of sound American leadership in foreign affairs. Rather, she said, national leaders should be able to identify potential conflicts and utilize diplomacy and negotiation to prevent trouble from growing acute.

Continually to mount such challenges to the primacy of power dealing in public life is important to the creation of a wider place for women in spheres of public authority, but it is important also for the whole society. Insisting on the importance of open exchange, consensual procedures, an ethic of inclusiveness in all the professions should help to create new forms of institutional life—forms that will allow and encourage the movement of humane values from the private to the public sphere where they might be practiced by men and women alike.[14]

First, however, the issue for women is to make firm their claim to an equal role in the making of the society's rules. And this means, most basically, making firm their claim to wholeness. It means making room in the society for women to develop a whole individual identity, releasing them from the confines of narrow, predefined roles.

The literature of the century by and about women poignantly reflects this struggle. The force of social constriction at the turn of the century becomes immediately clear in literary dramatizations such as Kate Chopin's novel *The Awakening* in which the heroine dies in the process of attempting change from a dependent to an independent persona. The other "solution" that literature is forced to, is for the heroine to go mad in her struggle, as in such thinly disguised autobiographical novels as Charlotte Perkins Gilman's *Yellow Wallpaper* and Antonia White's *Sugar House*.[15] From death and madness in earlier stories, we move to a contemporary literature of dislocation, novels of women who have cut old ties, moved out of constricted places, established an interior identity, but are left, in important ways, adrift. The society affords them some but not all of the vital connections—professional and personal—that they seek. Examples abound, including Marilyn French's *Women's Room*, Alison Lurie's *Foreign Affairs*, Gail Godwin's *Odd Woman*, all of Anita Brookner's heroines and most of Margaret Drabble's.

In spite of pressures to the contrary, what women seek is to be autonomous and whole, not somebody else's half, not even somebody's "better half"—not some gravity-defying vision of spirituality, the swan in the ballet *Swan Lake* (yet another dying heroine) forever being lifted out of her element, an object of adoration, by the hunter.

Epilogue

Four Lives

In the previous chapters we have identified a battery of danger points common to the experience of women seeking professional autonomy and authority. In doing so, we have clustered fragments of individual stories to develop thematic points. Here, in the compelling language of their own narrators, we reconstitute four stories in order to show how the various themes function in the full context of academic lives.

We have chosen stories that encompass these major themes, that reflect the experience of women in different generations, and that result in a variety of career outcomes—tenure, tenure track, part-time teaching, and career change.

What is important to note, however, despite the variations in individual lives, are the commonalities that run through the stories. For example:

> None of the women still in academe is at a major research university, although all four were at one point in their careers employed by such institutions in lower-echelon positions.
>
> Their self-perceptions, career goals, and strategies do not differ dramatically across generations, or across the seeming divide between tenured and deflected women.
>
> All of them, tenured as well as deflected, suffer serious compromise in the enactment of individual goals and values.
>
> Conversely, all four, deflected as well as tenured, accomplish important parts of their original professional purposes.
>
> In all of the stories, we see the recurrence of crucial benefits derived from the support of other women.

One

This tenured professor of philosophy was born in 1932, grew up in California, attended college on the West Coast and, a year after receiving the B.A., entered graduate school at a major midwestern university where she earned the M.A. and Ph.D. She was married before entering graduate school and had three children while completing her doctorate, which she received in 1961. Thereafter, she took teaching positions wherever her husband, also an academic, was located—first in California, then in Boston. Although some of the positions she held were part-time or non-tenure track, she spent no significant amount of time away from teaching and received tenure twelve years after finishing graduate school. She has published numerous articles from the time she received the doctorate to the present, and one book, a text designed for high school students.

The major themes in this story are the difficulties of shaping a voice of authority capable of expressing knowledge and insight that depart from rigid disciplinary norms. We hear in the interview about three book manuscripts—four including the doctoral thesis—that went unpublished, or, in the case of the textbook, was published but in unpropitious circumstances. Two of these manuscripts were interdisciplinary and on the "soft" edge of the discipline according to the interviewee. And two were aimed at a general, not a scholarly, readership—a design that requires a voice far different from that common to academic discourse.

This is, therefore, a classic story of "women's work" in the academy—choosing humane subjects, placing subject matter in a cultural context, transcending disciplinary boundaries, seeking social change through transformed consciousness, and paying the price. And it is a story both of creativity and of frustration, of work not brought to full fruition, of ideas not fully thrust into the exchange of the times, of attempts to educate a broad readership stymied.

[After graduating from college] I went to France to study French . . . and then while I was in France my then-friend and I decided to get married. And he said "Let's both go and apply to graduate school," so we did. . . . It was, in a way, his initiative. I think he sort of assumed that that was what I wanted to do and it was. But I had never given it very much thought. I guess he had made up his mind to go on for a Ph.D. in [physics] and it just seemed like a perfectly reasonable idea that I would go to graduate school too, in philosophy, which is what I had gotten the B.A. in. . . . My parents were very supportive. They paid for my education, even after I was married, but I don't think they, or I, or anybody else, ever even thought about what I might do with that education. . . . [I went into philosophy] because I loved it and I think that's something that is different between my generation and the younger generation. I really did it because I liked it, no other reason. Not because I thought it would be of any use to me later on. And I think that is a luxury that very few people, male or female, can afford anymore and in those days women could. I mean if you were privileged enough to be able to do something simply because you enjoyed it. You just don't hear anybody talk that way anymore. It's always vocationally oriented and it really wasn't for me.

Then once I started, I just went on. I certainly don't remember ever thinking of dropping out. Well, that's not true. When I started having children I guess I did. With the first one, I actually did drop out, but shortly afterward I found myself getting itchy again and so I got a position as a grader, and then I said, "Well, here I am. I'm back in it again. I might as well go on." By then I had gotten used to the arrangement of having a child and studying. The second one came just about the time I was about to take prelims and the third was born just as I was getting my Ph.D. It didn't interfere very much. It took me maybe a year longer. Obviously there were difficulties—practical difficulties, moral difficulties—but I think at the time the question was essentially how I solve these problems, not should I chuck the whole business. I mean, it was a time when there was a lot of discussion about working women and whether it was good for children and so on. It happened that a friend of mine in sociology was doing work at the time about how it was all right for women to be working and that it was the quality of the time you spent with your children and not the quantity, and it was very reassuring because you did get a certain amount of disapproval. . . .

My professors left me pretty much alone. I think in that way I benefited from sexism. I think on the whole they didn't take me seriously, that some of them were nice, but I certainly could not do what most graduate students did, which was to hang around all the time. There was a graduate student common room where they would play chess and hang out and talk and I was definitely not part of that scene. I mean, I would go to my classes and then I would go home. So I missed out on a lot of, not just the social life, but I think the things that sort of form the basis of the future professional connections and I think that's a real drawback. . . .

I didn't see an awful lot of my thesis adviser. He didn't really know an awful lot about my subject. After the preliminary defense of the topic, which was before a committee, I was pretty much on my own. That's what I mean when I say that I don't think they took me seriously. They didn't mind having me there. I wasn't holding anybody up, but nobody really took an interest in what I was doing and I think I was busy enough with other things of my own so that it didn't bother me. But, again, in retrospect, sometimes when I see people sort of hanging at their professors' doors with weekly appointments, I certainly never had anything like that.

One thing that I remember is that I did not follow the one bit of advice that was given to me, which was that you should pick someone to write about who was dead so that you could do this little nugget of a job and go on and do something else. My thesis was on theories of aesthetic inspiration. It was really creativity that I was thinking about—where creativity comes from. What I had discovered—it turns out that other people were working on the same idea at the same time—but I discovered that creativity is not one thing in art and another thing in science and another thing in other fields, but there really is some kind of human phenomenon that works across fields. No one in my department was working on this kind of thing. If I had been a male I'm not sure if they would have encouraged me to go on with it. I think they would have been more careful that you do mainline work. In general, aesthetics was not a very highly prized area of philosophy. It was not considered central to philosophy and it still, it's gotten closer now, but it was a woman's field. I think women tend not to go into the hard-core center of philosophy which I guess would be logic, epistemology, metaphysics. There were a few, but I think it was sort of expected that women in philosophy would be on the fringes with fields like aesthetics, or maybe philosophy of religion. It's comparable to what was going on in the sciences. I mean, in those days, it was nuclear physics that was the big area of physics, and you didn't find very many women there either, but you would find them maybe in biology or psychology. It was around the softer edges of the field. I think I have always had a hard time staying in the center of the field. It seems that I am always off at the edges. The outside person on my thesis committee was in psychology and in some ways he is the one who took the greatest interest in what I was doing. He and I became good friends and continued to be for a long time afterward, which was not true of the people in the department who were on my committee.

I just didn't consult much with anybody, and then at the last, when I was actually writing it, I wasn't there. We left because my husband took a teaching position in California. So I mailed them chapters now and then, and I think they were as surprised as anybody when I finished it and said, "Here it is" . . .

They were very nice. They scheduled the defense at my convenience which, since I was teaching, meant that it had to be during Christmas vacation. It was at night and I remember it all vividly because I was pregnant at the time and I was feeling horrible. But I had to fly back and there was a terrible snow storm and I got stuck in Chicago, and I barely made it in time to take the exam. And then one member of the committee forgot the exam and I had to call him up and so he was an hour late which meant that we were sitting around talking to each other. All of which meant that everybody was very benignly disposed toward me and then he came shuffling in, very embarrassed. The other people had relaxed a bit, you know we were sitting there talking to each other at night, alone and this snow storm building. I was feeling so rotten that I just wanted to go and throw up somewhere and the whole defense seemed like a joke. I mean, it was so silly, the formalities at that point. I guess I didn't really believe that at that stage they were going to turn me down and they didn't. But I have never had the feeling that anybody carefully read my thesis and evaluated it and argued with me and so on. I thought about publishing it, but I was really kind of bored with it by then so I thought, "Well, I'll just put it aside for a little while and then I'll get back to it," but I never did.

That's when we came out to Boston. What my husband had had before had been postdoctoral fellowships, but he had a real job in Boston, and I thought, "OK, now we're going to live like real grown-ups and we're going to have a house and so I will confine myself to that." At that point, I don't think I was seriously thinking of doing much of anything, even though I had the Ph.D. and had been teaching in California. I spent a lot of time house-hunting that year. I guess I realized pretty soon that I didn't want to be a full-time housewife, but I didn't think about just working on the revision of the thesis—turning it into a book. I don't know what happened to that. It just sort of slipped out of my consciousness I guess. Instead I started looking for work and found a part-time job at X College. I worked one day a week at first, and then one thing led to another and they began offering me more courses and all of a sudden I found myself teaching full-time.

At that point I began paying attention to what I was doing and realized that there were some choices to be made here. I really got professionalized in that job, mainly I think because the chairman of the department just acted naturally as if I *were* a professional, including me in discussions and so forth as if it were the normal thing to do. That's when I started writing and publishing. There was about a five-year period when I was feeling very professional and I went to meetings—I got a big kick out of the whole academic rigmarole. But by then it was too late to publish the thesis as a whole because several books on the subject had come out.

At any rate, another subject had begun to intrigue me and that was the philosophy of science. In the past that subject had been very narrowly focused on mathematical and physical kinds of questions, but it became obvious to me that there were whole dimensions that were not covered by that kind of reduction. For example, biology was a science and yet seemed to pose questions that were not handled in the classic philosophy of science which didn't deal with biology seriously. . . . I wrote a few short things about it, then somebody asked me to write a book which was to be part of a series of philosophy of science books for use in high schools or maybe even junior high schools. The guy who was editing this series had the idea that you shouldn't talk down to children. You should get competent people in the field to just say what they need to say and say it as clearly as possible and that ought to work. It turned out to be not such a good idea because we wrote books that I doubt would ever be used in a high school, certainly not in a junior high. They really turned out to be more difficult than that and also high school curricula were not really set up to deal with the kind of interdisciplinary approach we were taking. Finally the whole series folded. The editor left. They published the books that were written, including mine, but nobody was very interested, so they didn't promote them and they did it in the cheapest way possible and so the book never got much of a chance because it didn't fit into any existing scheme of things. . . .

It was not a good time in general. Just before I started writing that book I lost my teaching job—or rather I resigned because we got a new chairman with whom I didn't get along very well. . . . I could see that I would very likely not get tenure and I couldn't see the point of hanging on there for a little bit longer. It seemed reasonable to do something else.

Luckily, I got a fellowship at the Bunting Institute which was where I worked on the philosophy of science textbook. . . . but in fact it was a turning point because it gave me time to think about what I had done, to sort of review what I had done. It was really the kind of graduate student experience that I hadn't had before. I actually went to lunch with people. At X College, I guess, there were departmental lunches, but the idea that you would call somebody up and say, "Do you want to meet me for lunch?" . . . And the other thing that I could do was to sit in on classes.

While I was teaching, with three children, there wasn't enough time for things like that, but the Bunting Institute gave me a chance to look around a little bit and that was fun. And then I began thinking about women.

It's odd because that was 1968 and there were certainly people who were thinking about women's liberation and women's issues at the time but I was not in the forefront politically. I was involved in other kinds of political activities. That was also the time of the antidraft movement and civil rights and so on, and there were a number of women who were beginning to separate a women's movement out of that, and I was not terribly disposed to it, but I had to start thinking about it.

But the big turning point for me was a philosophical thing—the sort of funny experience that someone has at some point where something that you have been reading for years all of a sudden makes sense to you and I remember I was reading Kant's essay on the Beautiful and the Sublime. It is a horrible book in which he has a whole chapter about male and female characteristics and another chapter about national characteristics, and they are both just awful. It is really garbage—one passage is that women shouldn't trouble their pretty little heads thinking about geometry, that they might as well have beards. And I looked at this and said, "What does having a beard have to do with . . . geometry?". . . It just somehow over-whelmed me. . . . It suddenly dawned on me that maybe I'd better look at the rest of the philosophers and see what they were saying about women and I began doing that and it was appalling. . . . And I had read it before and it was just astonishing that I hadn't noticed it. This is what I find with my students now. They don't notice it either and if you call it to their attention, they try to defend it.

That is when I started collecting this material [passages in the great philosophers showing surprising prejudices about women] and I just pulled out the passages and put it together and I thought, "Well, I'll try to put an anthology together and that will be enough. Just put it out there in the world, and they will see. They will be horrified. The scales will be lifted." And it just wasn't like that. I couldn't get anybody to publish it. . . . I sent it to a few publishers. This was around 1970. I didn't have nearly enough determination. I sent it to a few and nobody was interested. . . . I thought all that would be necessary would be to point it out, and I just had no idea that even women would resist it. It was not just men who resisted it.

Such a book has since been published—in fact, two, at least, by other people—with selections pretty much similar to mine. They were pub-lished toward the end of the seventies. And I think by people who just had a lot more perseverance than I did. I'm really not much of a hustler. I mean I enjoy doing the stuff itself, but I'm not terribly interested in the business end of it.

I went from the Bunting to Y University in a way I would never have believed—through a convention. People actually do get jobs that way. It was all perfectly professional, but it is also true that Y University, which is a Catholic school, was undergoing a kind of political face change—it was becoming secularized, it was becoming liberalized, so the idea of hiring a woman and a Jewish woman must certainly have been attractive to them. . . .

As for the book on philosophers and women, when I saw that the anthology was not the answer, I decided to try a book-length discussion of the issues themselves, so I wrote that during my sabbatical year, but I couldn't find a publisher for that either. The trouble was that I didn't want the book to be a really scholarly book. I wanted to address a more general reader and so it's not full of a lot of documentation and footnotes. The result is that the professionals don't like it, but I tend to think rather abstractly, and so the ideas are obscure enough so that it is not really popular either. And so it sort of falls between the two. The problem is to find a way of talking to an inherently interdisciplinary crowd. You just want to reach normal, intelligent people. But I've used language that feels normal to me and then I see people looking at me sort of askew. "Oh, another philosophical word!" I was writing something for an art museum and I used the word "prescriptive." That sounds all right to me, but they objected. So I don't even know what is normal language anymore. But there is this impulse to reach the general reader. I just haven't really figured out how to do it.

Two

The woman in the following story was born in 1929, received her B.A. in American civilization and M.A. in English literature from a major university, then married, started a family of three children, and taught part-time before receiving her Ph.D. in American studies nearly twenty years after the M.A.

Subsequently, she published two books in American and women's studies, organized and helped run for several years a cross-university discussion group in her field, won two distinguished fellowships, and served as a visiting lecturer at several Ivy League universities. She has not, however, won tenure, or ever held a tenure-track position. The twenty-year delay in significant professional achievement was too large a barrier to overcome.

This long delay in professional credentialing stemmed in important part from the classic conflict of family and work—squeezing two lives into one. But in this case, the protagonist not only put family first, she also followed a transformational agenda to the point of virtual rejection of prudential concern for the "Rules of the Game."

At a number of turning points, she acted mainly out of love of her subject, giving little thought to the politics of the profession. Further, when she began her scholarship in middle age, she engaged in "Women's Work"—cross-disciplinary studies of women—thus placing herself yet further from the scholarly mainstream and the political protection of any discipline.

I think that I became aware of wanting to use my brain when I was very young because I was educated by Quakers in an all-girls' school. We never had a sense of cultural inferiority in the least. We were surrounded by pictures of Quaker heroines, and we knew the Quaker idea of the inner light that makes everyone equal in the same democratic sense that the culture as a whole does. So my education early reinforced my sense of my own capabilities.

I lived in a family where neither parent went to college. My mother was a very brilliant woman, but was never educated in any real way. The high school she went to pushed her into a bookkeeping stream because she was working class. She was trained to be a certain kind of servant to society. And I think she refused to let that happen to me, for which I am always grateful to her. She intuited the dangers of her own wasted mind and insisted on sending me to private school at any cost. She saved for my college education from my childhood on.

At the same time, there was certain tension. My ancient grandmother was in our house a lot, I loved her very much, and she, I think, didn't even graduate from elementary school. And there was a lot of inner conflict around the idea that I shouldn't be different from them. That I should be as domestic as they were—they were both marvelous cooks, for example. They made me feel that women who used their minds were queer, *at the same time as they were educating me to use mine.*

I went to a conservative high school where we had an excellent British-English education, but never read a word of American literature. In college, I discovered American literature with enthusiasm although the kind of elitism I was being educated in still did not consider many new

American writers worth reading, and hardly considered women writers at all. Still, my discoveries in American civilization enriched my identity. I found my education exciting.

At that stage, I didn't realize that I was a woman. I graduated from college Phi Beta Kappa, with a magna cum laude. I had worked with men mostly, there weren't many women in my field—actually only three in my class—it was considered an elite field at the time. There was no sense at all that we were inferior to the men in college. We knew well we were not. But also, there were no women faculty members, and summer study in an American studies program abroad was offered only to men. The *one* visiting woman scholar from England on campus at the time was the epitome of the glorious kindly old maid.

I don't think I focused my ambition at all, then. [Laughs.] I just loved what I was doing. I remember my parents asking, "What are you learning to help you earn a living?" And I would sort of ridicule that and say, "What a plebian way of looking at things. I am just so excited about what I am doing, it doesn't matter if I can earn a living!" Now that I look back, I think their point of view was surely wise, and I wish I had thought in a more serious way about vocation. Of course they also liked the idea of producing a woman of leisure who did not have to work. Women often receive more than one mixed message from this society.

Immediately after college, I got a Fulbright Fellowship, which was a kind of coup at the time. Then, after my year abroad, I returned to the United States and got my Master's Degree in English . . . but I hated the department. I got an M.A. in a year in English, because you couldn't get a Master's in American civilization, only the Ph.D. at that time. . . . The English department then seemed to specialize in setting up trivial obstacles, but you could get the M.A. by checking off requirements: three years of Latin, two foreign languages, etc., etc. No one cared if you knew Latin well or if you would ever use the second language. The rules seemed designed to drive out the imaginative. I had to write eleven papers in one semester all on different things; my sense of commitment was such that I couldn't bear that. I really felt, "If that's what you have to do, to be a professional, I don't want to become one." Now this may be a feminine reaction—an unwillingness to make compromises with reality. I felt I was just doing one picky little thing after the next, and I wasn't even doing them well by the time the year was over. I disdained the faculty because most seemed to be desiccated human beings. The one man I greatly admired enjoyed women more for their femininity than for their minds, but at least he was a real human being and a generous intellect. The other

English professors often seemed bored to death with teaching, or pedantic, lecturing on subjects like "Commas in Keats." No one encouraged women to be scholarly. No one even taught me about footnotes.

I was sort of whirling. And I thought, "The hell with it, I'll just get married."

I think what I see very clearly now is that what I did quite deliberately was to marry someone I thought I could live through and evolve through. And that doesn't work at all. But . . . it was exciting for a while to think that I could learn through my husband who went back to graduate school in history, help share his work, instead of having a career of my own.

I think many universities are so impersonal that just to be acknowledged as a human being in the system is a kind of triumph. Graduate school was a terrible atmosphere for me. Men need help there as well, but they get it from the *society* which is pushing them to complete their degree so that they'll be a member of the establishment in some way, whatever establishment they're working in. Allowances were made for men's part-time work that were never made for bearing children. Men get a lot of encouragement from society to contribute, whereas women get a double line. They're allowed in, and given some power, but at the same time they're told that they must be responsible for children. If I were a dean or president of a university, I would make sure all women got an extra amount of attention—because I think that's what *keeps* women in graduate schools. The idea of the mentor, the idea of the pusher is important in almost every woman's life who's ever accomplished anything. The slightest discouragement can reinforce the ambivalence many women feel and they drop out.

Well, I married in the middle of my M.A. year; my husband was drafted at the end of that year and I had completed my M.A., so I worked for the following year grading papers for a business policy course, a subject I knew nothing about. But the course made me realize that business policy involved more common sense than expertise. There was another more scholarly job I could have had, but the man who would have been my boss was noted for chasing his women research assistants around the stacks. On the advice of the woman who was leaving I avoided that position. . . . But I regretted losing the chance to familiarize myself with a valuable archive.

After teaching for ten years, part-time, I found the greatest trauma of my life when I tried to go back to school. By that time, I was eager to study for a Ph.D. in American studies. But I tried to get into a program, on a part-time basis, because my husband was not strong and I also had three children by then. I did not feel I could ask him to take care of the kids or do the things healthy husbands did to help if they had free time. There was much excitement in the air about Mary Bunting's support of older women—in their thirties—pursuing part-time studies. In fact, one of my earlier mentors told me it would be fine to come back part-time. I had always worked as a teacher part-time, never stopped working, as well as caring for children. I taught part-time at X University, and also at Y University, so I said I would also be willing to go on working to pay my own tuition for the Ph.D. I was rejected. . . . They said, "How can we admit a part-time student when we only have space for twelve serious *full*-time students?" Implicit of course was the idea that if you were part-time you were obviously not committed—perhaps too easily distracted by crude realities.

So, I took this issue to a female dean, who was outraged, as all the female deans at X University were—perpetually outraged and perpetually powerless. She called up the graduate office, which asserted that in spite of all the new talk no one wanted part-time graduate students. Which meant primarily excluding women. They still wouldn't be taking them, except that many older women can pay their own way. And the real question is often economic. When the establishment admits older women, it is because schools need the tuition or they need greater numbers of graduate students to teach the basic skills courses that professors don't want to touch. These graduate students play a useful academic role.

Anyway, at that point, I gave up and never reapplied to my "Alma Mater." Another university an hour and a half's drive away had an American studies program. I could have applied there but at that point I had lost confidence in myself. I had a three-year-old, and a husband who needed a lot of support to get through his own academic obligations . . . and I didn't feel I could commute too. The minute a closer university opened an American studies program, I applied, but by then I was forty. I really wanted to apply what I had learned to the society as a whole, and American studies seemed the best field in which to do that. I didn't want to go back into English literature, where they fretted over punctuation; or now about structuralism. And overemphasis on form seemed irrelevant to me. I'm a very practical person at heart. . . . I didn't want to concentrate on anything that seemed esoteric. So the minute the new program opened I applied, but this time I was cagey. I said I would go full-time, and then, when I was accepted, I went to see the chairman and said, "I can pay my own way if you let me go part-time and continue teaching part-time." So he did that; I always paid for my own tuition by teaching elsewhere.

But I loved my teaching job. . . . I was teaching American literature and I had good students, particularly at a suburban campus where a lot were older women coming back to school. Z University started a daytime adult women's degree program which was filled with people who had dropped out of colleges like Smith or Wellesley, or had moved East with their husbands from California. My students were challenging and highly motivated.

I didn't even think about tenure track because I was teaching in this lively adult program. I felt happy to be there and considered myself the luckiest person in the world to have such a part-time job. I can't believe how stupid I was. . . . my job seemed great because the students were very good, and the campus was only ten minutes away from my home so that when my children needed me—and sometimes they did—I could be there in five minutes. And the fact that the job wasn't tenure track, that it had no fringe benefits, that it provided no intellectual community, all those things seemed irrelevant to me at the time. When I finally went back to graduate school, I realized what I had missed, and that I had been, in a sense, exploited.

As a Ph.D. student, though, I felt the chairman never wanted to push me for any job. . . . I think he took me as a kind of experiment, and felt that people my age are really over the hill; and I think it still amazes him when anything good happens to me. [Laughs.] But he said he liked my book [published a year before this interview] and there were a few of us older women with kids in the graduate program, which was comforting to me. But I don't think we were ever treated in the same way the young hot shots were treated, or pushed for jobs, or even told when there was a job somewhere we should apply for.

Though once you're in and on the tenure track you have more trouble if you're a woman, age discrimination means that you're not even *interviewed* for jobs. Of course, most of the late entrants are women whose schedules are delayed by family responsibilities.

The tenure system as it's designed now, with levels of seniority, just wipes out people who get their degrees later in life, or their freedom to work full-time late in life. The system isn't adaptable.

There's a part of me telling myself, "Who wants their crummy jobs anyway?" but the truth is, I love to teach. Sometimes I'm envious of my husband [who has tenure], because they'll let him teach even if there are only two or three students in his class; I quit my job teaching extension courses at Y University because I couldn't go through with the anxiety of waiting to count heads anymore. One time there were nine students in one course I was teaching in American lit., and the school demanded ten, so the class was canceled. So I quit. I'm out of a permanent job, maybe forever.

My own peculiar attitudes have contributed, of course, to my final professional loss, though I wasn't aware of the loss at the time, or how it was happening incrementally. I always felt and believed, primarily from reading Emerson, that whatever one garners from life augments one's intellectuality. And I always believed [that to have] a variety of experiences was better, was enriching. From the very first I could see that the creepy man who was talking about commas in Keats—I had no husband and children then—was somehow a deficient human being, that I really didn't want to be like him at all. I felt that he might have been a better teacher of Keats if he had had more of Keats's passion. Now I have more doubts about that; obviously people can live their passions in the mind and not need to act them out. But I still think that experience adds to one's intellectual capacities in some ways . . . especially in the humanities. I was always working, always teaching, I felt that my career was not suffering terribly. But as I look back on it, I see much more now. I don't have the right jargon, I don't have the right connections. I don't even know the right people to review my books. Everything that pushes people's careers, that are so important, I lack.

I have a friend who over the years solidified her expertise on her subject so securely that when people want a certain thing, she's the expert. But I doubt if I could ever have become an expert in that way . . . maybe by temperament I'm an amateur in the good sense of the word. Making up a point of view like a patchwork quilt out of many pieces, I think of as a virtue, an ability—but such a skill isn't valued by society as a whole, now, in spite of all the talk about interdisciplinary this and that. I thought it would be [valued] more.

I think I was given a double message because the Quaker women among whom I grew up and was educated were discreet in some ways, but they were outspoken about many things. My grandmother was a feisty working-class woman . . . so I was always aware that there were other worlds beyond the local gentility, and the Republicans I knew at the country club where I played tennis. I chose the wilder truths to identify with. I did not want to see myself becoming genteel and non-wave-making.

Yet I think women experience great ambivalence about their choice of roles even today. In this culture particularly, where we preach "All men are created equal," women either must identify with men, or have had to until very recently, or stay in the background and be discreet, a supportive figure, an "angel in the house." But that's very hard when you've gone to a school that encouraged you to speak up in class, for example, and helped you to see yourself as capable.

But we're all conditioned . . . I was a great player with dolls and paper dolls, and had a world of people I took care of, I was made to ask which things were selfish and which were not. And even now, when I got a research grant to go to another university out-of-state my mother said, "Oh, now you're free to go, you don't have to take care of the children anymore." I think I was very much conditioned to believe that children whose mothers worked suffered greatly, not just became juvenile delinquents, but were deprived in some profound way. But I did always work part-time. On days when I wasn't going to be home after school, one of my children would always go to a friend's house, he didn't want to come in when I wasn't there. . . . And I catered to him. The sense of the children wanting you there is very strong. . . .

I think we look at our social responsibilities differently than men do. We often become very involved with the troubles of our friends. I think that one of the great virtues of a full-time job is that you don't allow yourself somehow to give so much of your energy to problems that might or might not be worthy of it. . . . You just don't know, of course, I think we are all a source of strength to each other, and maybe we need each other, but maybe we overdo it.

A full-time job gives you a different kind of energy with which to fight difficulties and problems. . . . And maybe it gives you a sense of your own worth in the world. And colleagues who value you—I think that must be a marvelous feeling to have that most of us never experience beyond a certain age. . . . I think you've got to find other sources of strength in life and not cling to your children as your emotional props. [That's] very hard when you're not wanted by the larger world, in a sense, as most of us are not.

I thought about starting a different career . . . but I realized that I was too old . . . if you're not wanted in the academic world because you're too old, the other world wants you even less. The world of ideas is willing, at least, to acknowledge you can think.

I thought of counseling students, but now you have to have a special degree for that. . . . I applied twice for counseling jobs without the degree but I was turned down [with my Ph.D.]. Clearly I didn't have what they were looking for . . . though what they require is probably hokey. . . . While applying I did do volunteer counseling for three years in a hospital, which I found interesting and I was good at it. My patients did well, at the time at least. But I think the whole business of having the right credentials is the thing I keep running up against in other fields. In any field where you'd have any kind of job of importance or value, credentials appear more important than ability.

And by the time you get to be too old to get credentials, it doesn't seem worth the energy to keep fighting, and knocking down doors. I just assumed that places like Digital or Wang wouldn't want me. . . . there comes a time when you can take only so many rejections. [Laughs.] But I did get invited by a woman editor of a series to write my second book, and I really felt that was wonderful. I felt grateful. . . . it's given me a little bit of status over the years to have some knowledge or capability that somebody wants. . . . My books are quirky, different, though I hope the compensation is a richness you don't get from conventional historical writing.

I've made an intellectual life for myself; I have a kind of internal sense that keeps me going. Somewhere I've gotten some ego along the way . . . but I also get very depressed, as I think we all do. It's very lonely to be working in your study day after day, wondering whether what you're writing is a lot of junk. . . .

There was a job in American literature at Q University, but they didn't ask me to apply, even though I'd been teaching there as a replacement. I'm good enough to fill in when somebody's sick, but for a regular position they want someone with letters from stars and now with a degree less than three years old. They have ways of not inviting you that make you feel terrible. You know when I taught there all last fall, they didn't invite me to *one* of the serious conferences where people gave readings of their work in progress. And that's also partly the lot of the part-time person; that's cruel and it makes part-time people feel even more worthless. You never really get used to it. . . . you yearn to have somebody say, "Come and listen to this paper."

I was so amused . . . X University did invite me to attend a conference, to hear a visiting scholar from Yale . . . but only after a male professor they had already invited said, "Why don't you invite the woman who's written a book about the very same subject the speaker is addressing?" [Laughs.] But they would never have asked me to speak, even though I was right there. There's a part of you that . . . somehow you get to the point when you ask how long must a woman put up with this? A friend of mine who's an anthropologist told me that in all the years Margaret Mead was living in Cambridge, they never asked her to talk at Harvard! But now a man has written a derogatory book about her, and they've invited him to talk about his book, and they tout his work as if it were a great contribution.

It's part of the great biological put down, I think, that Mead always fought! There are more women undergraduates, more women faculty, there are gestures toward women's studies, but it's *still a world in which women are considered inferior.*

Once I naively held all those myths about how academe is a superior world, and you didn't have to compromise yourself doing rotten things, and lie and cheat to get ahead and all that. But over the years I have come to see academe as every bit as corrupt and full of nastiness, and pettiness, and backbiting, and plagiarism . . . as any other world. I could never glorify it in any sense. . . .

I think that being in American studies teaches you that a lot of great work in American literature and American intellectual history has been done by outsiders, people on the fringe. . . . And I think that's a comfort. . . . People like Thoreau and Eakins. . . . And I still believe with Emerson that we can be creative and original, more so perhaps, by not being part of academe.

But at the same time I have terrible doubts about my own work . . . and I think the fact that it isn't given a stamp of approval by the same men who invited that professor up from Yale to talk about the subject of my book . . . is really insulting. [Laughs.] It's painful, even though I don't romanticize the academic world anymore. . . . there's no easy way for us to fit in. We make an eccentric world for ourselves.

It's still an experience of loss when September comes and I have no place to go. . . . I feel terrible. I've been trying to fill my life with other meaningful things . . . ways of not feeling useless, like organizing women's intellectual support groups. And I just keep working, making an effort to keep busy. . . . But it's true I do feel the need to make some connections in the world [besides my books]. I am a nurturing type.

Perhaps because my students were mostly adults, I keep up with a number of them still. That's meant a lot to me. I think that I have really valued all my students and learned from them. I will take almost any teaching job offered me anywhere now. I can never believe that what we have to give is inferior. But there's no doubt that we're not wanted; and you have to ask yourself, Why? Who's at fault? I think it's the academic world that's so false. They lose a lot by not having more of us around. . . . It's society's loss entirely, as well as our own, but we have to keep trying. For us married women who have support, there's at least a choice. We've invested so much in the intellect, we can go on using our minds as scholars. But there are also a lot of women who can't go on trying, who have no support at all, and we'll just lose them. They won't be able to play any active role in the profession. It's sad.

Three

This scholar of Romance languages and literature was born in 1942 and grew up in a working-class milieu. Through outstanding academic talent she won full scholarships to a prestigious and rigorous women's college and, subsequently, to one of the top graduate schools in her field. She married during graduate school and had three children. She taught continuously after receiving the doctorate, but always on two- or three-year contracts, as opposed to regular tenure-track positions. She has a half dozen published articles and a major book, published in 1985. At the time of the interview, after twelve years of teaching and publication, and with the prospect of an academic career limited to insecure introductory teaching, she has just left academe to enter the business world.

In all of our stories, there is no greater discrepancy between ability and professional status than we find here. What has happened, in addition to an extreme contraction in foreign language faculties in general, is the operation of a professional chronology that does not fit women's lives.

As we see in the interview, this woman did not quickly amass important professional credentials—particularly publication—which she would have to do to compete in a tight job market. And we also see the reasons why—reasons that run through many stories. Two important ones are working without essential support and encountering unforeseen trouble. But probably the most important is the interviewee's experience of creativity blocked, first by scholarly conventions, then by the difficulties pursuant to doing "women's work." Note her struggle with transcending disciplinary boundaries, defining limits to gender loyalty, and combining theory and reality. The result, thirteen years after she received her doctorate, was an outstanding book. But, measured by the prevailing chronology of academe, it came too late for substantial professional recognition.

I never made a clear decision to become a professional academic. It was one of those things that just, moved through . . . because I was very good at what I was doing. It seemed natural just to continue doing it, and my husband—well, my then boyfriend or fiancé—was already doing research, so it seemed very natural to go on to that track. I don't think I ever made a decision. I don't ever remember sitting down and thinking, "What shall I do with my life?" I just carried on doing exactly what I was doing. . . . Leading the life of an intellectual—that's the way I defined myself, unconsciously. That was me.

It was painful in high school. I was very plain. I was flat chested, skinny, intellectual, no doubt insufferable. I mean I didn't much like myself at all. . . . I wasn't lonely. I had friends. We did things together. But at the same time I *do* think I had some feeling of being a fish out of water to some extent. . . . It wasn't that I was actively unhappy all through high school. I had very good teachers. I was perfectly able to get along there, but I didn't have a social life with boys. Sort of did my homework, you know, produced the grades. I had very much a feeling that I had to perhaps be good with my mind because the rest of me was so unimpressive. And so you sort of develop that part of you which seemed to be winning some measure of approval.

But when I got to college, I found other people who [laughs] were weird like myself, and it all came together. Suddenly, the things that I was good at started to count as a plus instead of a minus. . . . I came from a basically working-class background. I was the first college generation in my family. My parents were extremely intelligent in one sort of way but basically not intellectual. No books in the home, really. And I was an intensely intellectual person. And so suddenly, when I hit that scene [she refers to college] it was like—it was like coming to a mother. I can't explain it. It was all the things that I liked.

I had a sequence of very, very strong women teachers. . . . It was our everyday experience that the top people were women. And I remember so clearly when I was a freshman, the criticism of my work was just amazing. I mean, we got the impression that nothing we could ever do would be any good. But gradually, as I held together, I ended up doing extremely well. . . . We wouldn't have been so good if the teachers were more accepting, I think. They ripped us up, you know. They really—at that college, women were worked to *death*. There was no messing around with those ladies because they knew we would have to be as good as or better than men to compete. I don't think they ever said that explicitly, but we knew—maybe not only to compete professionally, but to do whatever we were doing. . . .

[From college she went straight into graduate school.] Then I got married my first year as a graduate student. I was lucky inasmuch as I found a man who liked smart women, and I'm still married to him. And I had this idyllic life for two years. . . . He was in science and had a post doc at that point, and I had a scholarship so money was not a problem. Marriage just made my life more pleasant, changed nothing. I just had someone to do everything with. He made things much more interesting, much more fun. You did the same things that you would have done anyway. And I thought that life would always be like that.

[Her first major problem was the necessity to turn down a really good postgraduate fellowship because her husband couldn't move at that point.] The president of my college [a woman] was really, really angry with me when I told her. She felt that I was sacrificing my academic future, and she was absolutely right. However, I didn't take what she was saying really seriously. I thought it was just, you know, like going to the principal and getting a talking to, and then doing what I wanted.

Then when my husband finished his post doc, he got a fellowship here in Boston. I was going to apply for a teaching job, but then I couldn't because I was pregnant. You can't start teaching in September when you're about to give birth in October. Bad planning. I had no idea of how to do things. And I just had a hard time after that. We couldn't afford babysitters, and we had a very, very lively, unsleeping child, a new experience, and I was dealing with him. So I took a year off before starting to write my thesis. Then my husband got a job here so I settled in to work on the thesis. And I worked entirely on my own. My thesis adviser was in another country and, in fact, she was going through the same kinds of problems I did. She had two small children—her first child had a number of health problems—she was under an incredible amount of stress. Anyway, she never wrote to me, and essentially I had no guidance at all.

The thesis was on André Malraux. Terrible subject. Biggest male chauvinist in the whole world, and I'm writing about him. It was, in those days, in those deep, distant days, the trendy thing to be doing—existentialist stuff. Camus, Sartre, Malraux. My adviser was working on Sartre and she suggested that I work on Malraux—very logical at the time. I was analyzing his narrative technique. I was interested particularly in the uses of irony in fiction. Anyway, I completed this thesis and expected to be given an oral examination, but they ordered me to rewrite it. The reason was that someone else had written a book on Malraux and a lot of the stuff that I wrote did not look original anymore. Well, by that time, unfortunately, I had got myself pregnant again. [The interviewee then speaks poignantly about losing the child in an accident and her mixed emotions when she completed the rewrite successfully in the two months following the accident.] I completely rewrote it. I did everything differently. What I had done, I was really too nice. I was exceptionally nice in the first version. I kept saying, "Oh, there is this wonderful article by X. Z says this in such a superb way." Anyway, the second thesis I wrote was very nasty. I defamed *absolutely* everybody. I told everybody what I thought was wrong with their stuff. It was altogether much better, really. The second time was much better.

Then the problem was finding a job. I didn't look very hard. One of the problems is time. I mean, I was a successful mother, had a small child, having a decent married life, you know, and writing a thesis. So, when a friend of mine said, "I can probably get you a part-time job at [a local commuter college]," I said, "Wonderful." So for the next two years I worked there. I taught three courses a semester—that was part-time. [Laughs.] It was not a good move professionally, but it was convenient. Close to home. I could pick up my kid after school. And I wasn't completely inert professionally. I did submit my thesis to various places, but I had no idea what I was doing, no idea how to do it. The most important thing in my mind was to get pregnant again. And finally I managed it, the second year I was teaching. My husband was under a lot of stress, trying to get himself established. I was holding the home down, and being pregnant, and just convinced that everything was going to go wrong. Nothing did, it was a very uneventful pregnancy.

And then the next year we went to England on my husband's sabbatical, so I was out that year, but very happily. Again, when I think of all the mistakes I've made in my life, it's truly wonderful. Just before I was about to leave for England, the baby was about one month old, I got a letter from Yale University Press saying that they were really interested in my manuscript and they wanted some revisions. Anyway, this absolutely blows my mind. Essentially what I said to myself was "I don't have time to think about it. Maybe I'll think about it later. Too much going right now. Later on, I'll think about that." So the following year in Oxford, at a very leisurely pace, I revised the manuscript according to their recommendations. Finally sent it in, probably about six, seven months after they wrote. But they had changed editors. I had had a sort of provisional acceptance from an editor who left. And the new people said they didn't want it. And I wasn't even unhappy. I didn't realize that this was probably, you know, the death knell—that I'd *have* to have that book. I just was not on the ball. And I find it so hard to understand now, but I didn't realize what the hell was going on. It was happiness. I was just so euphoric at that point, you know? [Laughs.] I couldn't get myself down to it. . . . On the whole, the professional women that I've known who have made it in academia are gay, divorced, or childless. I have a feeling there's a general perception by the society and by the women themselves that having children in some way did indicate that you're out of it.

One of the good things in my life was that after I came back from England, X College laid me off. They were getting fewer language students by then. So I had to try and find another job. So I taught part-time at Y [a highly prestigious college] and they liked me, so they hired me full-time the following year on a two-year contract, although, they said, with no chance of tenure. They had a sort of revolving-door system. That's when I woke up intellectually. I had just been marking time, doing nothing extraordinary. I was no longer interested in Malraux. So there at Y College, I found people who were interested in feminism—a crop of assistant professors, mostly women, and we all got along very well. It was a very nice atmosphere. People were intellectually curious. I would be asked, you know, if I had read a particular thing. The assumption was that you had. Usually I hadn't. I was so behind. I had to scramble trying to work up structuralism. [Laughs.] I just loved it there.

But then various things on the home front started to go wrong, because my husband started to fall sick. He had a heart attack and he didn't get better, and so he had a triple coronary bypass and he was out of work for quite a while. My appointment at Y was nonrenewable, but I was offered a three-year appointment at Yale. It didn't look like a good time for me not to work, so for the next three years we lived with me commuting between New Haven and Boston and my husband looked after the children.

At Yale I was there all week and so I did an enormous amount of work. I think of it as my second postgraduate education, because I hit the real moderns and the Yale School of criticism. It was the biggest thing going, you know. But at the same time, I was not in a state to profit by Yale professionally in the sense of using it to forward me professionally. I was simply not ready. . . . I was trying to find my research link. I had published one article on Malraux, but that subject didn't matter to me anymore. So what I did, at Yale, and I had started it at Y College, was to get myself up to date on critical method and, at the same time, I decided, after a lot of to-ing and fro-ing, that I wanted to work in some part of women's studies. There were such wonderful opportunities in terms of lectures, just the general movement of ideas, talking to people. And I was living there during the week so I was able to—I think women never have the time, but when I was there, I was completely there, unlike when I was here when I was always running home. At Yale, I was available for everything—lunches, dinners, talking all night, that whole thing. It was like being an undergraduate again myself. I mean, I missed my family. They missed *me infinitely* more. [Laughs.] Miserable for them and very nice for me. It was stressful, very stressful, but it was enjoyable. And I got to know some wonderful women scholars. . . . So I started to really tick over. My old brain started to work again. And eventually I developed a research project—the translation that's coming out in a few months. . . . And I started to submit things to presses. By that time, I had smartened up on that level, and I just did sample translations and explained the project and set it up to see if it would fly, rather than do the whole thing and then have it rejected. And it was really beginning to look very hopeful. . . .

I mean things looked hopeful for publication. The job market (in the late 1970s) looked terrible. When my contract was up at Yale, I started applying for jobs in administration. It was an intellectual decision. I had gotten tired of teaching basic languages—it gets increasingly unrewarding. I wanted to focus now on scholarship. I didn't want to be spending all my professional time on language drills, so I thought administration—combining administration and research—was my best bet. I also applied for research money and got an NEH fellowship to work on the translation, and so I didn't push the administrative thing. Then I got to the end of that money and I finished the translation last June.

It was a very difficult project. It was an attempt to put feminism and the most advanced French critical thinking together. And it was born very much out of my feeling that, at Yale, I had been looked upon as second-rate—no major publication. And therefore I decided to attack something that was very hard, just to show people that I could do it, I suppose. Seems so pointless now. I really am just amazed by my own conflicts at times. So I was going to take on this absolutely blockbuster thing. It's a book of philosophy for starters. It assumes that you have a complete philosophical education which I absolutely don't have. And it was written in the most advanced poststructuralist idiom, which I actually dislike intensely. But, at one point, this famous professor at Yale said something to me about my not being able to learn that language, and I thought, "Screw you, baby!" [Laughs.] I may not write it, but it's not because I can't if I want to. So I learned the stuff and I think the translation is very good. And I learned an enormous amount. I got completely up in psychoanalytic criticism, for example, as well as philosophy. So, I put my mind to work, and at the same time, it's the work of a feminist philosopher. I think it is the deepest piece of analysis on patriarchies since Beauvoir in France. Also, there was definitely—for a long time I was floating. I was, how can I say, a scholar in search of a subject. And when I hit this work, there was a sense of my personal life and my academic life coming together. Suddenly those two linked as a unit instead of being juxtaposed, or clashing, or something. The way I saw my life, my view of the world, suddenly was integrated, and my experience, everything that I was, was relevant to this.

Still, if I had not decided to give up academic life, I wouldn't have pursued the theoretical stuff anymore. I mean, if you're interested in literary theory, you can't miss the French. They really have got it more together than anyone else. But having got through all that, it seems to me it comes out in exactly the same place where we started. That is to say, we have the male gods in our sky, and we're talking about male critics and male philosophers. The people on the platforms, the so-called men of letters—they're now the deconstructionist philosophers—they're all men. It's exactly the same. Nothing has changed. And they have managed to incorporate feminism in an extraordinary way. That's to say, now they are now preaching the gender-free theory that feminism has put forward. So now the male philosophers say, "Oh look, I'm writing like a woman. This is the great female text." . . . The conclusion is that Jacques Derrida can be more female than I, right? The argument leads to that. If you say that a feminist perspective has got nothing to do with biology, but it has to do with creating something other than the patriarchal system, then clearly the biological male has as good a shot at it as anyone, and in fact, a much better one! [Laughs.] Right? Nothing has changed! The males have simply moved up onto another level and we're still scrabbling. We haven't got any further along than we were, and I'm not prepared to go along with that. I'm just not.

I think it's important to recognize biologically based differences. I think that the shape of the female body, the functions of the female body, do have profound repercussions on all levels of experience. Now in some ways, that sounds very reactionary, but that is only because those intrinsically female values are, in fact, not valued. The point is to change, so you wouldn't have a society where only one sex determines the values, where you would have a truly bimodal system, two equal forces interacting, where both are necessary, equal partners in the whole. I think if one fails to recognize biological difference, one gets caught by it, one gets entrapped in the difference. If it were acknowledged, one could also see its limits. It need not be considered the be-all and end-all. That is to say, woman wouldn't be *only* a reproductive mechanism, but neither would she be *not* a reproductive mechanism.

But most of the women coming along now in literary theory accept the concept of cultural, not biological femininity and go around saying that Derrida and Lacan are "female" writers, and I think they're pursuing a dead end. It's really hard, or it was before I decided to leave the profession. I felt myself in a truly invidious position—someone like myself who is enormously obscure, has never produced anything of any great worth, ten years older than most of the people that I am critiquing, not a model feminist from the point of view of having sacrificed myself on the altar of family and children—and here I am in some sense accusing the new generation of young women scholars of having sold out. These are the women who are really making it in modern languages where it's very hard to make it, and here am I saying to these women, "You will triumph at the expense of selling out." That's a crummy thing to say. I have not felt good about saying it, haven't said it, of course, in print. My book doesn't go into this question. . . .

And so I have decided that there's not very much that's interesting in literary criticism at the moment. What I think is interesting now is real life. You see, I've come around in the picture. That is to say, biography, social science. . . . If I were staying in, I have an excellent project that I would work on—the concept of hysteria in women. I go into biology, I go into social history, medical history, with a very strong theoretical structure. I really have the theory together—don't have to worry about that. What I need are facts now, lovely facts. I love to read facts. But in order to do that, I have to have money, and I can't—I need, conservatively, $3,000 a year just to support myself in research. And, in fact, I also need intellectual support. . . . I really found it hard to be an independent scholar, finding people to talk to about your work. It is not easy, on the level that it has to be—I mean, not superficially, people who can really give you criticism. It's not that easy. . . . Last year I applied for this fellowship in women's studies, a new program for nontenured women. I really screwed myself up for it, and I got the recommendations, wrote the proposal, and I didn't get it. And it just made me think. I've got three degrees, I had a very, very good project. It was well written up. I had excellent recommendations from very good people, and just then there were so many good people out there. . . .

I mean, on one level I feel that I sort of want to rend my garments and tear my hair, and think, "What a waste. Four years of solid effort, intellectual effort, all down the tubes." [Laughs.] On the other hand, I think it probably doesn't matter at all, you know. . . . It's just that, professionally, there is no niche for me, I think, and because I have this basically humble view of this whole thing, not that I'm doing the most important work in the whole world, the world could tick over very happily without what I do, and so I have to get out of it now. So it's a conjunction of the fact that within my own discipline, everything is theoretical and seems to me to have reached a dead end, and the fact that there are no decent jobs. I'm not prepared to hang on teaching introductory courses, never having my own students, never having brighter students. . . .

So I'm going into business, real estate. I have to earn money. . . . I think I need to earn $15,000 a year. That's the amount I need to bring in, have always brought in. I'm very uncomfortable about living off my husband. I find that intellectually and emotionally, and in every other way, impossible. It's not him. He really has never pressured me at all about money. The pressure comes from inside. . . . It would be the same if my husband was pulling in $100,000 a year. I know a number of women who are actually doing private research with no support except their husband's salary, and I look at them and they're very happy doing what they're doing. They have no guilt at all about it. It isn't an issue for them. But for me it's a huge problem. I need to earn money for my own, well, for the financial status of the family, and I think for my own self-worth, or something. I don't know what it is. Maybe it's a class issue. Maybe it's my lower-class background coming out at me. I don't know what it is, but I simply cannot do it. I don't want to hang around doing research. . . . I can't see how they do it.

It's only in the last two months that I've acted on this decision. I had this symbolic. . . . this used to be my study and is now my husband's. We used to have two. I went into a snit and really thought, "This is it. I'm giving it up. *No more!*" So I moved all my files upstairs into the attic, and I changed. . . . I moved him down here. The whole house was in a morass for weeks. So I moved all my books to the attic and made his study into a spare bedroom. We can receive guests. That's actually very useful. And so I kind of, decided to make a new life of it.

But of course I haven't got into the next stage yet, you see. Haven't actually started on my real-estate selling [laughs] phase. I'm just learning about real estate right now. So who knows. I mean, I may go out of my tree, you know, playing tennis and selling real estate.

Four

This scholar of English literature was born in 1948, entered an Ivy League graduate school in 1969, and received her doctorate in 1973. She married while in graduate school and has two children. Like the previous interviewee, she entered a severely straitened job market in the mid-1970s and held a succession of full-time but non-tenure-track teaching positions until she decided to break this practice in 1982. From that point to the time of her interview in 1984, she worked as an independent scholar, writing a book on unheralded women in her field of literature.

The major theme in this story is a concentration on transformational values as opposed to prudential considerations in the building of a career. Again, like the previous interviewee, this woman did not build a record of important credentials quickly, but engaged intensively in teaching for the love of the subject. Continuing the parallel, she lost interest in her thesis topic and did not begin to publish seriously until, six or seven years out of graduate school, she found a feminist subject that she "recognized . . . immediately as mine." When she stopped teaching to work on the book, she was, again, working for the love of it, with little prospect of a future in academe.

We have, however, a postscript to this interview: in 1985 in an unusual turn of fortune, the interviewee was appointed to her first unambiguously tenure-track position and, several months later, had her book accepted for publication by a highly prestigious university press.

The sole reason I went to graduate school was that I wanted to be a university teacher. . . . I went straight from college to graduate school because my undergraduate professor advised me to, I got a fellowship. . . . I had been very determined . . . even though my family couldn't really afford college. . . . but I worked, I waited table, I was a chambermaid one summer, I got an office job at college . . . and I got scholarships. . . . I think I've been self-motivated, directed toward academe, since I was about eight. . . .

I had mentors in college . . . one a male, who really fired my interest in the Renaissance. Another was a woman, the only junior woman then in the department. . . . she was terrifically scholarly, but very warm to students. And I clearly felt she was the kind of person who could be a model. . . .

I went to college in the sixties and we were fighting very specific things, like getting student representation on various faculty councils, and there was an antiwar movement, which, you know, trickled back down into anger against the curriculum, against the kind of courses that were being taught. . . . It was not a disaffection with learning or scholarship or literature per se . . . and most of our arguments were to make literature more relevant, of course. And to [be offered] courses that were not so canonized. We were saying that literature was vital if you did it properly. And I brought that antiwar feeling, antiestablishment feeling, to graduate school.

My English department in graduate school at that time, mine was the first year they admitted any significant number of women, my class had twenty-five people, and ten were women. And that was a big improvement over the previous year, when they'd had two. . . . they didn't even have them every year, you know. It kind of filtered in. . . . I think they didn't have a clear policy of admitting women. So the place was incredibly male. There wasn't one woman faculty member in the department.

One junior faculty member came in in my second year, I remember well, and she created a terrific stir, not only because she was a woman, but because she was a feminist and she created more battles. Part of the problem was that the graduate students were very segregated from the junior faculty members, surprisingly enough. They did not see their interests as coalescing. The junior faculty emphasis was very very strongly on undergraduate teaching. . . . the graduate students were taught entirely by senior members . . . so we didn't know any women appointed as junior faculty.

The sexist discrimination was very subtle, and it took us a long time to figure out what was going on . . . the patronizing formulae . . . and I think what happened was that the ten women in that class became the most incredible overachievers. I mean it was basically a case of saying, "Ah, well, you think you know about women, do you?" The women in that class were the best students. . . .

I spent the last two years of my graduate school time in England, doing research and writing it up, and conferring with my thesis director in a series of transatlantic phone calls. Then he was over there for a term. . . . But, you see, I wrote the wrong thesis. . . . It was not only interdisciplinary, on literature and myth, but out of the mainstream. . . . I did a lot of iconography and art work and biblical study. . . . I spent months of my life in a theological library . . . but I loved it. . . . It didn't come clear to me for a long, long time that my adviser should never have let me write that thesis in terms of having something to turn into a book. . . . My thesis was absolutely impossible. . . . If he had been looking after my professional interests, which he wasn't. . . . To his credit, in a way, he was just interested in it for the sake of scholarship, as I was. . . . Working on it made me feel that I was following some great tradition of . . . medieval monasticism . . . or something . . . the scholarship. It's partly the thesis syndrome. . . . I mean I had to give myself a big kick in the pants to get out of the library and out of the art museum and everything and get my thesis written . . . because once you get into something, a great system like that, a myth. . . . investigating mythology . . . you can go on, it's like you become Mr. Casaubon in *Middlemarch*, and you're looking for the key to all mythologies.

I have trouble making five-year plans. My husband's very good at five-year plans. I sort of make a one-year plan, and that's interesting, because the way my career has developed, I had this series of one-year contracts. I think maybe there's something. . . . I saw myself as being very active as a scholar, but at the beginning, I think my first love was the teaching. . . . My first year of teaching [in graduate school] I was a preceptor for my Shakespeare professor. . . . I think it was the most exciting thing that had ever happened to me. . . . I knew then I was born to be a teacher. . . . What excited me, I think, was that momentarily . . . you were out of the scholar's cell, and you were passing on, or eliciting, or communicating, what you had found there to another group of people. And I think one of my strengths as a teacher, even early on, was class discussion. I always loved class discussion, I never enjoyed lecturing very much. In fact, I still don't enjoy lecturing, but I love the give and take . . . arranging a Socratic dialogue . . . or, let's see what happens when we do this . . . just that sense of exploring things, having an idea come up, and then hearing what other people have to say, and then who knows where you're going to end up with it. . . . That's the nub of what excites me in the classroom. . . . The course I set up for myself was becoming the catalyst. . . . So many of my teachers at graduate school, the ones I particularly loathed . . . came with yellowed notes, and just said, "This is what I wrote down twenty years ago; here it is, and be quiet and listen." And you know, you fell asleep in those classes. Why did you . . . ever bother to come? . . . Well, you had to, it was politic to come. . . . And I never wanted to have students come because it was politic. . . . I really just enjoyed the whole kind of melee atmosphere.

I got my Ph.D. in August 1973 . . . but I had spent the last two years in England so in a way I was insulated from the bad news [about academic retrenchment]. But it's funny, because even when I heard the bad news, I was quite convinced that I was going to get a job just by sheer dint of wanting one, and being aggressive, and getting one . . . and I went about it so systematically. . . . I compiled my lists and I wrote my letters, and I was quite sure at that point I would get something [in the city in which her husband was at medical school]. . . . And my thesis adviser made some phone calls, and I had some pretty God-awful interviews because of the people he called up who were clearly doing him a favor, and really had no intention of following through. . . . There were no jobs . . . and at that time, no female networking even existed.

So my husband and I drew a ninety-mile radius around his medical school, and I wrote letters, and followed up with a phone call saying, "I'll be in your town three days hence, could I speak to your hiring committee." And it worked out surprisingly well, and I got interviews and the chair of one department at a women's college was favorably impressed that anyone would have the chutzpah to call up and say, "I'm here!" and I had a very successful interview. We took to each other right away, and we had a meeting of minds. I mean, I really was excited at the idea of teaching in a women's college. There were lots of women faculty . . . my appointment was full-time, replacement for one or two years of someone on leave. And it was a wonderful time . . . I had very good friends . . . one of them was the scholar I'd filled in for, so she was in my field. . . . We had the last of the great students, the active ones, feminists, and the female faculty were terrifically close, the junior women. . . . We did courses together . . . and it's gone now.

I got kept on another two years, and I was commuting back to my husband . . . and every year I'd apply again for a job where we lived, it was a fall ritual . . . and nothing would pan out. . . . I think now it may have been because of the job I was holding down, that I poisoned myself [in the application]. I always felt that somehow, . . . I had to explain, why, with a perfectly good job, I was trying to get out of it and get to the place where I was applying . . . and you know, I always felt that putting in the business about not wanting to commute ninety miles anymore was somehow one of those female reasons for wanting to do things, not a professional reason . . . you know, to live with your husband . . . it made you seem lesser. . . . I did it four or five years in a row . . . it tends to blur now. . . . But nothing turned up and I kept commuting, it was the teaching that held me, and the sense of community . . . communication and support from other teachers. It was very intellectually stimulating . . . and they were a good bunch of friends . . . and the students were good.

When I was at undergraduate college, I was in an honors program. Almost all the students in this subject were women, and I had strong friendships. And then at graduate school, the people I was closest to were women, so although there was no role model on the faculty, I was used to having intellectual commerce with women . . . and that certainly was true in this teaching job. Later, another woman was important to my professional life. I was on a fellowship to study with a famous scholar the year after the first teaching job ended. There were about fifteen of us on that program . . . and she taught me an incredible amount about how to write. Now, I'd always prided myself on being a good writer, I'd always got A's

on everything . . . but she really tore my first paper apart. But I said, "God dammit!" and I sat down and redid that paper and in the process of redoing it and listening to her I learned how to write an essay, probably better than I ever had before. And I learned a lesson I should have known, because I've been teaching it to students for years, that you could always be better . . . and maybe she accepted me then, "you're a mensch." And I had this tremendous growth in scholarship . . . and confidence . . . . And she remained always very helpful . . . and wrote letters for me, and was always solicitous. . . . You know, I think it ended up being a very good thing for me . . . so I've gained a lot from other women, one way and another. . . .

I perceived myself in this first real teaching job as not being on tenure track . . . for my first few years anyway. Much later, I was told, of course you were on tenure track. Everyone's on tenure track here. . . . But nothing was ever spelled out . . . it was a gentleperson's agreement. . . . Later, at the time when part-time and temporary contracts became a legal nightmare, everything got very carefully spelled out, but I never even thought about it at the time . . . I mean I was much too naive . . . and I've never been hard-nosed enough to say, . . . "how am I going to get to my goal if I do this?" I seemed to be in a very nebulous position, and I accepted it, and I don't really know why . . . no one ever said, you ought to do this, have that manuscript done or be well on the way. . . .

Still, one of the things I hated . . . was the tendency of the Ivy League schools, and particularly women's colleges, to foster a perception of yourself as a sacrificer for the good of the school. . . . I remember the male president of the college actually said at a faculty meeting once, "you know, we'd love to give faculty raises this year, but we need more books in the library." . . . I mean you don't try to get things for yourself because you'll take them away from the students or the buildings . . . and that was very much in the air and it seemed immoral to me . . . that teachers were supposed to be different from anybody else as far as making a decent wage goes. . . .

And the older women faculty, the emeritae lived around the college and you talked to them and you heard it . . . you know, they were just devoted to that place body and soul, and they didn't care if they made two bent nickels a year, just so they were part of that whole institution.

My husband has always been the . . . mainstay. He has always been tremendously supportive . . . even at times when I've been ready to give up. He said, "You know, you'll hate yourself, and if you hate yourself, everybody else will hate you!" You know, he did most of the commuting for the first couple of years, he withstood that basically without a murmur and times when I think he must have driven on three hours' sleep after being up. And in fact . . . when I gave up a job at X University last year to finish the book, he was the one who basically pushed me to do it, and now he's taken the burden of the mortgage and everything else, because he said "You've got to finish it now, forget earning money, just finish it!" And that's always been his attitude . . . incredibly stalwart and supportive. Thank God!

I think the conflict came out at points where I wanted to apply all over the place to try to get a job. There came a kind of [natural] breaking point after he had finished his internship, when we could have moved, although he'd been offered a residency here . . . and everyone knows it's the medical center of the universe! And I had been following the job market closely and getting all the job information lists and everything . . . and we had a lot of strain over where we were going to end up . . . because to follow his research interests, he'd have to be near some major medical facility, some teaching hospital. . . . And you know, if there were an opening in my field in Asheville, North Carolina, what was he going to do there? He'd always been very fair to me, and it was a very big problem. Commuting that far was definitely not for us. . . . And then one morning, I woke up and said, "But *I* don't want to live in Asheville, North Carolina!" . . . I realized there were a lot of places I didn't want to live just for the sake of having a teaching job. And I struggled with that long and hard to decide whether that was a rationalization—I didn't have a teaching job while I was mulling this—but I truly think that's how I feel. I would not go anywhere just for a job, because I've realized that there are a lot of other things that I demand out of life now . . . the kind of place I want to live.

Then the year my husband started his residency, there were maybe six or seven jobs nationally in my field, and I applied for all of them. Everyone seemed to think it was good experience for me. And I got some nibbles, but when it came down to the bottom line, nobody wanted to interview me. This was a tremendous blow. . . . I didn't understand why . . . except that I had two things going against me at that time. My big problem was that at that time I had no publications. I had a wonderful teaching record, I had recommendations from all my X College experience, and from the woman scholar with whom I'd had the fellowship. . . . but I didn't have any publication yet. Also, I had chosen to write on women. "My next great work will be on women writers in the twelfth century!" Of course, everyone believes they don't exist . . . and nobody wanted me. So I went back to X College where I had had my first job, on a one-year appointment, but the handwriting was on the wall for me. Well, I don't know . . . I think now that if I had been willing to stay there and continue this mad commuting, I could probably have done all the right things and gotten myself in. But I didn't want to, now.

I found I didn't want to put all my eggs in that basket . . . I was really tired of the sort of round the clock nurturing of students, and I was very disappointed in the kinds of students that were coming through now. I felt that a different kind of person was being hired . . . people who were not interested in being collegial. . . . People who were basically looking out for themselves at the expense of the group . . . the opposite of the excessive devotion to the school of some of the older faculty. That's what the times were like, at that point.

But the new, competitive ethic, making education that kind of marketplace. . . . I know myself that I could never work at an institution or a company that worked solely for profit. I mean, obviously you have to have money to run the place, and I recognize there's a kind of naïveté in expecting a college [not to be] like that. But nevertheless, I want to spend at least half my day doing something that isn't figuring something with dollars. And I felt that college was becoming more like that. You can't teach this course because you won't have enough students, and we're wasting you by having you teach five students in this particular course instead of having you teach twenty.

And the kind of students who were coming in then, I felt the college began to foster things I didn't want to see fostered in young women . . . becoming *totally* professionalized. You know, you can go and work in a bank, young woman, and you can become a doctor, and you can become a lawyer. It seemed to be a message of opportunity, but it really disguised pushing women into competing in the male world, at the expense of developing what they were themselves. When I first started to teach there . . . the college didn't allow a studio art major. You majored in art history, and then you could do some studio art. And I had students who *fought* to be studio art majors, because they knew that was the best thing they did . . . not the only thing, but their best thing. And I wasn't seeing any more students like that, people who were trying to get out what was inside them, whatever it was.

So I got steadily more disillusioned. I got fed up with committee meetings. You know, committee meetings are a form of social activity there. . . . We decided to have a kid then, and I think probably the timing was not coincidental.

We'd been married seven years . . . and I decided I didn't want to commute having a kid, never knowing where the baby was. What was I going to do, drop it halfway between my home and my job? And I didn't want to subject a baby to that. Both of us had always felt flexible, that we could do whatever we wanted, short of moving to the other side of the country . . . but now I decided to move back to live with my husband and take my chances at whatever might come up.

I was still doing my regular fall ritual of applying for jobs. I spent most of that summer after I left my job applying for jobs around here. I papered the area with my vitae. And I got a job for the fall teaching freshman composition at a college nearby, and that suited me, because the baby was born in December. And I also thought that if I just taught freshman comp. I'd be able to work more connectedly on the book. . . . That didn't work out as I had planned, because freshman comp. is an incredible burden . . . and you really can't do anything else. So I taught for that one semester. . . . I didn't get to know people in the department . . . nobody in the department taught it, they recruited all the people they needed to teach freshman comp. from graduate students and part-time help. . . . There were gypsy scholars teaching three jobs, one course at three different places. It was a funny thing. . . . I was visibly pregnant that semester, and whenever anyone spoke to me, they brought up my pregnancy. Nothing else ever seemed to come up!

When I gave birth in December, I decided that I was going to wait until the baby was at least nine months old before I worked again. So I didn't push then . . . because all I could think about was the overwhelming thing of having a baby. I was pegging away at my book, going to the library fairly regularly, still doing my primary research . . . though I think at that point I still conceived of myself primarily as someone who did teaching better than scholarship . . . . And then the following summer, 1980, I again papered the area with my little airplanes of vitae, and this time I turned up a job. . . . and it was a very good job, full-time. It was a replacement position, a one-year contract, but the courses were yummy. I mean . . . I really needed it, because I'd had a kind of desert period for a while. So I went back in September when the baby was nine months old. And that year nearly killed me actually because I was still breast-feeding, I was staying up till one o'clock in the morning trying to get all my courses ready, I was teaching three courses each semester. And my husband took a picture of me, and I'm glad he did because I mean, it shocked me so much to see what I looked like. . . . I'd been living on coffee and chocolate bars . . . And I said, "Oh, my God, what have I done to myself?" But it was a wonderful year teaching. But the expense was enormous.

It was a classic case. I knew what the trap in being a superwoman was. I had told myself I wasn't going to do that. But what choice do you have, when you know you have to be somewhere to pick up the kid? I used to have the only calm moment of the day after I dropped the baby at her day care, and I had a fifteen-minute drive to school. I taught Milton a good part of the year first thing in the morning, and I would try to settle my brain and forget about diapers and everything, and try to think about Eve . . . and the angel Raphael.

Oh my God, it was a bizarre life, it really was. It was killing to try to live those two lives, really. I think probably with an infant, especially when you're doing something on-line like breast-feeding, it's impossible. . . . Clearly the trap is you want to be the *best* mother—and I breast-fed because it was the best thing to do—and the *best* teacher [laughs], and you can't stand to have a trade-off, so you end up trying to do both. . . . With an infant, the demand is encompassing, round the clock. And you become completely, you know, a split personality, just trying to continually juggle. I've felt great psychic freedom since our child has gotten a little independent. Now I'm doing it again [having a child], but I think you're probably wiser the second time around. You know what to expect. I think probably a real integration is impossible, as long as you're a mother. I think that's why women are leading these double lives, and it's terribly self-destructive.

I realized, before it was too late, what I was doing but I know women who still haven't realized what they're doing, to themselves and to their children, and I think . . . they're going to have a bigger crash than I had. I think the root of it [the superwoman] is in the way our society is built now, at least in the kind of institutions we have. Women are going to have to do it, I mean we're going to have to be the ones who, if we want to do these things, have to suffer, because nobody's going to put out a hand to us and say, "Oh, my dear, your lot is so difficult! Let us see if we can make it easier for you!"

My husband was a resident in a hospital when the baby was born. I mean, no one's first choice of someone to help would be a resident! Fortunately, he'd gotten the worst over before the baby was born. . . . he had to get up sometimes at 3 A.M., do seventeen-hour operations, he'd be on call every third night. . . . Fortunately, we've always shared things like housework. I mean, it's never been fifty-fifty, it never is, but he did the best he could. He always did a lot of child care, which he continued to do. He is sole guardian of our daughter on weekends, so I can have the whole weekend to write and finish the book. We couldn't afford to have nannies. . . . Without his kind of support, I wouldn't have been able to keep on. Just knowing he was involved at some level was terrifically helpful. . . . But I swear I'll never go through something like that again.

And I think of some of my close friends who were having kids about this same time. We were in touch by telephone, and if we hadn't been it would have been much, much worse for all of us. I mean you see people going through it . . . you're not alone. You get some inkling of what to expect. I think without the support of other women, it would have been an impossibility.

So, as I said, when the baby was nine months old, I got this wonderful replacement position . . . and I got a second year out of that . . . which takes us to last spring. At that point, I decided it was now or never with the book. I'd been working on it [part-time for four years] and it was time to finish it. And to do that, I was going to have to work on it full-time . . . not teach freshman comp. or night school, just sit down and write it . . . and fortunately, as I said before, my husband agreed with me. And he said, "Forget about earning money, just get this book done!"

The genesis of the book is interesting, because one of the generators was a woman. An early feminist critic came to the college where I was teaching and gave a lecture, and then we happened to share a long bus ride back here. I was commuting between my teaching and my husband then. And she [tried] to elicit what I was doing as a scholar, and . . . I said, well, I'm interested in the sister of such and such a poet, because she keeps popping up everywhere, but there's really nothing about her, and come to think of it, I'm interested in all these other women writers of that time I keep seeing in the Short Title Catalogue, and nobody has ever said anything about them. And she said, "Well, at the very least, you ought to write an anthology, you know." And then she said, "Come to think of it, why aren't you doing your scholarship on this? There's a whole field that's untouched." And by the time I got off that bus, I felt as if I were ten feet in the air! I thought, I've just discovered my life's work, . . . It was the most exciting day of my life . . . and I rushed over to the Boston Public Library and found everything I could, which was very scanty. And I recognized it immediately as mine . . . combining my interest in the period with my interest in women. . . .

You know, I spent the summer of '76 back in the Bodleian Library at Oxford. . . . My husband did a hospital rotation there, so we both had an excuse to go back. And I found so much stuff that summer, so much primary material, that I have filing cabinets full of notes . . . actually, everything about the women I could find. I had letters, diaries, works the patronage women carried out. . . . I had enough for five books.

It should be done by the summer [1983]. Seven years! the length of a standard apprenticeship . . . you know, labor for seven years. It should be done before the baby [second child] is born. . . . It's neck and neck right now. What the book has taught me over this last year of working on it full-time is that I now see myself primarily as a scholar and a writer, before a teacher. I realize the thing I ought to do most in the world is write, and I think I love to do the scholarly kind of writing. I have a feeling that my next book is not going to be a scholarly book, though. I cannot see another seven-year project coming up. But in the future, I can. I love to sort of sit in the library for hours and hours and hours and then come home to write something. I see that as a central expression of my identity. I mean, my dissertation topic was a carefully orchestrated thing. This research topic was going to necessitate disappearing into the Bodleian Library for two years. . . . it was trying to inhale as much of that life and language as I could. It was part of the monastic tradition. . . . What could be more like it than sitting in the Duke Humphrey Room [in the library] hour after hour in forty degree temperature! I remember looking up one afternoon in November, it was about two o'clock in the afternoon, and you know, those little reading lamps over the desks, and looking up and the whole room was completely dark except for those little pools of light over the desks of the readers, and all this huge mass of volumes that nobody ever reads, that are lining the walls of the Duke Humphrey. It was just an amazing vision of scholastic life. I loved it, I mean, they were some of the happiest years of my life. . . . the whole mystique.

Because I had spent all my time at college studying or working to make enough money to keep on going, I had no social life to speak of . . . and in graduate school, I was excused from a lot of my courses because I had done honors work, and I had fellowships. . . . In England, I had the sense of being a complete person for the first time in my life, feeling all kinds of different things, spending days in London at art galleries, going to the Continent, doing all the sorts of things I had dreamed about but never thought a poor scholar would do. And I met my husband, and we were married that year. We lived in England for a year. . . . it was not unstressful with both of us finishing dissertations, but we both remember it entirely romantically. What shape my future career will take I don't know, because quite frankly, what I've deliberately done is suppress all thoughts of what

I'm going to do with my life until I've had the second baby and finished the book.

I would still like to be in academia, but I think I've come to the point where it would have to be on my terms. I'm not going back to teaching freshman comp. here, there, and everywhere. That doesn't interest me anymore. I want to find something that will allow me to live the kind of life I want and to teach the kind of courses I want to teach to the kind of students. I think I've shifted the kind of students I like to teach now. I like teaching older students. . . .

I do think that if a student showed the least bit of political awareness, I'd probably be overjoyed. But I think [what puts me off] is that total self-absorption and the demanding of you to give endlessly. For the first time ever, in my last year of teaching, I sent a class home because they hadn't done the work. I probably would have been a lot more easygoing before, and said, "Oh, well, we'll sort of fake this. I'll fill in what you don't know. We'll talk about. . . ." This time I just felt I'd had it. . . . It may be because I knew how much it was taking out of me . . . and what I was giving up at home . . . to prepare that class.

Now, I think that to some extent what I've done is admit to myself and accept and even become satisfied with the idea that I may never work in academia again . . . like when I had the ridiculous feeling I'd get a job right out of grad school, now I feel I'll do something, I'll make something out of my life.

And I've spent a good deal of time in the last year being angry at academia because it doesn't live up to the dream, and I hate a lot of what it does to people. I find myself getting white angry, rage, full of rage . . . at what I see going on.

At the same time I went to the NEMLA [New England Modern Language Association] conference in April, and I was so impressed by what people were doing there, because it's not like the MLA [the huge national conference] at all . . . it's small . . . and everybody talks, and everybody's a participant. And people love what they're doing there, and there's none of that kind of clawing after position or throwing around of weight. There are very few big shots who go to NEMLA, it's really for the people! And it gave me a taste again of what I really like about the whole business.

I think that now we've reached the unfortunate point where people who have tenure have a kind of choke-hold on the whole profession, and that's using people up. They've been teaching the same course for twenty, thirty years. And it terrified me. . . . their tenure was like a jail sentence.

I think now it's the lack of ethics, the lack of morality, that's ruining it.

I saw it as a place unlike the business world, or the corporate world. . . . I didn't see it as an ivory tower, in fact I rejected it as an ivory tower. If it's going to be the place where the citizens of tomorrow spend four years of their life, it had to be a damn good place. And if what it's going to teach them by example is a lot of shady morality and this business, you know, of hiring people for three years, booting them out, hiring another . . . then it becomes a marketplace. And all these pretences at things like affirmative action, equal opportunity, I mean the whole thing becomes hollow. What are you passing on to the next generation?

Appendix

Background information on sixty-two interviewees at the time of their interviews, 1983–84. They include twenty-five tenured women and thirty-seven women deflected from the normal academic tenure track.

	Tenured	Deflected
Age		
34–40	6	13
41–50	11	19
over 50	8	5
Geographic Origin		
East	13	22
Midwest and West	6	8
South and Southwest	1	2
non-U.S.	5	5
Family Status		
Married	13	25
Single	5	7
Divorced	6	4
Widowed	1	1
Children	16	26
Field		
Humanities	12	25
History/Social Sciences	10	9
Sciences	3	3
Ph.D.-Granting Institution		
Ivy League	16	16
Other Eastern	6	13
Midwest and West	2	4
South	1	0
non-U.S.	0	4

Appendix

	Tenured	Deflected
Employment (Tenured–Type of Institution)		
Ivy League	2	
Private secular		
coed	5	
women	2	
Religious affiliation		
coed	5	
women	2	
Public	9	
Employment (Deflected)		
College teaching		
(part-time, non-tenure track)		13
Administration		
(academic, other education)		9
Academic or research services		
(editing, consulting, paid research, commercial writing)		7
Writing, independent		3
Business		5

Notes

Chapter 1. The Old Norms

1. See Jean Bethke Elshtain, *Public Man, Private Woman* (Princeton: Princeton University Press, 1981).

2. A number of books attest to the effective differential in power between men and women in the various professions. They include: Debra Renee Kaufman, "Professional Women: How Real Are the Recent Gains?" in *Women: A Feminist Perspective*, ed. Jo Freeman, 3rd ed. (Palo Alto, Calif.: Mayfield, 1984); Debra Kaufman and Barbara L. Richardson, *Achievement and Women: Challenging the Assumptions* (New York: Free Press, 1982); Cynthia Fuchs Epstein, *Women's Place: Options and Limits in Professional Careers* (Berkeley: University of California Press, 1971), and *Women in Law* (New York: Basic Books, 1981); Cynthia Epstein and Rose Laub Coser, *Access to Power: Cross-National Studies of Women and Elites* (London: Allen and Unwin, 1981); Emily Couric, ed., *Women Lawyers: Perspectives on Success* (New York: Harcourt Brace Jovanovich, 1984); Jill Abramson and Barbara Franklin, *Where They Are Now: The Story of the Women of Harvard Law 1974* (Garden City, N.Y.: Doubleday, 1986); Mary Roth Walsh, *Doctors Wanted, No Women Need Apply: Sexual Barriers in the Medical Profession 1835–1975* (New Haven: Yale University Press, 1977); Regina Markell Morantz-Sanchez, *Women Physicians in American Medicine: Sympathy and Science* (New York: Oxford University Press, 1985); Judith Lorber, *Women Physicians: Careers, Status, Power* (London: Tavistock, 1984); Leah Dickstein and Carol Nadelson, eds., *Women Physicians in Leadership Roles* (Washington D.C.: American Psychiatric Press, 1986); Jane Lesermann, *Men and Women in Medical School: How They Change and How They Compare* (New York: Praeger, 1981); Dorothy Rosenthal Mandelbaum, *Work, Marriage and Motherhood: The Career Persistence of Female Physicians* (New York: Praeger, 1981); Patricia A. McBroom, *The Third Sex: The New Professional Woman* (New York: Morrow, 1986); Liz Roman Gallese, *Women Like Us* (New York: Morrow, 1985); Margaret Hennig and Anne Jardin, *The Managerial Woman* (London: Pan, 1979); Harold H. Frank, *Women in the Organization* (Philadelphia: University of Pennsylvania Press, 1977); Rosabeth Moss Kanter, *Men and Women of the Corporation* (New York: Basic Books, 1977); Marion Marzoff, *Up from the Footnote: A History of Women Journalists* (New

York: Hastings House, 1977); Violet B. Haas and Carolyn C. Perrucci, eds., *Women in the Scientific and Engineering Professions* (Ann Arbor: University of Michigan Press, 1984); Ruth B. Kundsin, ed., *Women and Success* (New York: Morrow, 1974); Aasta S. Lubin, *Managing Success: High Echelon Careers and Motherhood* (New York: Columbia University Press, 1987); Sylvia Ann Hewlett, *A Lesser Life: The Myth of Women's Liberation in America* (New York: Morrow, 1986); and Sara Ruddick and Pamela Daniels, eds., *Working It Out* (New York: Pantheon, 1977). See also: the *New York Times*, May 7, 1985, p. 24, describing a law suit brought by women in the foreign service, alleging sex discrimination in job assignments, promotions, performance evaluations, and awards; and the *Bennington Quadrille*, October 1983, pp. 24–25, which presents statistics documenting male dominance of the higher echelons of the art world, in spite of the high percentage of women artists.

3. Of course, academic women meet also the remaining force of overt sex discrimination on which there is a substantial literature. See, for example: Joan Abramson, *The Invisible Woman: Discrimination in the Academic Profession* (San Francisco: Jossey-Bass, 1975), and *Old Boys, New Women: The Politics of Sex Discrimination* (New York: Praeger, 1979); Gloria de Sole and Leonore Hoffmann, eds., *Rocking the Boat: Academic Women and Academic Processes* (New York: Modern Language Association, 1981); Jennie Farley, *Academic Women and Employment Discrimination: A Critical Annotated Bibliography* (Ithaca: New York State School of Industrial and Labor Relations, 1982); and Jennie Farley, ed., *Sex Discrimination in Higher Education: Strategies for Equality* (Ithaca: New York State School of Industrial and Labor Relations, 1981).

4. Jessie Bernard, *Academic Women* (University Park: Pennsylvania State University Press, 1964); Alice Rossi and Ann Calderwood, eds., *Academic Women on the Move* (New York: Russell Sage Foundation, 1973). Angela Simeone, *Academic Women: Working Towards Equality* (South Hadley, Mass.: Bergin and Garvey, 1987), updates Bernard's statistical measurements of women's status in academe, concluding that "despite the perception of sweeping changes and dramatic progress, the status of academic women has not improved substantially since Jessie Bernard published *Academic Women* in 1964" (p. 144).

5. *Digest of Education Statistics* (Washington, D.C.: National Center for Education Statistics, 1983–84). Salary statistics are from the AAUP Annual Report on the Economic Status of the Profession, 1986–87, in *Academe* 73, no. 2 (March-April 1987). For other studies of academic women, see Helen Astin, *The Woman Doctorate in America: Origins, Career and Family* (New York: Russell Sage Foundation, 1969); Lucille Addison Pollard, *Women on College and University Faculties: A Historical Survey and a Study of Their Present Academic Status* (New York: Arno Press, 1977); Patricia Albjerg Graham, "Expansion and Exclusion: A History of Women in American Higher Education," *Signs* 3, no. 4 (1978): 759; Patricia A. Stringer and Irene Thompson, eds., *Stepping off the Pedestal: Academic Women in the South* (New York: Modern Language Association, 1982); and Emily Abel, *Terminal Degrees: The Job Crisis in Higher Education* (New York: Praeger, 1984). See also the special issue "Women in Academe" in *Women's Studies International Forum* 6, no. 2 (1983).

6. Literary scholars have both defined these plots and indicated strategies used by women authors to subvert them. Rachel Blau DuPlessis in *Writing Beyond the Ending: Narrative Strategies of Twentieth-Century Women Writers* (Bloomington: Indiana University Press, 1985), and Blanche Gelfant in *Women Writing in America: Voices in Collage* (Hanover, N.H.: University Press of New England, 1985), show women transcending the marriage plot, often by a quest for at least spiritual autonomy. See also Carol P. Christ, *Diving Deep and Surfacing: Women Writers on Spiritual Quest* (Boston: Beacon Press, 1980).

7. For a thoughtful treatment of ambivalence about dependency, see Colette Dowling, *The Cinderella Complex* (New York: Summit Books, 1981). An academic controversy, still unresolved, about women's "fear of success" began with work by Matina Horner, including "Toward an Understanding of Achievement Related Conflicts in Women," *Journal of Social Issues* 28, no. 2 (1972): 157–75. The question was reviewed in a special issue of *Sex Roles* 2, no. 3 (1976). For a recent study of the general issue, see Carol Becker, *The Invisible Drama: Women and the Anxiety of Change* (New York: Macmillan, 1987).

8. The problems of mothers and daughters have been explored in depth. See, for example, the works of Tillie Olsen who comments on the scarcity of writing by mothers both in *Silences* (New York: Delacorte, 1978), and *Mother to Daughter/ Daughter to Mother* (New York: Feminist Press, 1984); and Marianne Hirsch, "Review Essay: Mothers and Daughters," *Signs* 7 (Autumn 1981): 200–222.

9. Adrienne Rich, *On Lies, Secrets and Silence* (New York: Norton, 1979), p. 241.

10. See, for an excellent development of this theme, Rachel M. Brownstein, *Becoming a Heroine* (New York: Viking, 1982).

11. Barbara Welter's essay first defining "true womanhood" is still apt: "The Cult of True Womanhood: 1820–1860," *American Quarterly* 18 (Summer 1966): 151–74.

12. See, for example, Billie W. Dziech and Linda Weiner, *The Lecherous Professor: Sexual Harassment on Campus* (Boston: Beacon Press, 1984); Phyllis Franklin et al., *Sexual and Gender Harassment in the Academy: A Guide for Faculty, Students, and Administrators* (New York: Modern Language Association, 1981); Emily Abel, "Collective Protest and the Meritocracy: Faculty Women and Sex Discrimination in Lawsuits," *Feminist Studies* 7 (Fall 1981): 505–38; and, more generally, Catherine MacKinnon, *Sexual Harassment of Working Women* (New Haven: Yale University Press, 1979).

13. See Sandra M. Gilbert and Susan Gubar, *The Madwoman in the Attic: The Woman Writer and the Nineteenth-Century Imagination* (New Haven: Yale University Press, 1979); and Elaine Showalter, *The Female Malady: Women, Madness and English Culture, 1830–1980* (New York: Pantheon, 1985). Nina Auerbach sees "demonic women" not as vicious but as powerful in her *Woman and the Demon: The Life of a Victorian Myth* (Cambridge: Harvard University Press, 1982).

14. See also Sheila Delany, *Writing Women* (New York: Schocken, 1984).

15. For a highly illuminating discussion of the feminine hero, see Lee R. Edwards, *Psyche as Hero* (Middletown, Conn: Wesleyan University Press, 1984); and

Carol Pearson and Katharine Pope, *The Female Hero* (New York: Bowker, 1981). For a deconstruction of the term "women's nature," see Anne Fausto Sterling, *Myths of Gender: Biological Theories About Women and Men* (New York: Basic Books, 1986).

16. See Rebecca Bell-Metereau, *Hollywood Androgyny* (New York: Columbia University Press, 1985). Carolyn Heilbrun has labeled such exceptional women "honorary males" in her *Reinventing Womanhood* (New York: Norton, 1979).

17. Nancy Drew epitomizes a figure to whom Nina Baym ascribes the popularity of novels of a particular genre: in some 200 such stories a young woman between puberty and marriage achieves a level of economic and personal independence not apparent "ever after." See Baym's *Woman's Fiction: A Guide to Novels By and About Women in America, 1820–1870* (Ithaca, N.Y.: Cornell University Press, 1978).

18. For a further discussion of this concept, see Greer Litton Fox, " 'Nice Girl': Social Control of Women through a Value Construct," *Signs* 2, no. 4 (1977): 805.

19. For a suggestive discussion of this concept, see Rosabeth Moss Kanter, *The Change Masters* (New York: Simon and Schuster, 1983).

Chapter 2. Transformation

1. Scholars have suggested various causes for rebellion by some women, e.g., position in the family, the presence of role models, or membership in various ethnic groups. See the discussion of this issue in Angela Simeone, *Academic Women: Working Towards Equality* (South Hadley, Mass.: Bergin and Garvey, 1987), pp. 14 ff.

2. One finds a strikingly similar fictional account of a woman's flight from the restrictions of orthodoxy—in this case, Orthodox Judaism—in Rebecca Goldstein, *The Mind-Body Problem* (New York: Random House, 1983).

3. This was a period when academic authorities were still unguarded enough about women's issues to say such things as: "A woman teacher who marries creates a special problem for herself." George Gleason, "The Job Market for Women: A Department Chairman's View," *College English* 32 (May 1971): 929.

4. Barbara Erlich White, *Boston Sunday Globe*, October 21, 1984, B 15.

5. For a statistical measure of this proposition, see Lilli S. Hornig, "Untenured and Tenuous: The Status of Women Faculty," *Annals of the American Academy of Political and Social Sciences* 448 (March 1980): 115; and Simeone, *Academic Women*, pp. 54 ff.

Chapter 3. Rules of the Game

1. See "Academic Mentoring for Women Students and Faculty: A New Look at an Old Way to Get Ahead," issued by the Project on the Status and Education of Women, directed by Bernice Sandler for the Association of American Colleges; Jeanne J. Speizer, "Role Models, Mentors, and Sponsors: The Elusive Concepts," *Signs* 6, no. 4 (1981): 692; and Angela Simeone, *Academic Women: Working Towards*

Equality (South Hadley, Mass.: Bergin and Garvey, 1987), pp. 102 ff. For commentary on mentors for women in business, see Nancy W. Collins, *Professional Women and Their Mentors* (Englewood Cliffs, N.J.: Prentice-Hall, 1983).

2. *Harvard Gazette*, June 6, 1985, p. 3.

3. The story about the "old-girl network" is in *New York Times*, February 25, 1985, B 5; that about the Committee of 200, in *New York Times*, March 7, 1983, B 8. For an example of popular advice books, see Joyce Gabriel and Betty Baldwin, *Having It All: A Practical Guide to Overcoming the Career Woman's Blues* (New York: M. Evans, 1980).

4. And see Monika Kehoe et al., *Handbook for Women Scholars: Strategies for Success* (San Francisco: Center for Women Scholars, 1981).

5. See Nancy Hartsock's early essay urging a redefinition of power from domination to the exercise of energy and initiative: "Political Change: Two Perspectives on Power," *Quest* 1, no. 1 (Summer 1974): 10.

6. Jane S. Jaquette argues that women shun power in contemporary institutions because the matters at stake do not seem important, and appear rather as tokens contested in "a kind of male sandbox." "Power as Ideology: A Feminist Analysis," in *Women's Views of the Political World of Men*, ed. Judith H. Stiehm (Dobbs Ferry, N.Y.: Transnational Publishers, 1984).

Chapter 4. Voice of Authority

1. Professional women's difficulty in finding an assertive voice is an aspect of a general problem common to all women. See Robin Lakoff, *Language and Woman's Place* (New York: Harper and Row, 1978), the pioneering work on women and language; also Cheris Kramarae, *Women and Men Speaking* (Rowley, Mass.: Newbury House, 1981); and Sally McConnell-Ginet, Ruth Borker, and Nelly Furman, eds., *Women and Language in Literature and Society* (New York: Praeger, 1980).

2. *New York Times Book Review*, February 10, 1985, p. 12.

3. Phyllis Rose, *Parallel Lives* (New York: Random House, 1983); Adrienne Rich, *On Lies, Secrets and Silence* (New York: Norton, 1979); Tillie Olsen, *Silences* (New York: Delacorte, 1978); Elaine Showalter, *The Female Malady* (New York: Pantheon, 1985).

Two interesting studies of women struggling to write in sixteenth- and seventeenth-century England, in spite of their training in silence, are Elaine Beilin, *Redeeming Eve: Women Writers in England, 1521–1624* (Princeton: Princeton University Press, 1987); and Angeline Goreau, *The Whole Duty of a Woman: Female Writers in Seventeenth Century England* (New York: Dial, 1985).

4. Joanna Russ analyzes the many forms of denigration that effectively silence the voices of women writers in *How to Suppress Women's Writing* (Austin: University of Texas Press, 1983).

5. Alice Hamilton, cited in *Harvard Medical School Bulletin*, April 1985, p. 34.

6. See "The Classroom Climate: A Chilly One for Women?" Project on the Status

and Education of Women, directed by Bernice Sandler for the Association of American Colleges.

7. Rich, *On Lies, Secrets and Silence*, pp. 243–44.

8. That women have grounds for anxiety about classroom authority is affirmed by Elaine Martin in "Power and Authority in the Classroom: Sexist Stereotypes in Teaching Evaluations," *Signs* 9, (Spring 1984): 482–92. Nonetheless, we have direct evidence that experience with authority helps women to overcome even severe cases of classroom anxiety. The woman quoted about not wanting to get out of bed on teaching days wrote to us in 1987, several years after her interview, and remarked about her earlier comments: "I have recently returned to the faculty from administration and find these [classroom] tensions *dramatically* lessened. Being Assistant to the President taught me to say no without compunction and bathed me in enough controversy that I had to quit caring so much about how others saw me and just do what I thought best."

9. See for a collection of essays on consciously developed feminist teaching styles, Margo Culley and Catherine Portuges, eds., *Gendered Subjects: The Dynamics of Feminist Teaching* (Boston: Routledge and Kegan Paul, 1985).

10. Jean Bethke Elshtain calls this form of discussion "emancipatory speech" in "Feminist Discourse and Its Discontents: Language, Power and Meaning," *Signs* 7, no. 3 (Spring 1982): 603.

11. See for apparent confirmation of this point in a behavioral experiment, Sharon S. Mayes, "Women in Positions of Authority: A Case Study of Changing Sex Roles," *Signs* 4, no. 3 (Spring 1979): 556–68.

Chapter 5. Women's Work

1. Laura Lein, *Boston Globe*, June 6, 1985, "Living Section."

2. Women's verbal and men's mathematical superiorities seemed well established by the findings in Eleanor Maccoby and Carol Nagy Jacklin, *The Psychology of Sex Differences* (Stanford, Calif.: Standard University Press, 1974); but recent research seems to indicate there are no significant gender differences in initial cognitive abilities. See Janet Shibley Hyde and Marcia C. Linn, eds., *The Psychology of Gender: Advances Through Meta-analysis* (Baltimore: Johns Hopkins University Press, 1986); and Anne Fausto-Sterling, *Myths of Gender: Biological Theories About Women and Men* (New York: Basic Books, 1985). See also Ruth Bleier, *Science and Gender: A Critique of Biology and Its Theories on Women* (New York: Pergamon, 1984); Bleier and Fausto-Sterling agree that the much-touted gender difference in left/right brain function is groundless. The extent to which hard biological evidence influences the dictates of the old norms remains to be seen.

3. For an analysis of the major schools of feminist thought, see Hester Eisenstein, *Contemporary Feminist Thought* (Boston: G. K. Hall and Co., 1983).

4. For an argument on this point as it relates to creative writing, see the dispute between Elaine Showalter and Cynthia Ozick in the *New York Times Book Review*,

December 16, 1984, and January 6, 1985. See also Alicia Ostriker, *Writing Like a Woman* (Ann Arbor: University of Michigan Press, 1983).

5. See for an extensive development of these issues, Mary Belenky, Blythe McVicker Clinchy, Nancy Rule Goldenberger, and Jill Mattuck, *Women's Ways of Knowing: The Development of Self, Voice and Mind* (New York: Basic Books, 1986).

6. For detailed discussions of scholarship on women, see Ellen Carol Dubois, Gail Paradise Kelly, Elizabeth Lapovsky Kennedy, Carolyn W. Korsmeyer, and Lillian S. Robinson, *Feminist Scholarship: Kindling in the Groves of Academe* (Urbana: University of Illinois Press, 1985); Paula A. Treichler, Cheris Kramarae, and Beth Stafford, eds., *For Alma Mater: Theory and Practice in Feminist Scholarship* (Urbana: University of Illinois Press, 1985); and Devon Jersild, "Cutting on the Bias: Feminist Scholarship Today," *Boston Review*, September 1985, p. 10.

7. See for a probing and nuanced discussion of this phenomenon, Evelyn Fox Keller, *Reflections on Gender and Science* (New Haven: Yale University Press, 1985), as well as her biography of Barbara McClintock, *A Feeling for the Organism: The Life and Work of Barbara McClintock* (San Francisco: W. H. Freeman, 1983).

8. *Digest of Educational Statistics* (Washington, D.C.: National Center for Educational Statistics, U.S. Department of Education, 1983–84); *Fact Book for Academic Administrators* (Washington, D.C.: American Council on Education, 1981).

9. Shulamit Reinharz, *On Becoming a Social Scientist* (San Francisco: Jossey-Bass, 1979), pp. 11–12. See also, Jessie Bernard, "My Four Revolutions: An Autobiographical History of the ASA," in *Changing Women in a Changing Society*, ed. Joan Huber (Chicago: University of Chicago Press, 1973).

10. See Evelyn Fox Keller and Helene Moglen, "Competition and Feminism: Conflicts for Academic Women," *Signs* 12, no. 3 (Spring 1987): 493–511.

11. Adrienne Rich urges just such an agenda in "Toward a Woman-Centered University," in *Women and the Power to Change*, ed. Florence Howe (New York: McGraw-Hill, 1975).

Chapter 6. Life and the Life of the Mind

1. For a review of the literature on the comparative scholarship and status of married and single faculty women, see Angela Simeone, *Academic Women: Working Towards Equality* (South Hadley, Mass.: Bergin and Garvey, 1987), chapt. 6, "Marital Status and Academic Women." Research on women graduates of the Sloan School of Management at MIT reveals that women in business remain on a par with men in highly paid, fast-track positions for the first five years after graduation, but do not in these years begin families. (*Boston Globe*, December 29, 1985, p. 69.) Once they do, according to the study of Harvard Business School graduates by Liz Roman Gallese (*Women Like Us* [New York: Morrow, 1985]), they leave the fast track and establish themselves in some less highly paid situation. A study showing a similar pattern among women graduates of the Harvard Law School is Jill Abramson and Barbara Franklin, *Where Are They Now: The Story of the Women of*

Harvard Law 1974 (Garden City, N.Y.: Doubleday, 1986). But see Aasta S. Lubin, *Managing Success: High Echelon Careers and Motherhood* (New York: Columbia University Press, 1987), for stories of five women who have managed a successful balance.

2. For a detailed discussion of restructuring traditional domestic roles, see Gayle Kimball, *The 50-50 Marriage* (Boston: Beacon, 1983); for a collection of first-person stories about balancing dual academic careers, see Leonore Hoffman and Gloria de Sole, eds., *Careers and Couples: An Academic Question* (New York: Modern Language Association, 1976).

3. The cost to women of their double burden is drawn in detail by Sylvia Ann Hewlett in *A Lesser Life: The Myth of Women's Liberation in America* (New York: Morrow, 1986), and presented in a somewhat more positive light by Patricia A. McBroom in *The Third Sex: The New Professional Woman* (New York: Morrow, 1986). Stories detailing a variety of choices between the work and the life are collected in Sara Ruddick and Pamela Daniels, eds., *Working It Out* (New York: Pantheon, 1977).

4. This concept, developed in a broader context, is the by-now classic thesis of Jean Baker Miller in *Toward a New Psychology of Women* (Boston: Beacon Press, 1976). See also Florence Howe, "Women and the Power to Change," in *Women and the Power to Change*, ed. Florence Howe (New York: McGraw-Hill, 1975).

Chapter 7. Countervalues and Change

1. Coordinating Committee for Women in the Historical Profession, *Newsletter* 16, no. 4 (September 1985): 2.

2. *New York Times*, December 29, 1985, p. 20.

3. Cynthia Enloe, *Does Khaki Become You?* (Boston: South End Press, 1983).

4. Women's exclusion from an educated ideal that assumed public service automatically rendered their education of minor importance. For a discussion of the neglect of purpose in the history of women's education, see Jane Martin, *Reclaiming a Conversation: The Ideal of the Educated Woman* (New Haven: Yale University Press, 1985); and for a related discussion, see Barbara Miller Solomon, *In the Company of Educated Women: A History of Women and Higher Education in America* (New Haven: Yale University Press, 1985).

5. Geraldine Ferraro, *Ferraro: My Story* (New York: Bantam, 1985), p. 273.

6. For an excellent review of various (liberal, radical, socialist, third world, and anarchist) feminist theories concerning the nature and proper use of institutional power, see Janet A. Flammang, "Feminist Theory: The Question of Power," in Scott G. McNall, ed., *Current Perspectives in Social Theory: A Research Annual* 4, (Greenwich, Conn.: JAI Press, 1983). The essay includes an extensive bibliography.

7. See Virginia Woolf, *Three Guineas* (New York: Harcourt Brace and World, 1938), for an early plea for the same policy. See also Barbara Forisha and Barbara

Goldman, eds., *Outsiders on the Inside: Women and Organizations* (Englewood Cliffs, N.J.: Prentice-Hall, 1981).

8. For stories much like ours of women reentering the profession after time out for family responsibilities, see Irene Thompson and Audrey Roberts, eds., *The Road Retaken: Women Reenter the Academy* (New York: Modern Language Association, 1985).

9. For a radical analysis of the pathology of family demands on women and proposals for a more collective restructuring of domestic functions, see Michele Barrett and Mary McIntosh, *The Anti-Social Family* (London: Verso, 1982).

10. Coordinating Committee for Women in the Historical Professions, *Newsletter.* See also the excellent essay by Arlie Russell Hochschild, "Inside the Clockwork of Male Careers," in *Women and the Power to Change,* ed. Florence Howe (New York: McGraw-Hill, 1975).

11. *New York Times,* January 2, 1986, pp. 1, D 14.

12. *New York Times,* October 16, 1985, C 1.

13. Betty Friedan, *The Second Stage* (New York: Summit, 1981).

14. For a detailed argument for humanizing or feminizing bureaucratic institutions, see Kathy Ferguson, *The Feminist Case against Bureaucracy* (Philadelphia: Temple University Press, 1984).

15. See Susan Gubar and Sandra Gilbert, *The Madwoman in the Attic* (New Haven: Yale University Press, 1979).